HOW TO MAKE THE
BIGGEST
DECISION
of your
LIFE

Unlocking the secrets to a healthy, lasting relationship

Dr GEORGE BLAIR-WEST
and
JIVENY BLAIR-WEST

hachette
AUSTRALIA

To my ever-patient wife, Penny, who needed no one to teach her about true love and who played the dating game spectacularly well. Thirty-three years later I'm so grateful that one of us knew what they were doing!
– George

To my partner, Joe, for your undying support and encouragement. Being with you has taught me so much about love and what it means to be in a relationship. You make me a better person.
– Jiveny

And to those brave souls who have worked with us over the years. You have taught us profound truths while courageously confronting your fears as you work to understand this confusing thing called love. You inspire us.
– George & Jiveny

Publisher's note: People's names and stories in this book have been altered to ensure their anonymity.

hachette
AUSTRALIA

Published in Australia and New Zealand in 2021
by Hachette Australia
(an imprint of Hachette Australia Pty Limited)
Level 17, 207 Kent Street, Sydney NSW 2000
www.hachette.com.au

10 9 8 7 6 5 4 3 2 1

A catalogue record for this book is available from the National Library of Australia

ISBN: 978 0 7336 4501 3 (paperback)

Cover design by Christabella Designs
Typeset in Sabon LT Std by Kirby Jones
Printed and bound in Australia by McPherson's Printing Group

MIX
Paper from
responsible sources
FSC® C001695

The paper this book is printed on is certified against the Forest Stewardship Council® Standards. McPherson's Printing Group holds FSC® chain of custody certification SA-COC-005379. FSC® promotes environmentally responsible, socially beneficial and economically viable management of the world's forests.

CONTENTS

Authors' note

Sexual orientation

You will see in this book that we have used language based on a heterosexual orientation. Our work with LGBTQIA+ communities has shown that the bulk of the issues that we address in this text are relevant to couples of all orientations. For example, the fact that we will be attracted to people who are opposites in some ways, similar in others and that we need to have alignment in core values is largely true of all relationships. Equally so when it comes to defining true love and the commitment issues that need to be addressed if lives are going to become intertwined.

We are also acutely aware that LGBTQIA+ relationships often have an extra level of complexity due to societal bias. We hope that with the recent changes delivering marriage equality, that positive change is happening. Please know that you have our support.

Marriage

While this book is about helping people decide how to choose a life-long partner, and this typically results in a legal marriage, we do accept that a traditional marriage is not for everyone. Having said this, there appears to be something of a return to marriage in the wind. A large survey of 4000 couples from the UK, reported in 2017, gave us the following data: 95 per cent of couples would recommend getting married; 85 per cent of couples say marriage makes a relationship stronger; 83 per cent never felt any pressure to get married; 92 per cent feel there is less pressure to get married today than their parents' generation; and 73 per cent stated that they value marriage more now than they did as a child.

Whether you believe in marriage or not, what we do strongly believe is that a couple should consciously evaluate whether or not they want their relationship to be long term. Committing to this in some kind of conscious, ceremonial form is a way of clarifying and establishing the issues around the foundations of a long-term relationship. It is reassuring to see that in these UK findings, 91 per cent of couples choose to get married to demonstrate commitment.

As with all good health care, prevention should be paramount. This is the singular driver for this book. It is surprising how few measures are in place to prevent one of the most common conditions affecting humans in the Western world. Few life stressors compete with divorce in terms of the distress, pain and regret it causes for couples and the children who may be caught up in this emotional hurricane.

Research

There is a lot of research that sits behind or is referenced throughout this book. As this is meant to be an accessible read for the general population, we have not included full references on every piece of research. Nevertheless, we have attempted to include references on all the key research findings in the form of endnotes. Otherwise we have tried to provide enough information on any research such that an online search should allow more inquisitive readers to access the work. You will also find a bibliography for the books referred to along the way.

George and Jiveny

Preface

GBW

Our greatest joy – and our greatest pain – comes in our relationships with others.

– Stephen R. Covey

Love is giving someone the power to completely destroy you – and hoping they won't.

– Suzanne Wright

While Suzanne Wright's way of seeing love is not our favourite definition (we will come to that), it is one that nicely captures why so many of the people with whom we work are understandably apprehensive about loving. Whether it is our first love or following a painful divorce, we all sense the fullness of the power at play.

Since the beginning of recorded history, we humans have evolved to be in relationships. Girl with boy, Queen with King. Having a partner who has your back dramatically increases your likelihood of survival – after all, anthropologists have long known that a lone monkey is a dead monkey. Just one other person who cares enough to bring you water when you are too sick to get it for yourself, or to build a fire to keep you warm, is

1

not just twice as good; they can be the difference between life and death. Only in more recent times has research confirmed what cave men and women did not need science to tell them: those with partners are generally happier and healthier, and they tend to live longer.

For most of history, marriages were largely arranged. This brought benefits by creating strategic family ties, powerful alliances and greater combined wealth. In essence, marriage was driven by money and power, or for those further down the food chain, survival. With the Industrial Revolution in the mid-eighteenth to nineteenth century came wages that arrived independently of the family, allowing the children an equal degree of financial independence. Love marriages flowered as parental endorsement, let alone a dowry, were removed as obstacles and choosing a partner evolved from a luxury to a right. This right to choose ushered in new challenges.

One of the main challenges of life is mastering the complex, but critical, skill of finding a healthy and loving match. In arranged marriages, this skill was the purview of mature adults who were parents themselves. Starting with four parents, adding aunts, uncles, siblings and more into the mix, a mini-tribe of people was on hand to work out how well their two charges were matched. Collectively, they brought a century or two of life experience to the challenge.

Now we leave it all to two twenty-somethings with much less life experience.

This book attempts to fill the gap left by the mini-tribe. There is a bit to learn, but it is worth taking the time to do so. We would suggest that *there is nothing to life more important than relationships.*

Take away our relationships with partners, friends, children, parents, bosses, co-workers and customers and there's not much left. You are on a desert island – or a lonely planet. It is difficult to imagine a dream that could be fully realised without the involvement of others at some level.

The other key ingredient in a rewarding life is discovering, and pursuing, a meaningful purpose. But a meaningful career and the success that may follow can be hollow if you have no one to share it with. That's why we suggest that choosing a partner is the biggest decision of your life – bigger than choosing a career. Yet many people don't appear to think of it in this way.

It isn't that people don't recognise that choosing a long-term partner is a critical life decision. They get that, particularly if they're planning to have children together. It's that people typically do not tend to see it as a decision. They think that romance cannot be 'decided'. This isn't so surprising. As humans, we often tend to avoid making decisions – especially complex ones and, as we will see, the alternative romantic solution is particularly seductive.

The reality, though, is that *not* making a decision becomes a decision in itself. The fact that most people tend not to consciously choose their partner has dire consequences that pervade our culture.

So often our comedians nicely capture the unwelcome truths of our time. By the end of the twentieth century, divorce was statistically a normal state. Rita Rudner dryly observes: 'Whenever I date a guy I think, "Is this the man I want my children to spend their weekends with?"' This is a modern, sad but relevant commentary on the reality of relationships in the twenty-first century. It highlights how much of a dice throw we perceive partner selection to be.

But allow us to take a step back and speak to why you were drawn to these pages.

If you are over the age of fifteen, you have probably had some experience of the pain that relationships can cause. Chances are you have loved and lost and know this pain intimately. As a child, you may have been caught up in the whirlwind of overwhelming emotions that follow from watching two parents decide they can no longer live under the same roof. Otherwise, you've probably been witness to a close friend or sibling go through the loss of love and seen how soul-shaking and disorientating it can be.

Anger, guilt, hurt, grief, rejection, abandonment, regret and love, all swirling around and swapping in confused, emotional turmoil. Few experiences in life bring out the worst in people more than losing love. No experiences are greater drivers of suicide, homicide of partners and filicide (the act of a parent killing their child).

As a psychiatrist, I have worked with troubled couples for over 25 years to help them build what they got married for. Along the way, I have also provided psychotherapy to hundreds of singles, particularly those who have been trauma victims. Inevitably, the majority of these patients look to finding and making sense of love. My wife, Penny, is a psychologist who works in a similar therapeutic space; this has created an invaluable collaboration, for which I am very grateful.

Then, after graduating university, my daughter Jiveny decided to become a life coach. After studying at The Coaching Institute she decided to specialise in dating – and so our greater family collaboration began. This book is built on it.

Jiveny works largely with singles, with ages ranging from the early twenties to the late sixties. In this book, she brings the concerns of her peers and the voice of a generation who are currently confronting the question of marriage as a given. This book could not have worked without her.

In putting this book together, we had to choose between adopting a single voice or staying with our two, very different voices. As this book will be read by people getting married for the first time and people who have been divorced, we decided to maintain our two similar but different voices from our respective generations.

As with a good relationship itself, the richness of this book comes from these differences in thinking and in approaching the subject. Each of us has read the other's chapters and had input to the other's writing. Again, as with a good marriage, we are strongly aligned in our core values and beliefs; however, we think very differently and we believe this makes it a better book. After each chapter heading, you will see the author's initials, but by the end of the book you probably won't need them to identify each of us.

Psychotherapy and coaching are both focused on avoiding future regrets. Of the avoidable regrets in life, perhaps none is greater than losing love – particularly when children are involved. There are many books written about how to work on an existing relationship. Conversely, this book's focus is entirely about 'choosing the right person' and how best to set ourselves up for a successful relationship.

Every big problem was a small problem once. Prevention is most effective when you work on a problem while it is still small. Divorce is a big problem. Choosing whether or not to go on a fifth date and continue a relationship is tiny in comparison, but can potentially be life-changing. That is what underpins this book.

So, how do we define the 'best partner for you'? We will start with a simple definition: they are *the person who brings out the best in you*. And your job is to bring the best out in

5

them. When you do this for each other, you are off to the best possible start in a relationship.

Put another way, this book is all about how to make the biggest decision of your life: who will you choose as the other parent of your children? (And yes, the person who can bring out the best in you is going to be an excellent candidate for this role.) If kids aren't on your horizon, who will you choose to spend the rest of your life with?

To return to Suzanne Wright's quote, yes there is a power that we do need to give our partners. While that power can do us harm, it can also heal and create an institution of true love that can inspire and guide, not just a committed couple, but generations that may follow.

It's complicated:
The 'chosen one'

GBW

> You meet someone and you're sure you were lovers in
> a past life. After two weeks with them, you realize why
> you haven't kept in touch for the last two thousand
> years.
>
> – Al Cleathen, Comedian

Singer-songwriter Sahara Beck was only fifteen when she released her first full-length album. She was only nineteen when she won the Most Popular Female award at the music awards in her home state of Queensland, Australia. At twenty, she became responsible for this book finally being finished. Sahara is why I was invited to give a TEDx talk that, at the time of writing, has had several million views.

Even greater credit goes to my daughter. She encouraged me to put down in writing the collective wisdom I have been honoured to have been given by my patients over the decades. Jiveny motivated me to start it; Sahara motivated me to finish it.

Then Jiveny became a co-author of this book, to address directly the concerns of the current, upcoming generation of soon-to-be parents, her compatriots, our millennials. While millennials are the heralds of a brave new world, the most exciting aspect for me of this changing landscape is not the technology, but what is happening in relationships. This is the dimension of human experience that was thought to be relatively impervious to change. For example, while it still has a way to go, significant strides have been made around recognising gender diversity and same-sex marriages.

Moreover, how we meet, how we marry and when we marry is changing ... forever.

So, how did Sahara motivate me to finish this book after it had been languishing for five years? I was attending a TEDx event with an expectation of being inspired by the tech-savvy, erudite, well-researched and even better-spoken movers and shakers of our time. I was indeed inspired, and the speakers were all of these things. Yet I was also a little disappointed.

I had been asked to give a brief presentation on what I thought was an 'idea worth spreading'. I argued that while we know prevention is better than cure in all aspects of medicine, we have no meaningful prevention strategies in place for a condition that affects almost half of the population. This condition causes greater, longer-lasting emotional pain than most distressing human experiences. The condition, of course, is divorce. (Here I include the breakdown of any long-term love relationship – including same-sex relationships – particularly those involving children.)

I went on to argue that we need to go way back – before pre-marital counselling (who actually does that anyway?) and help people to become better at choosing their life-partners. My point was that much wisdom and many lessons are offered by research and clinical experience, and we need to turn them into common knowledge.

I proposed that while attraction is built on complex forces, most people have windows of time in which they make important decisions. Big decisions about choosing to move in together; the time of asking someone, or being asked, to marry; or planning to have children.

These 'decision windows' stand in front of events that will have major implications for our lives. When they arrive, they need to be enlarged to give us time to make better decisions. I suggested that once we recognise a window, there are ways to help people make better choices concerning these huge decisions.

Finally, I suggested that we need to appreciate the largely unconscious biases at work, so we can make more informed, conscious decisions.

As we walked out to lunch, I was chatting with a Gen X filmmaker who had spoken earlier. It only took a moment or two before she made the point I often hear: 'But we don't really choose our partners.' There it was, spoken like a true romantic ... ah ... filmmaker!

Another woman spoke to me of her mother being on her fourth marriage and her own recent divorce. This was delivered with a sad, 'well-that's-just-the-way-it-is' laugh. It was sadder than she realised.

At times like this, a part of me wants to shake people and rant, 'It does not have to be this way! Become conscious – awaken! Author your relationship destiny!' Another part of me knows that's not a cool thing to do at a TEDx conference ... or anywhere.

Several other women of middle-age – that is, Gen X and the last of the Baby Boomers – spoke with me, but there was the usual pervasive sense of, 'What to do? We don't really choose our partners ... it just happens ... it is not something you can control.'

In short, the belief in what I call 'romantic destiny' was alive and well, as usual. So I changed the subject, gave up on my hope of enlightening people and politely moved on. This book became even less published!

The myth of romantic destiny and 'the one'

Romantic destiny is the notion that there is some force at work bringing people together and creating attraction between them. This force works in mysterious ways and cannot be controlled. This notion of romantic destiny was built by Baby Boomers and those who came before them – a little known generation called, not too surprisingly, the 'Silent Generation', comprising those born between 1925 and 1945. Their voices were drowned out by the worldwide adversity of the great depression and then World War II.

How did romantic destiny gain such weight within our collective psyche? First, it is incredibly … well, romantic! As humans, we love a good romance: it's a movie in which we all want to star. While we could, quite fashionably, blame Hollywood, that would be a cheap shot. Hollywood simply gives us what we want for as long as we have an appetite for it. While it creatively stretches our attention in various directions, in essence it is a barometer, a reflection of our collective psyche. It is deeply human to want to believe in the romantic processes. This draws us to Santa Claus, the Tooth Fairy and the Easter Bunny from early childhood.

To understand the attraction of romantic destiny fully, we need to get to know its partner in crime: the myth of 'the one'. In its simplest form, this is the notion that once you find 'the one', you will live happily ever after. Romantic destiny invites us to wander down the road of life and in good time and, if we're lucky, in true Hollywood style, we will stumble across 'the one'. A physical stumble resulting in bodily contact is the best by far, as this is part of the process of 'falling' in love. The storyline unfolds, typically with both parties being on their best (read 'highly unusual') behaviour ... then bad behaviour ... then, finally, good behaviour again. Credits roll and they ride off into an eternal sunset on which the divorce sun never sets.

Here's the point: it was a scarcity of divorce that built the notion of romantic destiny and the myth of 'the one'. Those people growing up in a divorce-free world saw people find each other and 'appear' to live happily ever after.

What we now know from the research is that, unless there is obvious aggression or outspoken contempt for one's partner, even the children in a bad marriage will think their parents are happy enough. It was even easier for a marriage to look good from outside the house. The impression this left was that romantic destiny was bringing people together with 'the one' and they were living happily ever after.

The myth of 'the one' was also fed by the reality that Baby Boomers and those who came before had very little opportunity to date many people. So, it looked a lot like destiny put 'the one' in front of you, you married, and then lived happily ever after.

But they were not together, and did not stay together, because romantic destiny had led them to 'the one'. They were together primarily because divorce was socially unacceptable and financially devastating – particularly for women. This is why romantic destiny and the myth of 'the one' survived, unquestioned, for so long. The shift began in 1969 when Ronald Reagan, the then Governor of California, signed no-fault divorce into law. The greater United States and the rest of the world followed in the next several years.

The introduction of 'no-fault' divorce allowed a division of assets that gave women financial assurance, particularly as a greater share went to the carer of the children – traditionally accepted as being the mother. More importantly, the concept of 'no fault' introduced the term 'irreconcilable differences' as a valid reason for a couple to separate.

Blame and shame began to be dismantled as part of the divorce experience. This was a seismic cultural shift. As it became easier for women to leave a loveless or abusive marriage, they did – in droves.

Can I say categorically that there is no romantic destiny at work, bringing souls together? No, I cannot. The romantic in me would love to believe it is true. But if there is such a force, then the divorce rate would suggest it is not doing its job very well, and it needs some help.

The 'chosen one'

Maybe, if there is such a force, it brings souls together for a purpose other than marriage. Typically, when people meet 'the one', they experience the attraction as hot, intense and life-changing.

But what if a relationship with 'the one' is there to give us an intense, powerful, but short-lived romantic experience? An experience that ultimately teaches us not to be thrown off our individual life path by people who arouse strong emotions in us? Mark Antony and Cleopatra, and Romeo and Juliet undoubtedly felt they had found 'the one', but in the end it was suicide all round. Indeed, research suggests that often the more intense and earth-shattering the initial attraction, the higher the divorce rate.

Maybe after these intense relationships with 'the one', we need to more consciously choose our life-partner (and are now better equipped to do so). In short, we need to have a shorter relationship with 'the one' and go on to find the 'chosen one'. The 'chosen one' is chosen from a more conscious place with consideration to factors that we will work through in this book.

Another attraction of romantic destiny is that it requires absolutely nothing of us. It is dead easy. We just wander along in life and it happens. We just need to wait patiently for 'the one' to appear. The alternative to romantic destiny is complex; relationships are complex.

Not unreasonably, 'It's complicated' is now seen as a go-to explanation – or non-explanation – for relationship problems. This is a move in the right direction.

Why are relationships seen as so complicated? We psychiatrists, psychologists and other counsellors have failed to make this complicated knowledge more accessible. Why? I suspect it is partly because we have been caught up in a version of romantic destiny ourselves. Outside of a handful of curious research psychologists, clinical mental health professionals do not have the resources to scientifically dissect romance. More significantly, the exploration of normal human behaviour has always, understandably, taken second place to the research into mental ill-health.

Finally, there is a wide chasm between research and clinical practice limiting the spread of the latest research findings. Busy clinicians have enough to do between their clinical work and their requirements for continuing professional development. They don't have the time to wander through thousands of research papers to stay up to date on emerging findings. Indeed, books like this can help to fill this divide.

In turn, without guidance from the experts, the general public simply maintain their go-to explanations – some version of romantic destiny. As 'educated humans', we do not like feeling that we don't understand or know something. Our 'modern' schooling has been very unhelpful here. At school, not knowing something immediately qualified us as an idiot: not knowing was never a good look. On the other hand, the romantic destiny view makes us look like we know what is going on. It aligns with what most people think. It also makes us look more, well … romantic. In short, we are having a love affair with having a love affair!

I would suggest that, certainly among the older generations, the myth of romantic destiny leading us to 'the one' is among the most widely accepted misguided beliefs held by our species – at least in the West. It has not served us well, so it is time to upgrade this software. And this is already happening, which brings me back to my inspiration to finish this book – my run-in with my muse.

The big question

It was not until the very end of the cocktail party at the very end of the TEDx conference that it happened.

As I was heading to the door, having said my goodbyes, I walked past singer Sahara Beck, who had presented and performed in the afternoon session. With her trademark tousled blonde ringlets, she had sung with a sassiness and bellicosity that belied her petite frame and fragile beauty.

I complimented her on her presentation and her insightful, humorous lyrics about relationships. Her friend, aged twenty (as was Sahara), dived in with, 'So, how do we choose better partners?' There it was, the question that no folks of the older generations had thought to ask me – indeed, the *big question*!

I started talking, rattling off a couple of the simpler things to consider. Their enthusiasm caught me off-guard.

'Hang on let me write that down!'

So I waited while they dug out their smartphones and then picked up from where I had left off.

'What else can you tell us?'

I threw some more ideas at them, and they asked for even more.

It was not until I awoke the next morning that the full epiphany hit me. Generation Y, our dear millennials, who are now in their twenties and early thirties, have grown up with divorce as the norm. Indeed, Sahara said her parents had divorced when she was seven.

Gen X, immediately before Gen Y (strangely enough), were the first cohort to experience divorce, and its heartache, on a large scale. Before them, the Baby Boomers grew up when divorce was relatively scarce. In the Silent Generation that came before, divorce was about as common as rocking horse droppings.

Generation X bore witness to the beginning of the seismic cultural shift at the painful, sharp end. They reeled and recoiled under its devastation, but they were not yet ready to abandon romantic destiny.

Now, two generations into a divorce-ready culture, millennials are simply not buying it. They know from bitter experience how romantic destiny often ends. They know that 'the one' too often becomes the one suing for more child access and a larger share of the family home. Mostly, they are just too familiar with the raw heartache and soulful pain of marriage failure.

They say that alcoholism isn't a spectator sport – eventually the whole family gets to play. It is the same when a marriage ends. The whole family plays, whether they want to or not. No member of the family escapes the gut-wrenching hurt – even infants pick up on it. Indeed, nothing brings out the worst in humans more than a relationship breakdown.

The most violent of all crimes is a murder-suicide. The research tells us that 70 per cent of all murder-suicides occur in the context of disputes relating to termination of a relationship.

Gen X took time to process the fullness of the divorce epidemic as it broke around them. Another generation into a divorce-ready culture and our millennials are under no illusion as to what is going on – they are even more disillusioned.

But the fullness of my epiphany was that there is something else that defines millennials. They have grown up connected to information. There is a reason why they are not buying romantic destiny. Indeed, millennials are apparently the hardest group to sell to, because they are sceptical and quick to jump online and look for alternative products and services. While the quality of their evaluative resources may be questionable, they do not believe anything until they have comparatively researched it. This generation is changing our culture at a fundamental level. When it comes to relationships, I believe it will be for the better.

On top of this healthy scepticism, Helen Fisher, an anthropologist studying the dating behaviour of millions of Americans, tells us that millennials are concerned about being better parents, whereas the Gen Xers before them were more interested in having a better marriage.

If you are all about being a better parent, then the first step has to be avoiding the most damaging problem of all – a failed marriage and the pain that goes with it. It is an exciting possibility that the present generation of 'about-to-become-parents' could be more open to preventing divorce than any generation before them.

To finish the story, the very observant curator of the TEDx event, Juanita Wheeler, noticed the animated discussion I had with Sahara and her friend. Apparently she spoke to them after

I left. It was their interest in my work that resulted in me being invited back to give a TEDx talk the following year. Then my talk was picked up by the head organisation of TED and promoted internationally. The rest, as they say, is history.

So, how does attraction work? How do we make sense of the unconscious and conscious forces that lead us into our relationships? Why do we marry people with whom, in reality, we are a poor match? How do we not do that? How do we better choose the other parent of our children?

All meaningful change in life begins with a deepening of understanding, a raising of self-awareness and consciousness. This is the essence of this book: it aims to give you a command over knowledge, to make the unconscious conscious, to provide you with more power over your relationship destiny.

It aims to help you find the 'chosen one'.

From curious to committed

JBW

Getting married is a serious decision, because 50 per cent of marriages actually end up staying together!

— Alan Carr, Comedian

I burst into tears at the dinner table. I was out with my parents and we had only just finished our entrees. While I don't like to make a habit of crying in public, the emotions inside me needed to come out. I had been holding them in for far too long and it was becoming a heavy burden to carry. The question had inevitably arisen: was I seeing anyone at the moment?

I was still waiting to hear back from this guy I went out with on the weekend – the first guy I had dated since I had split from the 'soulmate' who had broken my heart. It was a year since we had parted ways and although I had taken plenty of steps towards opening my heart again, I was still left with a seemingly inescapable insecurity that I was no longer lovable.

Then, *finally*, I had met this guy with whom I saw new potential ... For me, he was a glimmer of hope on what had been a very bleak horizon in the aftermath of a broken heart.

And he had been pretty communicative until recently ... Yet the anxiety inspired by his aloofness was killing me.

As I let the tears fall, I came face to face with my fear. Underneath all my dating bravado, I was so afraid. Afraid that my time was running out, and I would never meet my match. Afraid that I wasn't worthy of the calibre of man I dreamed of partnering with. Afraid that I would have to settle for an unsatisfying relationship of compromise – or worse, that I'd end up old and alone and I would never get to start the family I had always dreamed of having. Should I give up now, get a clowder of cats or become a nun? Or should I just settle for that other guy who loved me freely, but who I knew didn't fully understand me and wouldn't be able to co-create the lifestyle I wanted for me and my future family?

That was me at 25, and I am *so* glad I didn't give up on dating and settle (as much as I like cats). Fast forward to now and I am in an *epic* relationship with an extraordinary man who ticks all my boxes, shares my vision for the future and is committed to co-creating a fantastic lifestyle for us and our future kids. But it was a journey to get here, and part of the reason why I am so passionate about this book. Because I know what it is like to feel the fear that I may live a life without love.

My journey

From as early as my late teens, I started to feel disillusioned.

Does romantic love even exist?

Is it really possible to find my own 'happily ever after'?

Will I ever meet a man who can meet me on all the levels where I crave to be met?

I wondered because, at the ripe old age of nineteen, I hadn't yet experienced anything close to what was depicted in fairy tales, love songs and rom-coms. Sure, I had my moments of attraction and infatuation, but nothing solid enough on which to build a real foundation of love.

I realised pretty early on that these desires weren't even based on a personal quest to be loved. I'd had people willing to love me and I *still* came out dissatisfied. What I needed was someone *to* love. Someone who saw themselves as worthy of being loved well too. Someone who could inspire me to show up fully in a relationship, to give *and* receive love – a two-way street.

In the years since, I have sampled all kinds of arrangements, from fleeting romances to committed partnerships, open relationships to toxic dependencies, friends with benefits to 'soulmate' connections.

I fell in love. I fell out of love. I chased love. I renounced love. I confused lust for love. I ignored love for lust. Sometimes I broke hearts. At other times my heart got broken. Still, I soldiered on, seeking a loving connection that could weather my storm.

Then, at the age of 24, I thought I had finally found the perfect man to create my future with ... until it all fell apart. Badly apart.

It took eighteen months for me to find my place in this world again. So many sleepless nights as I lay in bed alone, ruminating over our relationship. Playing things over and over in my mind. Trying to untangle our roles in the demise of what once seemed like the ultimate love story. Asking myself what I had done wrong. Where was he at fault? How could things have worked out differently?

While I had developed a hunger to better understand love and relationships back at nineteen, it was the pain of this heartbreak that really forced me to dive deeper, show up, look within and do the work.

After that taste of what a relationship could be, I wasn't ready to give up on dating altogether. However, I was clear that I did not want to go through any unnecessary heartbreak again.

Still licking my wounds, I kept the man of my next relationship – let's call him Tom – at arm's length. Despite the magnetic sexual chemistry and his obvious affection for me, my recent, raw pain limited how much I was ready to engage. Besides, Tom was a talented but jaded musician, angry at the world and seemingly unmotivated to take responsibility for his adult life. I was ambitious with big dreams and an optimistic outlook. Because of this great divide, there were some parts of each of us that remained off limits. They had to be, in order to keep the peace.

As this became clearer to me, I grew painfully aware that without aligned vision and values, he would never be able to share with me the life I truly wanted. I also noticed something had changed in me. Whereas in the past I was often quite happy to let things unfold without much talk about what the future might hold, I found myself thinking more and more about wanting to start a family at some point. It was time to get serious about finding a life-partner.

Over the years, I had witnessed the plight and struggle of single mums who had long been abandoned by their at-the-time lovers. Often it was a story of boy meets girl, falling in 'love', her getting pregnant and, not long after, the couple waking up to find that they were in love with a fantasy. While I related to my female friends more closely, I know this was just as challenging for the fathers too. Then there is the child's experience. It was a mess all round.

While I admired their womanly strength, I decided that, if possible, I would like to avoid such a fate. That meant that, while knowing there were no guarantees, I had to choose my partner as consciously as possible.

Yet the more time I spent with Tom, the closer we got. Sometimes I would lie in Tom's arms thinking *what if?* What if I gave Tom a proper chance? What if I allowed myself to fall in love with him? But then, *what if I got pregnant to him?* I imagined us living together in his share house with his three housemates who seemed to be constantly partying. That wouldn't work for me – too much noise, too many late nights and a constant flow of visitors. So then what? Maybe we would go and live with his mum? We wouldn't be able to afford a decent place on our own unless he started working again. I imagined Tom working – coming home tired and resentful after an eight-hour day on a minimum wage. Eventually either quitting or getting fired followed by another period on the dole. And then with a kid? Maybe he could be a stay-at-home dad? I imagined him being good with kids. But then I would get resentful if I had to be the primary breadwinner and miss out on my own kid's childhood. I knew I wanted more equality in my relationship.

Ultimately, I had to face the fact that staying with Tom meant settling for less. Equally, I was also holding him back from a relationship that could be a better match for him. Unless I found the strength to say goodbye to him once and for all, it would be difficult to find a more suitable partner.

I realised it was time to part ways. But breaking up was hard (I'd already tried with him twice). Having grown so used to each other's company, we often found ourselves drawn back together in our loneliest moments. Finally I decided that I needed to make a clean break. For years I had been contemplating moving to Melbourne as I had friends living there who loved the city. The draw of a new place with new possibilities was strong. I also wanted to study to become a life coach and Melbourne had some great opportunities for doing that. Finally, I decided to go for it.

After settling into a wonderful share house with two great housemates in Melbourne's inner north, I once again plunged into the modern world of dating. Here there were plenty of fish in the sea. In fact, with the added novelty of internet dating, the choices were downright overwhelming. To complicate things further, for the first time in my life I was playing the dating field with the conscious goal of finding a life-partner – *no pressure!*

Clearly, it was time to get smarter about dating, but where to start? In those first few months in Melbourne, I went on plenty of dates and came to a disconcerting observation. Throughout my adult life, most of the men I had dated fell into one of two 'types'.

I had this pattern of dating men who were sexy, playful, dazzlingly creative, incredibly emotionally intelligent and most of all broke and directionless. It was fun and they were easy to connect with, but they also seemed a bit aimless and considering I was now looking for the future father of my children, this scared me. In their company I felt seen – indeed often worshipped – but I knew starting a family with them would be a struggle as I yearned for them to become more ambitious and self-motivated.

When those relationships eventually ended, the pendulum would quickly swing the other way. I would find myself dating men who were charming, driven, financially successful and frustratingly emotionally distant. Dating them, I sometimes felt more like an accessory than an actual partner. In terms of true intimacy, we barely scratched the surface. Eventually this lack of connection would send me running back to exhibit A.

In neither scenario was I satisfied. I was dating two halves of my dream man, and it left me wondering whether I would have to settle for less.

There were times when dating felt hopeless, as if I would never find a man who could meet me in all the ways I wanted to be met. Were my standards just too high? My expectations too grand? Or maybe I was just too messed up for love? These were the insecurities that haunted me in my darkest moments.

Luckily for me, I had resources. Not only did I have a psychologist and a psychiatrist as parents, they both specialised in relationship therapy. Growing up, the intricacies of intimacy often made for casual dinner conversation, but it wasn't until this later stage of my life that I started paying more attention to their insights.

I knew it would take work to identify and understand the patterns I had been playing out in my dating life, so I jumped right in. Any chance I got, I picked my parents' brains clean on their thoughts on relationships and dating. I read every decent book I could find on the subject. I bought online courses and watched countless hours of YouTube videos. I went to workshops that encouraged me to understand myself better. I started more conversations with friends (and sometimes acquaintances) about their own relationship experiences and what they had learned along their travels. Throughout these conversations, I also gained some profound insights into the hearts and minds of men.

Most of all, I sat with every disappointment along the way and questioned, 'What role did I play in this? What could I have done differently? How can I learn to grow beyond this old pattern?' And 'What do I want to experience next?'

Lo and behold, in the midst of all of this, it happened – I attracted my whole dream man.

Now I look back on all this relationship questing with a smile. Romantic love does exist. It is not hopeless and I didn't have to lower my standards.

Of course, that doesn't mean this journey was easy. It took around five months after meeting my partner, Joe, before I decided to date him exclusively. *Talk about a slow burn!* The truth is, I suffered from a classic case of commitment phobia. This meant I spent a lot of time distracting myself from the brilliance of the man in front of me by looking over his shoulder for the next best thing. At times, the more he made himself available to me, the more I pulled away. His healthy emotional intelligence and open communication were confronting at first, but now these are some of my most treasured qualities.

In the beginning stages of getting to know each other, I wasn't sure if we would ever be more than friends. But looking back, my healthiest relationships have been those with unassuming counterparts – those who were not picture perfect but the more I got to know them, I discovered a mind, heart and soul I deeply resonated with.

I had so many conversations with friends about Joe those first five months. *Should I invest myself more? Shouldn't I? What if it doesn't work out?* And the even scarier question to contemplate: *What if it does?* Eventually a friend of mine gave me a book to read called *An Uncommon Bond* by Jeff Brown. It is in this book that Jeff writes about what he calls 'the unavailable/available pattern' which described me at the time to a T.

'It's where you convince yourself (and others) that you are available for a relationship, but you always find a way to stop short. That stopping short can manifest in many ways: choosing unavailable people, looking for excuses to run, focusing on a lover's imperfections rather than their appealing qualities, getting lost in the excitement of ecstatic possibility until the first glimpse of real vulnerability sends you packing. It's the addiction to possibility and the fear of intimacy all rolled into one.'

That's when it hit me – five months in. I'd spent all this time looking for the reasons why it wouldn't work with Joe, rather than considering the reasons why it would. This point became even clearer over dinner with a close friend where we were discussing the qualities we really wanted in a life partner. As I shared my core values, I realised *Joe actually ticks all of those boxes, so why am I holding myself back?*

Something shifted in me after that conversation. The next time I saw Joe, I started to look at him differently. In the five months we had been casually dating and hanging out as friends I'd gotten to know him reasonably well. From that, I already knew we had aligned vision and values, that he was emotionally intelligent and someone I genuinely enjoyed spending time with. He was good at making me laugh and I had always enjoyed his hugs. All in all, we were very compatible. And as I focused more and more on those facts, the floodgates flew open.

My appreciation and attraction towards him climbed quickly and steadily as I opened myself up more, invested more and allowed myself to get to know him on a more intimate level. Turns out that chemistry does not have to be there right from the beginning. For me, it was something that grew and intensified as time went on.

By the time he proposed to me three years in, I said yes without a doubt, knowing that since I had decided to commit to him my life had been better for it. To this day, he brings me so much joy, pleasure and support and looking to the future I feel confident that we will continue to enjoy each other's company for decades to come.

But enough of a smitten love-rant from me! My point is that applying the concepts my father and I have put together in this book has resulted in the most nurturing, fun, sweet, sexy, secure and sustainably passionate relationship I've ever known. This is a relationship where I finally feel safe to go all in, invest and express all parts of me because: (1) I got really clear on what I wanted in a partner and how to heed the warning signs before getting hurt; and (2) I've observed the consistency of my now husband's character over enough time to trust him with my whole heart.

Perhaps the biggest lesson I've learned from this journey is how to make better decisions. After all, we do not go to a therapist (or read books like this) so that we are given 'the answer'. Instead, it is all about shifting our mindset and raising our consciousness so we can see ourselves more clearly and become more self-aware.

After completing my coaching certification, I started my practice as a dating and attraction coach, working with single men and women to uncover the blocks and barriers keeping them from a healthy long-term relationship. My study and experiences have shown me that from brutal self-awareness and the growth that follows, we can learn to make better decisions.

This foundation of making a considered, conscious decision has since become invaluable for laying the bedrock of a healthy and sustainable long-term relationship, for both myself and my clients. And I look forward to sharing it all with you.

Head over heart in love

JBW

To love oneself is the beginning of a lifelong romance.

– Oscar Wilde

Being single is awesome, and not just because we get the whole bed to ourselves. It is awesome because it is an opportunity to truly get to know ourselves, and from understanding ourselves better we can become clearer about where we want to go in life, and what we want to create and experience. When we are clearer about what that path might be, we can make more of the (sometimes difficult) choices that will help us to experience it.

Not everyone takes up these opportunities for self-discovery. Many simply turn their focus to filling up the empty side of the bed again.

Nevertheless, I believe singledom is an important rite of passage in any person's life. It's valuable to take the time to figure out what drives us – who we are and who we want to become – independent of anyone else's expectations. To get in touch with our needs, wants and deepest desires without external influence. To befriend and nurture ourselves into someone we are proud to be. Singledom is a time of creativity and self-expression. Trial and error. Adventure and growth. An invitation to reflect on past mistakes and choose differently, instead of repeating old patterns over and over again.

All this is hard to achieve when we are impulsively jumping from one relationship to another. It is precisely in our lonelier moments that we really get to know ourselves. And it is through the time we spend connecting with ourselves alone that our own love affair begins.

Other perks of being single include being able to flirt with good-looking strangers, move to the other side of the country on a whim, stay up until sunrise talking with a new acquaintance (or, for introverts like me, leave the party early). We are untethered and the possibilities are endless. In short, we can pretty much do what we want, when we want, with whom we want. This is true freedom.

Having said that, relationships are great too. They hold a mirror up to our blind spots and ground our self-knowledge in experience. After all, we can only do so much personal growth when we are single. No matter how much we think we have evolved, relationships put all that 'personal growth' to the test. It is easier to be a Zen master when you don't have a partner to trigger you. And it is easier to be 'a good person' when you don't have to make hard choices between what you want to do and what your partner needs from you. When we're alone, selfishness can rule unchecked. In short, life is generally more comfortable without compromise.

Even so, 'single' and 'taken' are essentially two sides of the same coin: both experiences acquaint us with different facets of ourselves. It is through singledom that we find our independence and through relationships that we learn what it is to be a part of something bigger: a couple.

Being happily single is an important foundation for a healthy and fulfilling relationship. It is from singledom that we learn about authoring our own life and through a relationship that we learn about commitment to another. Both experiences teach us what we are really made of. Neither is better than the other. Both are worthwhile.

If you are recently single, my suggestion is to slow down, settle into it and embrace your time as a free agent. As with all of life's opportunities, the trick is not to waste them. The better we use our time as a single person, to explore and define ourselves and our priorities, the better we can set ourselves up for a meaningful and fulfilling lifelong relationship.

Love and used cars

Choosing a life-partner with whom to settle down is a big deal. There is no decision that will have a greater impact on one's life than who we choose to give our heart to and share our emotional, parental and financial life with. Much of our future happiness and sorrow will be determined by the person we choose and how deeply we allow them into our life. There are few choices in life that have the same long-term impacts as this one.

Choose the wrong job – hey, people do that all the time – and you can get another one. Choose the wrong house and two years later you can move. Rent the wrong house and you can move within months!

But choose the wrong partner, and then have kids with them, and even with a divorce you are going to have to interact with that person for decades at least.

In contrast to what we are told in fairy tales, *sometimes love just isn't enough.*

Yes, we can fall in love with all kinds of people, yet *realistically* some of them simply won't be compatible with the life we want to create for ourselves. What we don't want to do is waste years on a relationship based on the hope and fantasy that *one day* this person will change into the person we want them to be.

With this in mind, it is important to recognise that (like it or not) dating is an evaluation process that should lead to a conscious decision about whether to proceed.

It is the phase for us to get to know someone and *then* decide how much of our lives and valuable time we want to invest, while taking note of how willing they are to invest in a life with us in return. This 'evaluation process' is obviously going to take more than a few dates to figure out. For best results, we need to keep our eyes open all the way up until we choose to have kids together, because after that point we are locked in for life, irrespective of whether the relationship prevails.

But what does it mean to 'evaluate' a potential partner? As crass as it might seem, let's take a moment to consider how we might buy a car ...

When we're looking at buying a car, there is a lot to consider. Often we will start by looking at our budget: what are we willing to invest in it at this stage of our lives? How long do we expect to have this car? Is it a long-term or temporary investment? If it is a used car, we'll also want to know a bit about its history: is it safe and reliable? Does it have any ongoing issues? And why did the previous owners want to get rid of it?

Then we'll take it for a test drive to see how it handles ...

If we are really doing our homework, we will also find other options to compare it with – and maybe even take those out for a test drive too.

Ultimately, a car sale is only made when we know it meets our needs and desires, improves our lifestyle and our perceived value of it equals or exceeds that of the price tag attached.

That's how we buy cars that we may only drive for a few years. If later we discover it is not quite right for us, we can often sell it on quite easily. But relationships are a bigger investment, which is why we need to put *at least* this much thought (if not more) into choosing a life-partner.

This is what we will be unpacking in this book – more specifically, the kinds of things you might want to consider before marrying your life to someone else's – things like:

- the psychology of attraction
- the relationship life cycle
- the key relationship turning points that often go unnoticed
- what 'true love' really entails
- a mindset for modern love
- how to make the most of online dating, as well as offline dating, opportunities
- how opposites attract and similarities bond
- the importance of having aligned core values
- six specific qualities that help to support a healthy long-term relationship
- the power of vulnerability
- the importance of breaking up well
- how to tell when men are ready for marriage (they have a clock too)
- and finally, how we can use all this information to make a good decision.

But fear not. Approaching relationships with a little more of our head doesn't mean we have to lose any of the heart. Nor will we need to abandon the romantic within (mine is certainly still alive and thriving). This isn't an either/or equation.

What we are really working towards in this book is an integration of the head *with* the heart as we become more conscious in our decision-making process. The problem is when people choose a partner without stopping to make a considered, conscious decision. It's *all heart*, and the results can be devastating.

So let us bring some balance to this equation as we peel back the layers of what dating means in this exciting new era of love.

Doing battle with our unconscious: Banfield's insight

GBW

Someone is sitting in the shade today because someone planted a tree a long time ago.

– Warren Buffett

One factor determines success in life more than any other. It is more powerful than family background, education, intelligence or having influential contacts. It was defined by Professor Edward Banfield of Harvard University when, in 1970, he published a book entitled *The Un-heavenly City*.[1] Banfield was a sociologist who was interested in why some people got ahead in life while others did not.

His journey to discovering this critical insight into human nature began with his work in the 1950s while undertaking research for the University of Chicago, where he earned his doctorate. He and his Italian-speaking wife spent nine months living in, and studying in great depth, a small town named

Chiaramonte in Italy. This community was defined by its elevation of commitment to family above all else.

Surprisingly, Banfield found that a culture of unmitigated devotion to family led to widespread problems, particularly feuds, simmering resentments, pervasive unhappiness and poverty: 'From the cradle, the family socialized children ... to follow the old ways, stay close to home, and distrust others.' For example, there was no charity for those outside the family, as each family was expected to care for its own. As sons were made to follow in their father's line of work, trades grew because of this, rather than because of an economic need for them in the town.

The writer Kevin Kosar noted in 2016 that Banfield's 1958 book, *The Moral Basis of a Backward Society* 'was a watershed in poverty studies, one still read in college classes today'.[2] In particular, he noted that Banfield's research 'revealed astonishingly low levels of individual agency'.

Individual agency is all about one's capacity to be effective and achieve in the areas of life in which one wants to succeed. Back working in the United States, it was Banfield's work in Italy that inspired him, over the next couple of decades, to further explore and understand the very basis – the pure essence – of individual agency. He concluded that the single greatest factor that determined success in life was what he called a 'time perspective' – more specifically, a long-time perspective. He came to believe that whether it was financial success or more general career or life success, those who rose above were those who considered the long-term implications of what they were about to do. They brought their future into their present.

It was all about 'the amount of time that you take into consideration when planning your day-to-day activities, and when making important decisions in your life'. The longer the timeframe considered – five, ten or even fifteen years – the better. At the extreme, he identified highly successful people who were even 'planting seeds for trees they were not going to sit under'.

Applying the long-term view

My patients who look well down the track as they make important life decisions are the ones who do the best in psychotherapy ... and life. Conversely, at the other end of the spectrum, people who are driven by a need for immediate gratification reliably tend to be under-achievers.

Applying the time perspective test of, 'What will this mean for me in a year, or five years?' flushes out three things. First, issues that have no real long-term impact are immediately revealed for what they are – that is, of low priority or significance.

Second, considering the problem from this angle will often reveal the direction we need to take. A decision to go to university and study engineering, law or astrophysics is driven by a time perspective. A decision to take the first job that comes along, offered to you by a friend of your parents, is not. Thinking about the implications of a decision you are about to make in five years from now will often change the decision you might make. Do I put the $15,000 I have saved towards buying a new car or do I buy a cheaper car and save for a deposit on a house? Introducing a time perspective would highlight the fact that a car is going to go down in value over time, whereas a house will typically go up.

Third, and most importantly, a time perspective gets us to look past the fears and anxieties that often stop us from doing something that is better for us in the long term. Nearly always, in my experience, fear-based decisions are poor decisions.

Thinking about the longer term implications of going down path A or B will get us past the fear that can hold us back. For example, applying a long-term view will allow you to see that giving that presentation at work, while nerve-wracking, will allow the visiting big boss to appreciate the high-level work you have been doing.

Okay, but what happens when we apply Banfield's insight to making the biggest decision of our lives? I would suggest that this is where it has its greatest application. Thinking about life, five and fifteen years down the track with a potential partner, is a sobering and thought-provoking challenge. If you are having a great time partying with your partner several nights a week, thinking about how they will adjust to being a parent and growing older can be revealing.

The concerning thing for me as a relationship therapist is that when I ask people how they evaluated someone before living with them, letting them become the other parent of their children and/or marrying them, I do not hear reassuring answers. Yes, the people I am asking are seeing me because their relationship has failed or is failing, so they can teach us about what *not* to do.

What I typically find is the opposite of Banfield's insight. Not only did people not apply a time perspective to their decision making; they actually often did not make a clear decision at all. Sure, when her partner gets down on one knee it looks like she has to make a decision, but in truth the decision is more often a foregone conclusion after a series of non-decisions. Indeed, when men get down on one knee in public – and worse still on television – there is even less room for a decision to be made. Women in these situations feel compelled to say yes because the rejection would be even more dramatic and damaging. So, they say 'yes', thinking, 'I can change my mind down the track'.

But what happens next? The news of the proposal (and acceptance) spreads like wildfire, fanned by the strong winds of social media. I have seen a number of women who have been caught up in this process and kept putting off cancelling the wedding.

A woman who came to see me a decade into her unhappy marriage explained, 'I was looking for the right time to say I had changed my mind and try and let him down gently, but it never came. So, I decided to do it quietly a few months after the wedding. By then I was pregnant.'

One of my more insightful patients made the point, 'I now realise there is never a good time to cancel getting married!'

This need to align with the expectations of others, rather than do what you want to do, has a name in psychology research: it is called a 'demand characteristic'.

Early experiments in psychology failed, as the participants worked out what the researchers were looking for or what they thought they were looking for. They then behaved in a particular way, which was not normal for them, to meet this supposed 'demand'. This was the reason why 'blind' studies were developed. This is where the participants do not know whether they are receiving the treatment condition or the placebo condition. 'Double-blind' studies, the best of all (and the most expensive) are where neither the participants nor the supervisors know which is the treatment condition or exactly what is being studied.

The point is that going in a direction expected by others is, literally, a force of nature that needs to be reckoned with.

I have not been able to find any research data on the number of people expecting to get divorced *before* they got married, but I would not be surprised if it was a significant number.

While I am sure that not many people go into marriage expecting to divorce, I know that many more people go in with some serious concerns which they repress from their awareness. This word, 'repress', brings us to a necessary discussion about how our unconscious mind works if we want to fully understand what is happening in our mind as we choose a partner.

Understanding your unconscious mind

The power of a demand characteristic at work is self-evident. We have all had the experience of responding to, and going along with, peer group pressure in at least some of its different forms. And we know the bad decisions that can follow from this.

But why would we not take notice of serious concerns – especially when they can lead to the enormous pain and hurt that goes with separation and divorce, particularly when children are involved?

To understand this, I need to give you a crash course in understanding the unconscious mind. This will also help you to understand the significance of Banfield's work. In simple terms, your unconscious mind is the part of your mind that does everything else except the things that you consciously think about. And that is a lot. It runs our body's systems while allowing us to walk (a surprisingly complex activity – ask any twelve-month-old) and chew gum at the same time (not so complex).

Indeed, it makes many more decisions in the course of a given day than we do consciously. Researchers have suggested that only around 5 to 10 per cent, or even less, of the decisions we make in a day are actually made with our conscious mind.

By making so many decisions for us, our unconscious mind frees our mind up to make conscious decisions throughout our day. And while we might like to think that these are the most important decisions in the day, I have some bad news. Decisions we make consciously are those that we would like to make – the ones we are most comfortable with, rather than the most important ones. Even more disconcertingly, our unconscious mind is way more powerful than our conscious mind, as it can do multiple tasks at the same time. In contrast, our conscious mind can only do *one* thing at a time.

While people look like they are multitasking with their conscious mind, the truth is they are quickly switching between tasks. This has been tested by looking at the brain wave attentional patterns of people who appear to be able to do two complex tasks at the same time – say, doing mathematics at the same time as playing piano. What they found was that the mind jumps quickly from one task back to the other. On the other hand, your unconscious mind is quite able to do several complex tasks at the same time.

Scientists estimate that our five senses send up to 11 million bits per second of information to the unconscious mind for processing. Our conscious mind can only process around 50 bits per second. Stop and think about that for a moment – that is a huge difference!

To use a computer analogy, our conscious mind is like the keyboard on a computer. It is nowhere near as powerful as the CPU (the brain in a computer) that equates to our unconscious. The good news is that while the keyboard is relatively under-powered, it ultimately has the ability to control what the brain of the computer does. Becoming more conscious means bringing more understanding of the forces at play, and decision making, into our conscious awareness. That is why you are reading this book.

Moreover, while we might like to think that our unconscious mind can only make simple decisions, in fact they can be decisions that require quite a lot of complex calculation and judgement. If you doubt this, think about the experience of driving a car. I could spend many hours in my office giving you a conscious, intellectual understanding of driving a car. We could go over and over it until you have it completely clear in your head. Then I could put you in a car for the first time and give you the following instructions: 'Drive up to that five-way intersection, take the second right while you sing along to the song on the radio, chew bubble-gum and wave to your friend on the opposite corner as you make your turn.'

It would be a rare person who could do that on their first drive. Our conscious mind is simply not able to attend to these different tasks *at the same time.* But after only a few years of driving, we can all do that – literally 'without thinking about it'. The difference is that, over time, our unconscious takes over more and more of these tasks, leaving our comparably puny, conscious mind to do a simple task, like wave at a friend.

Now think about the challenge of turning in front of oncoming traffic – particularly two lanes of it. It is quite a complex calculation to work out the speed of oncoming cars and your own speed as you turn in front of them. Your unconscious mind processes this data and makes a decision for you, without any difficulty, after it has had some practice.

Indeed, insurance and car rental companies know that we all become much better drivers as the years go on, because our unconscious is learning at a constant rate, so by the age of 25 we represent a much lower risk.

I remember being late for work one day and thinking, 'I will drive through this particular intersection on the yellow light, as it is such a long wait on the red.' I was distracted and my unconscious mind, very annoyingly, stopped me on the yellow light because I was not consciously in control. This was when I realised that my unconscious mind was a better driver than I am! More to the point, I want you to appreciate how my unconscious mind was actually making a decision here – without my awareness.

Three jobs

Our unconscious mind applies this power to three main jobs. It is that part of our mind that we share with every other animal on the planet. Job number one is pretty obvious. *First and foremost, keep us safe.* Staying alive comes before sustenance. There is no point in looking for dinner if you're about to *be* dinner.

Once safety is covered, then it looks to find food and water – sustenance to survive. Once that box is ticked, it looks for gratification – job two done. Nicer food, maybe alcohol rather than water, and some sex is a good day's work for one's unconscious mind. Note that both of these primary tasks are 'here and now' tasks. This is a critical point in understanding the unconscious mind. It does not look for gratification in the future, no it looks for it now, immediately.

Your unconscious mind has no concern for the future. Zip. Nada. If it can keep you alive in each successive 'now' it has had a great day/week/year. Job done.

We have to make a conscious effort to get our brains to consider the long-term implications of what we do, and the decisions we make, in our present. This is why Banfield found that a long-term view is what defines the small percentage of people who are successful. It is not the default position for human beings.

Understanding our unconscious mind's immediate focus also explains why it is that we are more concerned about what our peers, friends and family think we should do now. Being aware of what those around us want us to do is a critical part of ensuring our safety in the tribe. We cannot afford to piss off our tribe. Remember, a lone monkey is a dead monkey.

So, our unconscious mind – the most powerful part of our mind – literally has no concern for the future beyond making sure that we are safe, fed and having a good time *in the now*. It is built for immediate wellbeing, and then immediate gratification. In particular, unless very loud warning bells threaten our immediate future, our mind is built to soften these bells to a gentle tinkle … if we can hear them at all.

It is also important to appreciate that the language of our unconscious is not logical thought; it is emotion. This is simply because logical thought is too slow when our life is at risk. Our brain is designed to recognise and to respond to fear, long before we can work it out cognitively. As humans, we feel first and think second.

Ironically, emotions are also the threat. In a world relatively free of sabre-toothed tigers, or other unpleasant beasts, our mind's number one threat today are unpleasant emotions. (And the fear of rejection comes close to the top of the list!) The greater the negative emotion involved, the more our unconscious pays attention. While it is interested in positive experiences too, because its job first and foremost is to keep us safe, it is most interested in experiences that are likely to cause us some form of pain.

This ties in directly with our unconscious mind's third job, which after safety and immediate gratification, is recording all of our behavioural routines, as required, for different life situations. This starts when we are babies. There is no greater single field of information recorded than that around our interpersonal interactions and relationships.

If you bring all this together, our powerful unconscious mind spends a lot of time studying and recording how to respond to relationships from the perspective of keeping us safe. Most problematically, it learns from relationships among which we grew up; these are likely to be very, very different from the relationships that we will have as adults. We need to learn to override these automatic behaviours and recordings to come up with new strategies for our adult relationships.

In particular, our unconscious mind will keep us in familiar relationships rather than choosing to look for new ones. At the end of the day, our unconscious mind would rather keep us in the swamp where we know all the crocodiles by their first name and are familiar with where the quicksand lies. Just across the blue water, we can see a beautiful palm-fringed island with white crystal sands, but our unconscious mind will stop us from swimming across to it for fear of attack by sharks and being torn up by the coral.

Familiarity is much safer than 'new'. This is why not only do we need to fight our unconscious mind to leave unhealthy relationships, but we need to fight it to change our social and life patterns to increase our chances of meeting a healthy partner.

The problem with safety is it leads to sameness, which leads to regret, which in turn leads to unhappiness. Like drinking alcohol, staying safe feels better today, but will leave us more depressed tomorrow. *Safe is sad*. Banfield's insight essentially means that happiness and success come from doing battle with our mind's need for safety. Because its language is emotion, our unconscious mind does not get us to do this through logical argument; it simply makes us 'forget' about heading over to the beautiful palm-fringed beach or has us feel that it would be ridiculous to do so. That beach is for other people, not us. This swamp is perfectly fine, thank you very much.

Anybody who has walked into a shop saying to themselves, 'Don't buy the chocolate', and has walked out with their favourite treat, understands how this works. Emotions win over logic most of the time.

Fortunately, it is not hard to work out the programming of our unconscious mind: we just have to look at our patterns over time. Recognising our particular patterns provides important clues to how we might be holding ourselves back from a healthy and fulfilling relationship.

Every big problem was a small problem once

As we have seen, our unconscious mind actually makes decisions without our awareness. One of the ways in which it gets us to make important decisions is by encouraging us to not make a decision. It does this very simply by getting us to 'forget' – or, more technically, 'repress'.

Our unconscious mind controls where we place our attention, what we forget and what we remember. Collectively, these powers give it enormous control over us. Just think about how much power I could have over you if I could control where your attention was focused, what you remembered and what you forgot.

Let me give you an example from one of my patients, in terms of how our unconscious mind can make major decisions for us in this way. Let us call her Tina. Tina worked in administration at a nearby university and was wanting to move into a research assistant role. A friend of hers gave her the name of a professor who was looking for a research assistant and paved the way for her by giving her a good rap. She handed Tina a piece of paper with his name and number on it, with the warning that she needed to call him within a week as he wanted to hire somebody quickly. When they next met, she asked my patient how it had gone. Tina responded, 'Oh my god – I completely forgot about it!' By then it was too late.

In therapy, Tina worked out that there was a part of her that felt that she did not deserve to work in an academic space. Despite her university degree, she didn't feel she was smart enough and so her unconscious mind kept her safe from the risk of failure.

Our unconscious mind will often make us 'forget' more important things that we would expect to remember because there is some aspect of the thing that makes us uncomfortable. We all do this. Think about tasks on your 'to-do' list that you seem to keep forgetting to deal with. Typically, they will be the harder jobs, or maybe those that involve us having to deal with someone that could lead to conflict. Your unconscious mind thinks it is helping you by getting you to avoid the task.

Banfield's brilliant insight is that those of us who are best at overcoming the unconscious mind's preference to not look at the future consequences of our actions will do best at life. Indeed, it is knowing the longer term consequence that pushes a task onto our to-do list in the first place.

Every big problem was a small problem once. If this is true (and it is), then you can see how your unconscious mind can happily turn small problems into big ones – just by getting you to not deal with them.

In the sabre-toothed tiger-deficient world we now inhabit, the unconscious mind generally keeps us safe by continuing to do what we are already doing. The devil you do know is safer than the devil you don't.

You can see how this powerful process applies to continuing in unhealthy relationships.

Better the devil you are dating ...

Every big hurt was a small hurt once.

I want to finish with eight words that are perhaps the most profound eight words I have come across. They also marry perfectly with Banfield's insight.

Easy choices, hard life;

Hard choices, easy life.

These are unsettling words if you sit with their sagacious symmetry. To know they were spoken by an alcoholic, Jerzy Gregorek, who went on to win four world weightlifting championships, gives them real ... weight.

Just remember, while you make easy choices in the here and now, essentially by letting your unconscious rule, you are lining up for a hard life. Now there's a long-term view to look out over. And it's not just who we choose to have as a partner. These principles apply to who we choose as friends and business partners.

In the next chapter, we will look at research exploring how this tendency to avoid decisions plays out in relationships.

Sliding versus deciding: Chaining ourselves together one link at a time

GBW and JBW

> In any moment of decision, the best thing you can do is the right thing, the next best thing is the wrong thing, and the worst thing you can do is nothing.
>
> – Theodore Roosevelt

> If you could kick the person in the pants responsible for most of your trouble, you wouldn't sit for a month.
>
> – Theodore Roosevelt

Perhaps one of the biggest reasons why we don't always make the best decision when it comes to partnering is that we spend too long in unhealthy relationships.

The decade between the ages of 18 and 28 is a critical part of the life cycle, with specific developmental tasks. It is a decade of experimentation when it comes to both careers and relationships. First, as Jiveny has nicely highlighted, it is a time to define ourselves through singledom. Then it is a time for us to experience different relationships so we can become clearer about not just what it is that we want from a relationship and a partner, but also how to be in, and bring our best self to, a relationship.

Clearly, you cannot complete this developmental task if you only have one or two long-term relationships during this decade. Ideally, we want to have several very different relationships that last somewhere between six months and 24 months.

We are certainly not talking about having as many partners as you can. If you allow for a few months between relationships to get over them, reflect on them and grow, over this decade people typically have between three and six significant, at least medium-term, relationships. One or two of them may be live-in relationships.

In the last chapter, we explained how our unconscious mind will keep us on a familiar path because it feels safer. Better the devil you are dating ... As our social structure and culture change this is becoming even more of a problem.

Sliding through milestones towards a worse marriage

In a report sponsored by the National Marriage Project, titled 'Before "I Do"', Galena Rhoades and Scott Stanley outlined some of the key cultural shifts that have changed the way people approach dating and relationships today. In the past, marriage was considered a very intentional decision, which usually came before cohabitation and having children. According to this report, the sequence has now reversed, with a society-shifting 90 per cent of couples having sex, and 75 per cent living together, before marriage. In addition, approximately four out of ten babies are born to unmarried parents.

'This relationship sequence – with sex, cohabitation, and sometimes children preceding marriage – has become the norm in our society. But it raises some interesting questions,' comment Stanley and Rhoades.

'Sliding versus deciding' is a theme that came up again and again throughout their findings; it points to a concerning trend as more and more couples enter relationships by default rather than as a result of conscious choice.

'Relationships go through various important milestones – like having sex for the first time, moving in together, getting engaged, getting married and having children. Each transition involves consequential decisions: Do we move in together after we're engaged or before, or do we wait until after we marry? Do we have kids before we get married or after? Do we want to have a wedding or elope?'

Stanley and Rhoades highlight that:

How couples handle these choices seems to matter. Some make definitive decisions that move them from one stage of a relationship to another. Others are less intentional. Rather than consciously deciding how and when to transition to the next stage of the relationship, they slide through milestones without prior planning.

Which brings us to the kicker finding in their research: 'Our findings show that couples who slide through their relationship transitions have poorer marital quality than those who make intentional decisions about major milestones.' The danger here is that couples slide into marriage (and parenthood) mostly because it appears to be a reasonable and natural progression.

To better understand this, let's drill down on one particular study by Rhoades, Stanley and Markman – you will appreciate its relevance by its title, 'Should I Stay or Should I Go?'[3]

What made this study so informative was that most prior research had been done on both de facto as well as formally married couples. Unfortunately, there has been much less research into romantically involved, unmarried couples in the early stages of a relationship. It is these early relationship stages that are so critical to understanding why people are happily together, or unhappily divorcing, a decade or two later.

In a large study of nearly 1200 people, Rhoades and her colleagues looked at what factors, from early in the relationship, made it more likely that they would continue as a couple. What kept them together? Was it how much they loved each other?

Only to a degree. Yes, commitment to the relationship was one indicator of relationship stability; however, the other factors that kept people in a relationship were nowhere near as romantic – indeed, they were somewhat concerning.

Before we dive into these findings we need to unpack the underpinnings of this kind of research. Unsurprisingly, research has found that there are both positive and negative forces that keep people together. The negative ones can be grouped under two headings – 'constraints' and 'investments'. Let's start with the core positive force.

What makes a relationship a true relationship goes beyond feelings of being attracted to your partner. It is when we back it up with a degree of commitment, or dedication, to the relationship, not just in the present, but also as a probability in the future. It is about having a clear sense of being a 'couple' rather than two separate individuals in a relationship. A dedication to the relationship is about making the all-important shift from 'me' to 'us' to find out if the relationship has potential.

Chaining ourselves together

After the positive forces of attraction, we have the negative forces that hold relationships together. These are the things in a relationship that sit on the other side of the equation. They make it harder to leave as they chain us together. The more chains holding us back, the harder it is to leave. These are the 'constraints' on leaving. For example, the moment a couple move in together and they have no alternative home to go back to, they have created a constraint. Constraints make it harder to exit a relationship.

Then there is the third and final group of factors at work, which make up this triangle of forces that progressively trap us in a relationship: our 'investments'. These could be both tangible investments, such as setting up a joint bank account, and intangible investments, such as disclosing our sexual proclivities and having our partner still accept us anyway.

It was these constraints and investments – the negative forces that chain people together – that most interested Rhoades and her co-researchers.

So what were the most common ones? Here is a list of the things that gently slid couples down a slippery slope of greater engagement:

- signing a rental lease
- paying for each other's credit cards
- sharing a debt
- having a pet
- having paid for future vacations
- making home improvements together
- owning a house together
- having a joint bank account.

Some of these, like paying for a holiday, are links in larger chains. Others, like buying a house, are chains in their own right. The actions that sit behind each of these chains are often undertaken without careful thought to their long-term implications. The more constraints and investments, the harder it is to leave – even when it starts to appear that the match is not a good one. Stanley and colleagues described it in this way:

> Constraints creep up on cohabiting couples, creating an inertia that favours relationship continuance regardless of the quality of the match between partners, which in turn reduces options and alternatives before partners realise it.

The key words here are 'before partners realise it'. It's the old boiling a frog metaphor. Drop Kermit into boiling water and he jumps out. But put our friendly, green ectotherm into a pot of comfortable spa-warm water, then gradually heat it and, so the theory goes, he doesn't see his early demise coming and happily enjoys his bubble bath until ... well frog legs will be served momentarily.

Couples allow one thing to lead to another until they are well chained and invested in a relationship and then ... the baby. The greatest chain of all.

We cannot even begin to apply Banfield's long-term view to decision making, if we don't first realise when we are making (or not making) critical decisions as we wander along our relationship journey.

But first we need to step back and look at how we are attracted to each other in the first place.

Matchmaking in the twenty-first century: The psychology of attraction

GBW

A good way to get to know your date is to ask about their first pet, favorite movie & mom's maiden name, then login & read all their emails.

– Christopher Hudspeth

We girls complain about guys using us for sex, but sex is awesome! Start bitching when he uses you for laundry, or as a human shield.

– Stephanie McMaster

Chris Wainhouse, a particularly masculine male comedian gives us a joke that nicely illustrates the perils of meeting online. 'Let me tell you a bit about myself. I'm a tall girl. Yes, I'm very beautiful with large, perky breasts. At least that's what I told Peter, my online boyfriend in Canada. I can't wait to see his face when he comes over in June to marry me. He says he has a good sense of humour … we'll see!'

While how we meet is changing dramatically; how attraction works, not so much. Attraction is built on a DNA-laden psyche and how it evolves from birth. While there are many paths it can go down, the underlying principles are relatively stable. Nevertheless, let's start with what is changing.

More than any other development in the history of human beings, online dating has radically transformed how we meet potential partners. Back in 2013, I attended my first iDating conference – it was a decidedly unusual beast. I have attended many medical conferences and even more relationship therapy seminars since qualifying as a psychiatrist, but this event was a totally different planet. Maybe what gave it away was the delegates' mud-wrestling activity from 10.00 pm until midnight. I cannot recall seeing that on an Advances in Modern Medicine conference program! Where was it held? Las Vegas of course! The real eye-opener, however, was the sheer magnitude of the dating machine of the twenty-first century. Dating coaches, matchmakers, online dating sites and myriad companies marketing to 'that' target market – the single human – were in abundance.

We now all recognise that, with the increased use of mainstream apps, online dating is no longer for 'losers and nerds' (the response I got for many years when I would suggest it to my patients). I was surprised to learn, among many things, that way back in 2009, social sub-groups got the power of this machine with 61 per cent of same-sex couples finding their partner online.

At the conference, there were sessions on all aspects of the dating process. From New York we heard about how a dating coach would stalk his client and eavesdrop (literally!) on his date to give him feedback; from Los Angeles we heard of how a makeover team would style, dress and groom you to within an inch of your inner magnificence; from three young 'iDaters' living in Las Vegas, we heard how they would not look at a possible date if there was no photo – a message that came up again and again. The world believes that appearance is King.

It was at this conference that I met Julie Ferman, professional matchmaker. How professional? Oh, about US$15,000 for-just-a-handful-of-dates-no-guarantee-of-success professional! She is one of the world's small group of elite, highly paid professional matchmakers. Where's she from, where's that market? The city of angels, LA, of course! She is, indeed, a kind of angel.

My knowledge of matchmakers was so limited that my only reference point was a musical from my childhood. My parents loved *Fiddler on the Roof* so much that my mother bought the vinyl album (yep, that's how far back we're going). Set at the very beginning of the 1900s, before cars arrived to usurp horses in this tiny town in eastern Europe, the movie tells the story of a Jewish family with five daughters of, and approaching, marriageable age.

The village matchmaker, Yente, looked at this family and saw a nice little earner for some years to come! You can guess where it goes. Little does our matchmaker realise, but she and her ilk are about to become a whole lot less busy. The battle for love-based marriages is about to begin.

Around a century after Yente and her colleagues joined the unemployment queues, Julie and hers were riding a resurgence of the craft. Julie has been matchmaking for twenty-plus years. In her early fifties, she is an energetic, cheerful, attractive voice of clarity in this over-hyped space. Julie is also a self-confessed, incorrigible flirt, which makes her a great match for her own work. In her flirting, she is modelling to her clients this key skill in dating.

It is a few years since anyone greeted me with a bright, twinkle-in-the-eye 'Hello Handsome!' on our second meeting, but for Julie her flirtatiousness is her calling card. Her green eyes sparkle with an intelligent desire to connect and explore ideas. She is unaffected, fun and engaging. She opens a later email to me with, 'You are too cute' – many could not get away with it, but Julie is a natural. (And, yes she had already met my wife – we had interviewed her together!)

Her flirting is often how she finds clients. Men are attracted to this energy and when she drops in that she is married, she then smoothly follows with, 'Now, let me find you someone who isn't!'

As Julie answered my questions about her work, she told me how, unlike many of her peers, she takes on female clients. If you reacted to that statement, so did I. Would not all matchmakers take on female clients? Was that not half the business?

Nope.

'Female clients are much more difficult, so many of my colleagues only want to work for the men,' she explained. 'Women are more likely to complain, write critical reviews, want refunds and want to sue you much more often when you do not find them their perfect match. They take it much more personally than men do. So, I do take on women – but I charge them more.'

I had to ask the obvious question, 'How much more?'

'Oh, around [US]$5000 more.'

Hmmm, a 30 per cent premium for the female factor.

Maybe it was an American thing?

She continued, 'The men are much more straightforward and generally clearer in what they want.'

Maybe she was saying that we blokes are simple. I'm fine with that. Hey, we blokes have to leave room in our heads to think about important things, like cars and football, not to mention complex matters like the impact of boutique beers on our drinking heritage. Maybe it isn't an American thing – except for the suing.

[I would agree, we men are less complicated when it comes to the mating game. Unfortunately, we make up for this though by being less communicative, and often less able to express more complex emotional issues, making it harder for our partners to work out where we are at.]

She continued: 'Men increase in their romantic value as they age.'

This was not a term I had heard before. As it turns out, there is a spectrum of romantic value (RV), with the sexually inexperienced, awkward nerd at twenty carrying the lowest RV. At the other end of the spectrum, we have the greying, but fit, 50-year-old chairman of the board – the equivalent of the silver-back gorilla (who may well have been the awkward nerd of twenty).

Julie said: 'A woman's RV to a man, typically but not always – these are big generalisations – sits around her capacity to be sweet, loving, kind and attractive, and typically peaks at a younger age.'

Refreshingly, Julie was not concerned with political correctness; she was just telling us how it works in the weird and wonderful world of high-end matchmaking.

Before any older woman reading this feels too discouraged, there is good news here. As Julie went on to explain, while a man's RV increases with age and a woman's decreases, it is easier for a woman to get in touch with being more caring and loving, and to make herself more attractive, than it is for an older man to make himself more successful.

This reminded me of research by John T. Molloy on why men marry certain women. (We will revisit his research later in more detail.) By interviewing men and women who marry over the age of 40, he found that men were attracted to women who took care of themselves, presented well and were socially skilled. To be clear, it was not how beautiful they were, it was more about how much they took care of themselves. Which any woman can do. I believe the power of this comes from it sending the message, 'I care about myself and I will care for you too.' Caring is central to loving. Importantly, while how beautiful you are (however that is defined!) is not under your control, how much you care about yourself is.

Typically, after a phase of dating much younger women, they actually married women much closer to their own age. A particularly important point was that these women allowed their caring side to emerge. Many older men said they married women aged over 40 because they had demonstrated their capacity for kindness in one way or another (e.g. when they had the flu).

In short, older women can increase their RV in ways that are more difficult for men. (Interestingly, Molloy found that men increased their RV through their preparedness to accept feedback from these older women on how to present and function socially.)

I was not surprised when Julie explained:

A majority of the successful men I work with want, as one of my clients put it succinctly, to come home to 'a soft, warm landing'.

My high-powered, successful female clients want the same thing. They want to come home to a supportive, caring husband, but then they will want their partner to be independently successful and strong too, which makes for a confusing message.

And then while these women want to come home to their soft landing, they do not want to give it. It is as if they see it as weakness, or subservience to be warm and caring.

Balls can be helpful on a woman in the board room, but not so much for greeting you as you walk in the front door, and certainly not in the bedroom! As this problem becomes obvious to the male client, I'll get the 'I won't be seeing her again' call.

So I am often counselling women on how appreciating and responding to a partner's needs does not have to impact on their own sense of self. A soft landing will leave us with more respect for the pilot of the plane, not less!

And then, of course, we have the women who lose their identity as they try to be what they think their partner wants – which is just as big a problem.

Did I mention that Julie breaks it off for her clients too? It's not just about saving her client the discomfort. Asking 'Why?' gives Julie valuable intel into what went wrong and while she garners this valuable feedback, she will then make a decision about how helpful it is to pass on to her client. There is no point passing on feedback about things you can't change, like being too short or not smart enough. Nor will she pass on feedback to change something that Julie knows is a peculiar issue for the individual offering the feedback and not helpful to her client:

There is no space in my work for what is right or wrong in a person, just what works between a man and a woman to make the match. Even the women who do not want to create a soft landing for their partner, who don't want to change anything about themselves, can find a match, but they will have a smaller pool to fish in and it will take longer.

And of course, time here equals significant dollars. After a couple of decades of working in her craft, Julie brings a pragmatism that cannot be ignored. Which was what made her next point so intriguing.

The wrong look

I asked Julie about how important photographs were in her work. At this point, she dropped a small bombshell – something I have waited so long to hear that I had abandoned all hope.

This is what she said: 'I never show either party a photograph of the other before they meet.'

What!? This did not make sense in a world where looks rule. Didn't she listen to those three Las Vegas iDaters?! 'But sometimes they must want to see a photo?' I pushed.

'I require them to trust my judgement. They know I have taken the time to work out what they're looking for and they just need to let me do my job. Photographs get in the way of the process.'

Hold the phone!

'Photographs get in the way of the process?' I repeated as I leaned in. Julie replied:

> I have to find a partner that has the kind of look that my client is looking for, particularly the men. There's no point introducing them to a blonde with large breasts when they prefer a brunette with smaller breasts. I listen carefully and get the big-ticket items right, but looks are not what real attraction is about. As I said, photographs get in the way of the process.

What was 'the process' to which Julie was referring? As I drilled down further on the issue with her, what she said aligned with a truth that I have seen in my clinical work.

People think they know what they are attracted to, but too often it is a construct, an illusion, that is either not their own or, if it is, it is what they *think* they want. Often the person they find themselves most attracted to is quite different.

As she held fast and wisely refused to allow her clients to look at a photo before they met, Julie prevented them from putting too much weight on physical appearance. She knows from experience that this can screw up the best laid matchmaking plans. The truth is that while people think physical appearance is important, it is much less so than people think. *The greatest crime ever committed on single people is the belief that attraction is first and foremost about looks.* In the online world, this translates to one word: 'photo'.

Let's go back to 'the process' to which Julie was referring. I could see she had a clear sense of something at work that was quite different from how most lay people think of attraction. To understand the nature of this dynamic, we need to take a step back and look at the psychology of attraction. How do our minds work when it comes to what we see, or don't see, in potential partners?

The psychology of attraction

An awareness of many aspects of human psychology has filtered down to the general population, but not so much with the psychology of attraction. So let's dive in here.

Let's start by looking at the early theories around how attractiveness works: what are called the 'matching' and 'assortative mating' theories. In a nutshell, we are attracted to a partner of similar ranking. First and foremost, as a general rule of thumb, good-looking people match to equally good-looking people. Then, once looks are in order, educated people and those with a similar socio-economic standing will find each other attractive. Non-smokers and gym junkies will hook up, while short, balding, fat, unattractive, financially challenged men and rich supermodels should, theoretically, not.

This way of seeing attraction is inherently ... dare I say it ... attractive. When I was aged ten, we all decided to rank the boys and the girls in my class in order of attractiveness. We then matched them up such that the number one boy got the number one girl, the number two boy the number two girl and so on. Of course, out of almost 30 kids only the first two, or maybe four (myself not included) gained any satisfaction from the arrangement. Tellingly, hardly any of us went on to marry our 'ranked' partner!

These theories did allow for a little complexity, such that younger women are attracted to older men – the silverback gorillas who can bring home more than their fair share of the kill. Correspondingly, older men are attracted to younger, apparently fertile women with clear skin and obvious breastfeeding capacity who can continue their lineage.

In essence, if you are up with what our advertising industry defines as attractive, you are up to date on these theories. Advertisers love these theories because they can now sell you things that will improve your looks and your status, and thereby your attractiveness. Accordingly, dating sites match people up on looks and similarities. Photos are a must.

When university students are studied, they generally find that they select potential partners in this way i.e. based on aligned rankings. Many studies of this kind proved that matching theory does explain why a student will choose a particular student as a date. Put photos of the opposite sex, along with some brief bio information, in front of a student and ask them who they are attracted to and voila – matching theory is confirmed.

The better-looking people pick the better-looking photos. Even the better-designed prospective studies, which follow a student's behaviour so it does not rely on their memory or what they think they would do, found the same thing. Physical appearance accounts for a lot.

We need to hope that matching and assortative mating theories are flawed; otherwise, people with beautiful minds and souls but no Hollywood-defined good looks to match will be relegated to life's crappier partners and lifelong unhappy relationships. Fortunately, there appear to be some critical glitches in these theories.

Speed-dating research shows that who people choose to date in real life has little correlation with who they would have picked from photos. It is simple research. They get people to choose who they would like to date from photographs, then they introduce them through speed dating. They choose quite differently. In real life there is a different force at work which determines who people are attracted to. It is not about looks. There is something more at work here.

As Julie says, *photographs get in the way of the process.*

Matching theory debunked

As you might have guessed, most of the research into matching and assortative mating theories was done on university students and looked at *who they thought they would be attracted to, not who they were attracted to in real life.* The speed dating research exposes the flaw.

But there is one key insight that follows from these theories. They explain how younger people negotiate attraction. Teenagers and young adults, who have yet to trust their own developing judgement, look to their peers for validation of their partner choice. This is why we find that 'social status' is core to these theories from research done on young people. When you do not trust your own judgement, you turn to what is socially defined. While eighteen-year-olds will 'find' someone attractive based on what their peers find attractive, this is much less the mechanism at work at 28, and rarely at 38.

Yes, it follows that if you see a 45-year-old man clearly choosing a 'trophy wife' twenty years his junior, he has not matured and is still operating from a playbook that was designed for teenagers. We are also looking at one of the contributors to why divorce is much higher when people marry young. They have chosen a partner based on what society defines as attractive rather than what they themselves find genuinely attractive.

With this in mind, let us return to my discussion with Julie Ferman and the small bombshell she dropped towards the end of our interview: 'I never show either party a photograph of the other before they meet.'

Julie could see that we are attracted to a person's 'gestalt'. This German word refers to 'an entity's complete form', which is more than the sum of its parts. In our current context, it means that people are attracted to everything that makes up the person *in combination*, not just their face or their body. It is about seeing one's wholeness.

Your personality, how happy or sad you are, your energy level, your optimism – these are all critical elements that, together with your physical appearance, create your 'attraction gestalt'.

Because one's attraction gestalt is much more difficult to define, people and researchers – who very much need to quantify things – focus on the components of attraction that are the most quantifiable, such as looks. In real life, however, it is not so much about how a partner looks, but how they make us 'feel'.

How someone makes us feel when we are with them is a function of *all* of them – their attraction gestalt. How good the person on our arm looks gives us social standing, *but nothing could be more irrelevant to a happy long-term relationship.*

Eleanor Roosevelt, the longest serving First Lady of the United States, and 'First Lady of the World' (a tribute to her human rights achievements) had something to say on this matter. She was well qualified as she grew up being recurrently reminded of, as she said, 'being without beauty' in her autobiography of 1961. Her beautiful mother repeatedly highlighted Eleanor's 'plainness' and openly called her the truly cruel nickname of 'Granny', such that she 'wanted to sink through the floor in shame'.

As a young woman, well before her fame, she wrote an essay entitled 'Loyalty and Friendship'. She proposed that, 'It may seem strange but no matter how plain a woman may be if truth and loyalty are stamped upon her face all will be attracted to her and she will do good to all who come near her and those who know her will always love her for they will feel her loyal spirit and have confidence in her.' A lack of commas and a very long sentence aside, she became living evidence of this salutary truth.

While one is drawn to beauty, one stays for character.

Valuing beauty above all has become socially instilled in us from a young age. The job is to grow out of this too-common thinking. As we mature, we slowly but surely need to build our own personal views of what we want in a partner. *Indeed, the decade between 18 and 28 is the time to experience enough different relationships so you can accumulate this knowledge about what you want in a partner's character.* Equally, it is a time for you to experience enough relationships so you can work out how to bring the best '*You*' to a relationship and be the best partner you can be.

Unfortunately, in an online world, we cannot get around the emphasis on the image – the photo – as the total summation of you. We can use this to our advantage. Have the photograph share something about who you are rather than just what you look like. If you're an outdoors person take a photograph of you out bushwalking in some hard to reach place. Be true to yourself. Do not put up a photograph of you with a puppy if you are not a dog lover!

How can the research behind the assortative and matching theories be so wrong? At medical school, we were taught to start a critical analysis of a research study by looking closely at the sampling method. Any researcher knows that if you get the sample 'right', you can prove almost anything you want. For example, if you want to show that your new psychotherapy technique works, it is easy. Choose people for your study who are emotionally intelligent and committed to change. Better still, in the name of 'study purity', exclude people with annoying accompanying problems like alcohol abuse or a personality disorder. This problem is called 'sampling bias'. Asking university students how they work out who is attractive took us down the wrong path from the start.

When we look at the research into what makes a couple happy in longer term relationships, we find that physical appearance is much less important. If I was to summarise this research, the longer the relationship, the more it becomes apparent that how your partner makes you feel is way more important than how they look. In a study I found fascinating – because my wife and I agreed that we both did this – it was found that couples do not see each other as they are. When they think of their partner, their mind's eye sees them as how they were when they were much younger – how they looked when they fell in love.

This finding means that we will not appreciate our partner's ageing as much as we might expect. In our mind's eye we will see the version of them we were initially attracted to – their whole gestalt.

A 2012 survey, commissioned by Medicis Aesthetics, polled over 1000 men and women to get a detailed insight into the role physical attraction plays in long-term relationships. The most important finding for me was that concerns over a partner's ageing appearance are highest among couples whose relationships are experienced as unsuccessful. This might suggest that as people lose their looks, their relationship goes downhill. No. If this happened there would be no happy older folks! In truth, it tells us that people who have not matured beyond a focus on the superficiality of looks are less able to build successful relationships. As the partners age, the flimsy foundations of the relationship are exposed.

This is exactly what I have seen in my clinical practice. Your partner can be the most gorgeous Playboy model on the planet, but if she repeatedly makes you feel like shit, no matter how great she looks, you will not be able to stand the sight of her. Not terribly surprisingly, it is the same for women married to the handsome, self-centred, gym-addicted executive.

Maybe you have tried selecting a partner based on them being one of the 'beautiful people'. If you are reading this, then it would appear that this went the way of most relationships built on problematic foundations! The good news is that once we grow out of choosing partners the way teenagers do, the divorce rate goes down.

However, if matching and assortative mating theories don't explain attraction, at least in more mature folks, and it is more about the feeling a partner gives us – the attraction gestalt – then how does that work? Let's dig a little deeper.

Imago theory: How attraction really works

JBW

> When we meet an Imago match, that chemical reaction
> occurs, and love ignites. All other bets, all other ideas
> about what we want in a mate, are off. We feel alive and
> whole, confident that we have met the person who will
> make everything all right.
>
> — **Harville Hendrix,** *Getting the Love You Want*[4]

Love is claimed by some to be the most powerful thing in the
universe; it's 'what the world needs now', it's 'all you need', it's
'the answer'. However, love is a complicated beast. Attraction,
excitement, reliability, familiarity – all these and more have
described love in action, yet the fundamental processes that
drive the course of romantic love can be quite paradoxical.

Over the years, therapists and researchers have created a
number of models that assist in making sense of the process
of attraction. These help us to understand why certain people
come together and why some relationships work out and
others do not. The various models have related foundations,
so that no one person can claim total ownership of this space.

However, one of the clearest, most sophisticated therapists and writers in this space is Harville Hendrix PhD. (While he has written a number of books, the interested reader should start with *Getting the Love You Want*.)

Imago theory

The beauty of Hendrix's model, on which he and his partner, Helen Hunt PhD, collaborated, is that it explains why we have a tendency to choose partners who will inevitably challenge and upset us to varying degrees.

In a nutshell, Hendrix reminds us of how we are all born into this world as a vulnerable infant. In this innocent and defenceless state, we are influenced and programmed by the love and attention of our caregivers whom we must rely on to survive. Unconsciously, from the moment we are born, we begin to create an internal 'map of love' based on what we experience love to feel, look and sound like, and what we need to do in order to receive 'love' and attention.

Growing up, our primary caregivers (usually parents, but could be grandparents, aunts or older siblings) play huge roles in building our 'maps of love' – so much so that these relationships become the model of behaviour we seek in our future relationships. From an early age we enter a dance of sorts, where we try different behaviours to elicit more care and less negative reactions from those caring for us. Indeed, this task dominates early childhood.

As we continue to grow up, we build an 'Imago' that records both the positive and negative aspects of how we experienced 'love' throughout our childhood. The pleasure and the pain. The nurturing and the toxic. The healthy and the dysfunctional, along with our role in triggering these and other emotions. These patterns of relating also tend to get passed down from generation to generation, unless consciously addressed and healed. For better or worse, we learn to equate 'love' with what feels familiar and in alignment with our early experiences of relating.

This means that many people do not have a very healthy foundation for understanding how true love feels to begin with. In many cases, our internal maps can be based on a version of love built upon very difficult terrain. When habits of dysfunction are passed down from our caregivers, it leads us to believe that dysfunctional behaviour is a normal part of what love entails. Unfortunately, without the experience of healthier love, it can be difficult to know what else to look for.

In addition to our family life, as we grow up we inevitably get wounded in different ways. For example, being left out or bullied by our peers at school leaves its mark and also gets imprinted onto our map of love.

In an effort to protect ourselves from these hurts again, we often unconsciously create different strategies – guards and defences – to keep our heart safe. And while these strategies might have helped us avoid more hurt in our youth, as adults these same strategies can actually get in the way of us experiencing healthy love. Paradoxically, our unconscious mind tends to seek out partners who will recreate some of the most familiar and often painful scenarios of our childhood.

Why would it do this? Our mind, like our body, has inbuilt healing mechanisms. We know surprisingly quickly after meeting someone whether or not they can love us (and potentially hurt us) in a way that is familiar to us. When we find out they can, we are often drawn to them. Our unconscious hope is that we will recreate the loving space we experienced in our infancy with a romantic partner who exhibits the best – and the worst – traits of the people who raised us.

As irrational as it might seem, we often invite people into our inner circle who could really hurt us. We often feel that this time 'it will be different', as we are now an older, potentially wiser and more capable human being. *This time* we will get them to love us and cherish us in the ways we always wanted – in the ways that did not happen the first time around. And, if we succeed in this mission, we will be healed, finally.

This is why we are often most attracted to people who are likely to challenge, hurt and trigger us in similar ways – because they embody the most challenging attributes of our caregivers, which also feels familiar to us. We are drawn to these people in part because we know how to 'fit in' with them.

This entire process happens unconsciously. Unwittingly we will consciously think we are drawn to someone because of their blue eyes or their 'great sense of humour' while these forces work away in the background leaving us feeling drawn to the other. This familiarity is what leaves us with a sense we have known the other for years, only days into a relationship.

Attraction driven by familiarity and the promise of healing is not a good thing. It can mean we are too comfortable around the bad behaviour with which we grew up. Our warning bells might not ring. Red flags may be ignored. It can also mean that we line up to help people who cannot be helped. Remember that personal change must be driven by the self – no amount of good intention can make someone change who is not motivated to do so.

One common example of Imago theory at work is when a woman, who grew up with an alcoholic father, goes on to marry an alcoholic. The red flags do not deter her as the sense of familiarity outweighs them. Instead, she focuses on his potential and tells herself he will change for her. Slowly but surely, the relationship turns to shit as he does not realise that he is supposed to be saved, make the most of this fabulous opportunity and then live happily ever after. Unfortunately, he has no motivation to give up the booze as this was not what he signed up for.

A particular fallacy of this strategy is that in such moments of confrontation with our Imago playing out, we often regress into the same childhood state we were in at the time of wounding. In this regressed state, we cannot access adult tools to help us heal or take the relationship in a healthier direction. So, our woman married to an alcoholic has no capacity to influence her husband in a healthy way. Indeed, her anger at her father is more likely to rise up and push him further towards the booze. This is how toxic patterns of relating transpire and tend to repeat themselves until the lesson is learned, or not – or people give up on relationships all together.

Building on Hendrix's philosophy, my father and I have often discussed the delusion of modern society: how we glorify the feelings of intoxication and infatuation, sending us searching for a strong sense of chemistry from the first date, hunting for a fire when all we need is a flame. So often, this lustful search for love can result in a short and painful affair, with disappointment quickly replacing hope.

Why is this a familiar and damaging pattern? Because greater attraction often comes with a greater capacity to cause pain.

Beware the nines and tens: All we need is a flame

Consider attraction on a scale of one to ten, with one representing a complete lack of attraction and ten signifying overwhelming chemistry. Many people launch into the dating world seeking the nines and tens; these are the people who inspire intense passion and lust, and get us inebriated on the fantasy of an idyllic future.

As we have discussed, the reason we feel so strongly towards these people is because they feel familiar and dangle the promise of healing under our noses with every kiss. The problem is that we often mistake this familiarity for 'romantic destiny' and jump to wild conclusions in the process. The most dangerous belief of all is that the intense attraction of a nine or a ten will give us our 'happily ever after'. With these passion-driven, rose-tinted glasses on, we have a tendency to ignore the red flags and warning signs and may unwittingly sign up to a challenging future of extreme ups and downs.

Here is the thing about nines and tens . . . Yes, they represent an opportunity for self-healing. But they also rate so highly *because they have the greatest capacity to treat us in the worst possible way*. In fact, nines and tens tend to carry high levels of the traits that caused us the most pain in our formative years. Still, it is our unconscious hope that they will bring about our deepest healing – which brings us to the rub ... *Unless both people are getting therapy or are unusually self-aware and uncommonly good at personal growth and self-healing, there is nothing that will stop them from simply playing out the problematic pattern again*. The intensity of attraction means that we tend to jump into bed quickly with them. With passion overcoming reason, we often speed into a relationship that would better have been avoided.

How often have you been intensely attracted to someone who makes themselves unavailable to you? This is a common dynamic because it is not infrequent to grow up with a parent who was not there for us when we needed them. As much as our parents might love us, they have a life too, which means they will inevitably not be there for us at some critical times. If a parent was particularly unavailable, for whatever reason, these experiences can leave us drawn to people who will not be there for us – which I am sure you can agree is not a good thing.

With the nines and tens you are playing with fire. Remember, all you need is a flame – a raging blaze we can do without.

The slow burn

A safer and more reliable method when looking for a mate is to aim for a slow burn. Using the scale of attraction mentioned above, a six, seven or eight (in terms of initial attraction) can often be a better choice in the long term.

In the range from six to eight, there is enough to keep us coming back for more without losing our better judgement along the way. Our head is in the game and we can identify dysfunctional behaviours before we get too involved. This also allows us to really get to know the person in whom we are interested in, without projecting a fantasy upon someone who is driving us wild.

Generally, a seven is the sweet spot, as some eights can be too close to the problematic level. Consider an eight if they are unusually self-aware and interested in personal growth. Move on if they are not.

And you want to know the good news? Aiming for a six, seven or maybe an eight, does not necessarily mean sacrificing the highs of lust and passion in the long run. In fact, many couples who start with a slow burn report reaching similarly high levels of passion down the road as they wholeheartedly fall in love with their partner. Indeed, we will see this happening when we look at the research into arranged marriages.

Ultimately, with self-awareness comes choice. Without understanding how attraction works, we are its slave. Once we understand our patterns and become aware of what our nines and tens look like, we can avoid them. Think back over your life. Who were the nines and tens for you? What was the pattern? What did they have in common?

We *can* update our map of love to reflect a healthier model of relating by reflecting on our dating history and learning these lessons now. The trick is to remain open to dating the sixes, sevens and maybe even some eights as you build on that slow burn.

There's a few more than 'the one': 350,000 potential partners

GBW

> [In the 1960s] People were willing to leave if they were unhappy. Today people leave if they can be happier. This notion that we deserve and we are entitled and we must be happy on earth is part of the perfection [story] … I would urge people that today it's less about finding the right person and more about being the right person.
>
> – Esther Perel

Writing a book is a great way to clarify one's thinking. Sometimes it shifts it dramatically. Researching and writing this chapter (and a later one in which I interview two Pakistani men about their arranged marriages) consolidated a shift in my mind with which I have flirted for some time.

I have always been struck by how people who have been happily married for decades met after dating a handful of people and then married a workmate or a friend of a friend. In hospitals I watched doctors marry nurses with whom they worked closely. I married a psychologist in the unit I worked on. Maybe the universe organises partners we can be happy with to be in our immediate vicinity. Or maybe there is something completely different at work. This chapter will explore this proposition.

Earlier, we spoke about romantic destiny and how our society has fallen in love with the idea of 'the one' – that special person who will make you blissfully happy forever – without much effort on our part. Both men and women will ask their friend after a new date, 'Do you think he/she is "the one"?'

As we have touched on, the concept of 'the one' is incredibly seductive. Nothing could be simpler. You do not have to think or evaluate once you find 'the one', because there is no other competition. Just one soulmate each, and once you find them you are set for life. Friends are less likely to ask you, 'Do you think he is one of your potential soulmates?' If you can just find your one and only soulmate, things will go swimmingly. This is the real promise behind the soulmate conceptualisation.

It is always helpful to understand where ideas that pervade our culture, and exert such a hold over us, come from and if they still hold value for us.

The origins of the seductive soulmate myth

You do not have to look too far to appreciate the metaphysical premise of the soulmate – the name gives it away. It is not a 'sole' mate – that is, a single mate. No, we are talking about a meeting of 'souls'. We are talking about a concept that is as deeply embedded in the metaphysical as the concept of God. Indeed, it is fascinating that such a profoundly spiritual concept has embedded itself in our culture to such an extent that even committed atheists will happily use the word in discussion.

If we do not see it as a religious or spiritual concept, then it becomes a magical concept, because what underpins it is a process that suggests that, as we wander through life, we will just happen across 'the one' meant for us. It is built around the presence of some metaphysical force that will bring us together. This form of 'luck' is attractive – it is so much easier to stumble across 'the one' than to sift through dozens of potential applicants, thoughtfully evaluating each one.

Friends may not help. Often they get a form of battle fatigue. Rather than help you work out whether the latest one is the right one, they can be inclined to bring the process to an end with a 'just pick one already' approach. There is also a double entendre around soulmate. In spoken language, no distinction is made between 'sole' and 'soul'. The 'sole' mate version is also attractive as it reinforces the notion that we will luck across 'the one' – and only one.

Richard Bach is fairly representative of the spiritual version of soulmate thinking. You may remember him as the author of *Jonathan Livingston Seagull* and maybe the more overtly spiritual book, *Illusions: The Adventures of a Reluctant Messiah*.[5] While I enjoyed *Illusions*, I am not buying everything Richard tells us. Here is how he describes our soulmate:

A soulmate is someone who has locks that fit our keys ... we feel safe enough to open the locks ... we can be loved for who we are and not for who we're pretending to be. No matter what ... with that one person we're safe in our own paradise. Our soulmate is someone who shares our deepest longings, our sense of direction.

Wow! Who would not want to buy into that? Just think – all you have to do is wait until your chance encounter where you discover that your key fits their locks. As a bonus, if you are not sure of your direction, find your soulmate, see where they are going and follow on, because they will share the same direction!

Now don't get me wrong. I actually believe much of what Bach is promising here is attainable for some, but for reasons we are going to come to, I don't think this particular spiritual perspective helps us to get there.

Understanding how to build a healthy relationship, be our vulnerable self and take the risk for being loved for who we are is the goal for every relationship. Often there is not a key to unlock this, but rather we build the relationship over time.

Second, you actually want a soulmate who 'respects', but not necessarily 'shares', your deepest longings and your direction. This is because you want them to have their own longings and their own direction that is different from (but not incompatible with) yours. You want them to be an individual with their own life and desires. In this way, they will enrich your life and take you to places that you did not know existed as you share not their longings, but their experience of pursuing their longings. (Later we will talk about how you do need to share certain things, particularly core values.)

Whether or not you accept these spiritual notions of a soulmate is not particularly important to where we are going here. The point is that we need to understand where it comes from and why the idea of the soulmate is so seductive. It promises someone who will love us as we are, with the sub-text: find the right person and little further work on the relationship is required.

Then there are less romantic, more helpful versions of a soulmate. These are the ones that I am inclined towards.

Elizabeth Gilbert, author of *Eat, Pray, Love*, sees our partner as a mirror ...

who shows you everything that is holding you back, the person who brings you to your own attention so you can change your life.[6]

For me as a relationship therapist, Gilbert's understanding is much more valuable. It speaks to the need to change and grow and how our partner can help us do this. More than that, it sets us up with the right expectations. It tells us that in going into a relationship, even with a soulmate, we are going to be confronted by our partner to become more, to become a better partner and to become more of who we can be.

For those who are spiritually inclined and are comfortable with reincarnation, we find another perspective again. This one offers a deeper spiritual notion of the soulmate. For this perspective, let's turn to Michael Newton's book *Journey of Souls: Case Studies of Life Between Lives*.[7] In Newton's view, it goes something like this. A soulmate is someone with whom you have been in relationships before. You come together in this life to work through any unresolved issues that you need to make sense of, that are holding you back. And you don't have to spend the rest of your life with them. They could be close friends, or they could be a partner with whom you are together for just a few years.

Most of all, there will be fireworks! In this telling, a soulmate (there could be more than one) is someone who you have unresolved issues with, and you are getting together to work them out, hopefully, this time around. Just because they are a true soulmate, marrying them does not mean that a painful divorce is not a likely part of the story (again and again). What is most helpful is the idea that soulmates have something for us that we need to learn.

While I don't think we should take much relationship advice from Madonna, she may be right about this: 'Your soulmate is the person that pushes all your buttons, pisses you off on a regular basis, and makes you face your shit.'

My personal favourite is the view of the ancient Greeks, who put it this way: marriage is where you find a partner who will get to know you well enough, to teach you what you need to learn about yourself to be the best person you could be. The problem arises when we don't realise this is the deal. As our partner begins the lesson on our shortcomings, we can respond in a way that at school would get us sent to the principal's office. Nevertheless, if we are open to it, our partners can be the best teachers of that all-important subject: how to become a better person.

Hollywood has made billions of dollars out of promising us all a soulmate. Few popular movies make it to an airing without a 'love interest', and almost never is a 'love interest' found by dating a few people and choosing the healthiest one (admittedly most storylines do not have time for this sub-plot). Typically, our would-be lovers bump into each other on a busy footpath with someone spilling coffee, or some other fluid, and someone apologising profusely until they look into each other's eyes.

Imagine if we bought cars based on the myth of 'the one'. In our next car accident, it might go something like, 'Why weren't you looking where you were going … hey, that's a nice-looking car you have there. Is it for sale? But you'll need to knock the price down for that dent in it!' There is a reason why we don't buy cars this way. One reason is because we know that there are lots of cars out there, of all different kinds. We do not want to limit ourselves to those we bump into – we want to make the best decision possible.

Manufacturing love from nothing

If we put bumping into our soulmate at one end of the spectrum, at the other end we find the work of Dr Robert Epstein. He is a relationship researcher and professor who earned his PhD at Harvard University. I love the story of how he found himself studying how we can artificially and deliberately manufacture 'falling in love' with a stranger.

He was a university researcher looking for a research project. Importantly, for reasons that will become obvious, he was single at the time. She was a woman looking for a research partner and a project. He found her particularly attractive. In a genius move, he suggested they see whether they could deliberately fall in love with each other and write a book about it.

Apparently, 'she loved the idea, but her boyfriend wasn't as thrilled'. It would appear that the boyfriend's position won out. Not prepared to readily abandon the most novel pick-up strategy that an academic has ever come up with, he wrote an editorial about it in *Psychology Today* in 2002. The media picked it up and more than a thousand women from six countries offered to see whether they could deliberately fall in love with our professor. At this point, he graduates from genius to legend.

In fact, dozens of researchers have looked at this phenomenon of 'artificially creating' love. Back in 1997, Arthur Aron and his co-workers published, 'The Experimental Generation of Interpersonal Closeness'. After hearing that one couple involved in this research fell in love and got married, Mandy Len Catron took this work to a popular level when she wrote an article in the *New York Times*' Modern Love column in 2015: 'To Fall in Love with Anyone, Do This'. She listed 36 questions that promote intimacy, which many of us found in our inboxes as it went viral.

You see, Mandy had decided to see whether, over a few beers in 2014, she could 'manufacture love' with 'someone I knew, but not particularly well' – and she did. She fell in love. She was still with Mark when she published her book, *How to Fall in Love with Anyone*,[8] in June 2017.

Epstein suggests that the key factors that can create love from almost nothing are:

- commitment to the relationship
- effective communication
- accommodation (not as in living together – being sensitive and making allowances for the other)
- vulnerability – finding the courage to let people into your true self with all its shortcomings
- sharing adventures
- sharing secrets
- spending time inside the other's personal space
- joking around.

This explains why secretaries marry their bosses and doctors marry the nurses with whom they work. Think about how many of these boxes you will tick by working on a big business deal or saving a patient's life together – especially if you work long hours late into the evening and have to 'grab a bite' together. If you are joking around as you do this, it is already looking a lot like a date.

Then someone, often unwittingly, makes the killer move. Maybe after working those long hours together, they share their vulnerabilities about whether they really can pull this big a deal off, or are they really making the best decisions for the patient? What if they are wrong and the patient dies? Powerful intimacy-building forces can be found in workplaces. Vulnerability is the essence of intimacy, and builds closeness and belonging.

A quick side note on being vulnerable. Too many people miss opportunities to build lasting relationships by 'not wanting to burden' a friend, or potential friend, with their problems. More often than not this is about a fear of being vulnerable. Moreover, friendships only deepen around having problems. Personal problems to a relationship are like fertiliser to a plant – both are a bit shitty, but their absence results in much slower growth.

We all find it rewarding to help a friend. The only way you can allow them to enjoy this reward is by 'burdening' them. Don't share your problems and you deny them the opportunity to enjoy the reward and you stunt the growth in the relationship.

The same applies to potential partners. As we will see when we define love in the next chapter, we really only feel loved when we have shown our shortcomings and vulnerabilities to the other and, despite them knowing this about us, they still want and care for us. We need to find the courage to gradually show more of our real self. It takes courage, because we risk painful rejection. But without the courage to be vulnerable, we can never connect, we can never be intimate.

One of the 'love-building exercises' that researchers in this space use involves purposely invading another's personal space. For most of us, that is around 45 centimetres. Subjects were asked to move progressively from outside another's personal space to well inside it, so they were as close as possible without touching. (For hormonal university students, this exercise apparently 'often ends with kissing'.) Think about doctors and nurses working on patients in an emergency room, or a boss and a secretary poring over a document, or two students – or indeed any two sexually compatible human beings looking at the same device.

Our legendary Professor Epstein has calculated that there are approximately 350,000 of 'the ones' in the world, with whom you can fall in love and have a good relationship. The point he is making is that there are many, many people with whom we can 'manufacture' a successful, loving, intimate relationship. 'The one' is just the one of these with whom you choose to build such a relationship.

How many of the 350,000 live near you is another question – though, even if 99.9 per cent of them live somewhere else, or are in a relationship (like the woman of his genius idea), this leaves 350 potential partners – and guess how many you need for a happy life?!

The Indian paradox

It is something of a paradox that marrying for love has gone hand in hand with a dramatic increase in divorce rates. Marrying for love has swung the pendulum all the way from medieval times, where marriage was about property and building interfamily relationships. Back then, love was not just considered irrelevant; it was thought to be a silly reason for marriage. The decision was made by the parents – because they would not get caught up in the emotion that would otherwise confuse young lovers. This still happens today in many countries, particularly India.

The lowest divorce rates in the world occur in India, where only around one in ten relationships ends in separation. Why is it that arranged marriages have a much lower rate of divorce than love marriages? You might argue that this low divorce rate is because of the cultural sanctions against divorce. This is certainly part of it, so it becomes interesting when we look at Indians who have moved away from their own culture and live somewhere in a culture that is very accepting of divorce, such as the United States.

Indeed, one could even argue that divorce rates might be higher for couples who were 'forced into' an arranged marriage but live in a culture that almost encourages divorce. Unlike India, America has a culture where you can find friends and future partners who are completely accepting of separation and divorce. But no, the Indians who live in America still have low divorce rates.

The 2008 US Religious Landscape Survey found that Hindus (80 per cent of Indians are Hindus) have the lowest divorce rate of any group in the United States. Are they unsophisticated people blindly following their religion? The survey found that they have the highest level of education in the country, with 48 per cent having postgraduate degrees.

One might argue, 'Okay, but surely their cultural expectation that you do not divorce might still be at work, even if they live in divorce-ready California? Their family and friends back home (and any that have moved to California) will still frown on them getting divorced.' The real question is whether people in arranged marriages are more in love?

Professor Epstein also researched arranged marriages to answer this very question. The research shows that when you get couples to rate the amount of love in their marriages, one typically finds in love marriages that it is high around the time of tying the knot, then declines fairly rapidly. In arranged marriages, not too surprisingly, it starts off at a low level, but by five years in, the couple's feelings of love have exceeded those found in a typical love marriage. By ten years into the marriage, the love is twice as strong as it was! So clearly it is not that arranged marriages have a low divorce rate because they do not want the shame of divorce. No – they are genuinely happier in their marriages.

There is a truth to be learned here. What is it? Arranged marriages do not start with a lot of love. Conversely, they do start with a lot of commitment. Yet they end up with more love on average – indeed, a lot more love – than a love marriage. What is the key? Epstein puts it plainly: 'The most important factor was commitment.'

What is the nature of this commitment in an arranged marriage? In essence, the expectation at the time of marriage is that, 'There is no love now, so we must commit to co-creating it.' As M. Scott Peck puts it in *The Road Less Travelled*, it is all about how love is built on fully committing to just one other. Peck makes the point that we can love many people as we go through our life, even simultaneously. The heart is big enough to love multiple people at once, but our time is a finite resource and the more partners we adopt, the less quality time we have to really be there for each one. Consider all the other day-to-day obligations most of us have and we can see how impractical it is to be there, to be fully present when needed, for two or more partners. (And there you have the core problem with polyamory.)

So what can arranged and 'manufactured' relationships tell us? The key seems to be a mutual commitment to each other, and each other alone. The one you happily spend the rest of your life with is not the one you feel the most love for and so you then commit to them; rather, it is the one you commit to and then the true, lifelong love follows.

That is so important, I will repeat it. *The one you happily spend the rest of your life with is not the one you feel the most love for; it is the one you commit to.* Commitment, in turn, is about holding a course despite whatever bad weather comes along. No matter what. No explorer would ever cross an ocean to their new land if they did not stay the course. A lifelong love will only be there, once we decide to commit, if both partners hold true to the plan.

If it was just about finding the one we love the most, we would have to continually move on to find out whether the next potential partner is someone we will have a greater attraction to. Indeed, many people are confused about this and, when the honeymoon is over, head off to where the grass might be greener.

This strategy is doubly dangerous given what we came to understand about dating the nines and tens when we discussed Imago theory. Remember that the people to whom we are the most attracted often take us into the most conflicted relationships. It is triply dangerous when we also factor in that a more powerful initial attraction leads to more relationship breakdowns as the couple rely on this to carry them through challenges, in lieu of commitment.

There is one final finding of note from Epstein's research. Studies in the United States routinely find the arrival of children to be a threat to the amount of love between the parents. In contrast, more couples from arranged marriages reported that their 'love grew' when they had children. Consider, for a moment, how this will profoundly change the experiences of children who are born into a relationship where love is growing rather than declining. It will resound through the ages. It will change the sense of love and family for their children and their children's children. Epstein proposes that this too goes back to the expectations being brought into the marriage.

I would suggest that a big part of the commitment that couples bring to an arranged marriage is that they expect there will be problems along the way and *they will have to build their love for each other as they face them.* Among other things, this means they are more patient and forgiving of each other as they tackle life's problems as a more united team. The fragility of the love means they are more considerate of their partner's opinions and feelings as they set out on the epic journey of marriage. This mindset is much more able to respond to the demands of parenting.

In a love marriage, the love that is already on the decline from the point of marriage onwards is further assaulted and diminished by various demands. Few problems will demand more from us, and will cause us more worry, than children. The love married couple are shell-shocked to find the love they thought would see them through until death, is falling away as the demands on them mount. They feel cheated and often blame their partner.

So, where does all this leave us? The take-home message is that love is not found; it is built. Surprisingly, we can build it with more people than we think – a lot more than 'the one'!

In a later chapter, as we start to look at how to choose a better partner, we will return to look at what we can borrow and steal from the arranged marriage. We will do what we can to move towards its spectacularly low divorce rate.

First, though, let's consider what long-term love really is.

Redefining love: 'True love'

GBW

My feelings of love may be unbounded, but my capacity to be loving is limited. I therefore must choose the person on whom to focus my capacity to love ...

True love is not a feeling by which we are overwhelmed. It is a committed, thoughtful decision.

– M. Scott Peck, *The Road Less Travelled*

'He treats me pretty badly. It's left me pretty unhappy for the last few years. He's often impatient and rude to me. I can't rely on him to turn up to pick up the kids from school as he'll often call me saying he's catching up with workmates after work ... but he's not all bad. I know he loves me in his own way.'

After hearing versions of this over and over again, I realised that I needed to come up with a clear way of defining love – not just in a way that made sense to me, but in a way that made sense to the people, unhappy in love, who came to see me.

Too often, these people would also tell me a similar story about their experience of love at the hands of their parents.

Even after relating the most horrific stories of how their parents had abused them emotionally, physically and/or sexually, they would finish with a version of, 'but I know they loved me in their own way'. Their claim was more about hope than loyalty, let alone reality. They desperately hoped that their parents loved them. As humans, we have a surprising preparedness to believe that another loves us despite clear evidence to the contrary.

Like most things in psychology, the capacity to love falls under a bell curve – tall in the middle with small groups at either side. While most people sit around the middle, at one end you have people who are incredibly loving and at the other end those who are simply incapable of loving. Typically, these people had parents who were damaged by their own parents (who were damaged by their parents and so on ...) who left them hurting, angry and incapable of healthy love.

Unfortunately, fertility is the same across the bell curve. The truth is that terrible parents can still have innocent, lovable kids. So children are born to all groups. Growing up without love can leave us too ready to accept the same from a partner. This is the familiarity of Imago theory.

Even more problematically, being brought up by parents who cannot love leaves the young child feeling unlovable. The perfectly normal egocentricity and limited mental capacity of the young child prevents them from attributing the lack of love to whom it really belongs – the parent/s. The damage to the vulnerable child's self-esteem is monumental.

For couple therapy, I could see I needed a way to help my patients to clearly and objectively work out whether they were being loved or not. It is not just about resolving the confusion, there is a critical reason why we need to work out if we are being loved or not. Why?

Because we will blame ourselves for not being lovable if we wrongly think that someone is loving us when they are not. It is not just the young child that makes this error.

This is a tragic problem, and you cannot fix a problem until you diagnose it correctly.

After some months of couple therapy, one of my more insightful patients pointed out quite poetically, 'So what I see here Doc is that it's a matter of working out whose shit is whose.'

It can be very freeing for people in unhappy relationships to realise that their feelings of not being loved were accurate, and this had nothing at all to do with their lovability.

To do this we need to be clear on what love is – what I will call 'true love'. So, I went looking to define love.

My review of the historical and current definitions of love over the next several months left me cold. Any romantic view was just that and little more. The philosophers I read had clearly never had to explain it to a patient sitting in front of them. The writers on whom I focused, who were looking at the impossible-to-define-objectively *feelings* of love, left me with nothing I could use clinically. Any definition had to provide indisputable, clear evidence of whether love was present or not.

Why true love can't be built on feelings

When it comes to defining love, it is important that we let go of the sense that it is emotionally driven. I do realise that this seems to be not only counter-intuitive, but at odds with how most people think of love. The reason why 'true love' – the love that fuels a long-term relationship – cannot be driven by feelings is simple: feelings come and go. Indeed, few things in life are more impermanent than a feeling.

If we based long-term relationships on feelings, they simply could not survive. If my wife and I based loving our children on feelings, then Jiveny would have been out on the street by eighteen months of age after decorating our kitchen with yoghurt ... again. Seventy-five per cent of teenagers would be homeless by sixteen.

Equally, no one will piss you off more than your partner. Remember that the Greeks saw marriage as being about your partner getting to know you well enough to teach you how to be a better person. This translates into, 'Your partner will piss you off more frequently than anyone on the planet.'

In a healthy relationship our partners will react to and pull us up on our shortcomings – hopefully in the privacy of our relationship. This will, in that moment, kill not just feelings of love, but most positive feelings. Normal humans become defensive. Many respond by attacking their partner.

So, while our partner does the Greek job of showing us our shortcomings, there are going to be a lot of negative feelings churning around the relationship. And then there are the myriad external stressors on a relationship – work, financial, friendship problems and so on.

Emotions are in a constant state of flux. They are ephemeral, which is why true love cannot be built on a feeling. The more I read the more it became clear to me that any working definition of love could not be based on ever-changing feelings. So what was the foundation for true love if not feelings?

My search to define love ultimately took me to M. Scott Peck's *The Road Less Travelled*. As a fellow psychiatrist, he appreciated the need for any definition to be useful in practice. His chapter entitled 'Love is Not a Feeling' grabbed my attention, with lines like, 'When love exists it does so with or without a loving feeling.' Peck explains that our partner being our 'constant and stable ally' is central to love. He defined love as being a commitment to nurturing spiritual growth in both oneself and the other person. Commitment – there's that word again. It is so much more than committing to fidelity i.e. not having an affair – emotional or sexual – with another person. It is about committing to love *in spite of how we feel*.

This commitment is not at all about sticking it out with a partner until death do us part. An unhappy, let alone abusive relationship can be a desolate place to spend the rest of your life. A commitment to nurture growth changes everything. I dare you to have an unhappy relationship if both you and your partner are genuinely committed to both your own growth and that of your partner's.

I shared Peck's way of seeing love with my patients, but I could see that they didn't quite buy it. There was something missing. I realised that no allowance for the feeling factor was too big a leap – and they were right.

We all know there is a special feeling quality that goes with being in a deeply caring relationship. I have come to believe that this feeling is more about a sense of belonging and *acceptance*. As I pondered this, I realised that it is acceptance that takes us to the essence of belonging.

We all want to belong. There is a big difference between being 'part of' a group or tribe versus feeling that one 'belongs' to a tribe. You feel a sense of belonging – that the group wants you in it – only *after* you have been brave enough to be vulnerable, to show more of the real you. If you *continue* to find that the group still *accepts* you, that is true belonging. The powerful feeling behind this is acceptance. It is a quieter feeling. Lovely, soft and warm, it is a far cry from the rampaging rapids of lust and passion.

And you don't need to have it with a large group. A group of two is just fine. You can sit there with a friend of ten-plus years who has proven their friendship through tough times and quietly enjoy the deep satisfaction of knowing they accept you and care for you despite your shortcomings.

Another issue with Peck's definition that I could see was a little problematic for my patients, was the term 'spiritual growth'. Australia has lower levels of both religiosity and spirituality than America, such that this term was discordant for many.

So, with deep respect to Peck's thinking, I felt the need to build on his work and address these issues. It is very much an example of standing on the shoulders of a giant.

I would suggest that we redefine love, or at least what I would call 'True Love', as follows:

> True love is the feeling of being fully accepted by another who knows you intimately and who is committed to nurturing both your personal growth and their own.

This is written in a way that refers to the experience of being loved – the *receiving* side. It allows us to be clear about whether or not what we are experiencing is true love.

To point it in the other direction, from the *giving* side, we would word it in this way:

> To truly love another, you make them feel safe enough to be vulnerable as you fully accept them and commit to nurture their personal growth as well as your own.

Of course, the best way to inspire another person to give us true love is to become expert at the giving side.

Unpacking true love

While this way of seeing love is driven by commitment, not feelings, there is one feeling that is central to it. Feeling fully, deeply accepted by another is special. Inherent to it is a sense of safety. If people know our shortcomings and still care about us, then we are safer than if they do not know our shortcomings and care about us – simply because of a fear that if they 'find out' about us, their care for us could be in jeopardy.

It is about being fully accepted, without judgement. You can experience this feeling in many relationships: it may be at the hands of a lifelong partner, an adult child or a good friend.

You may think you feel love after a few intense days or weeks together, but no, it simply is not possible. Infatuation yes, true love no. Getting to know another's shortcomings occurs with intimacy, which can only be built over time. You simply cannot get to know the majority of another's shortcomings without months of interacting with them. This is largely because of that word 'interacting'. Most of us either are not aware of our own shortcomings or, if we are, we are reluctant to tell others about them. It takes time for sufficient trust to be built for us to be comfortable about sharing them. If your partner runs late, misses rent or bill payments or has a tendency towards scraping the car, these things will only become apparent over time, as you interact with them. What we fail, or refuse, to share will inevitably be revealed over time. Time is the ultimate truth serum. A tendency to anger, to drink too much, to avoid conflict – all will be inexorably drawn out and put on display given enough time.

The feeling of true love builds in direct proportion to the increasing intimacy. The better someone knows you, the more powerful the feeling of being loved. As Jiveny will discuss in more detail in her 'Power of Vulnerability' chapter, increasing intimacy requires the courage to be vulnerable. Early in a relationship, the love must remain in doubt because you know that the other person does not see the fullness of who you are: strengths and weaknesses, aspirations and fears, capacity to do good and to do otherwise. Over time – over years – the other cannot help but see the fullness of you. As true love grows with time, and our partner gets to know us, warts and all, it becomes more and more indestructible.

Which brings us to nurturing personal growth. Is it not a conflict to accept someone just as they are, warts and all, but then want them to grow and change into something more? At first glance, this might seem to be so, but then there is that important word 'nurturing'. Sun, soil and water do not demand the flower to blossom, but they are there to make it possible.

This means we are not demanding of another's growth. We do not require it, but we will be there to support our partner when they wish to take on their next personal challenge. Alternatively, we may help them with a long-standing issue they want to overcome. They may have to give a presentation that they find particularly anxiety provoking – we will find time to be there for them, to listen to them practise and to encourage.

The simplest way to nurture a partner's personal growth is to create a world where they feel safe and cared for by someone who understands both their immediate needs and their longer term desires. The sun, soil and water are eternally patient. In the same way, we need to be patient in a relationship, ready to nurture our partner when they desire growth.

'Patience' is an important word in relationships. Indeed, patience is one of the greatest virtues. Impatiently pushing someone to grow when they are not ready will not only fail, it will delay them coming to this desire themselves – sometimes for years.

I really appreciate it when my wife gives me space to write undisturbed. It's even better when she prepares lunch for me after I have been writing all morning. But when she says to me, 'Shouldn't you be writing? Don't you have a publishing deadline soon?' I can be less gracious, as she highlights my avoidance of confronting the keyboard.

At times, some well-placed, gentle encouragement is appropriate, but do not always expect it to be greeted with open arms. We bought a piano for my wife after she expressed her desire to return to the lessons she had started in primary school. It sat there, rather quietly, for many months afterwards. In what I thought was inspired, for her birthday I gave her some lessons with a teacher who came highly recommended. She responded to this gift with somewhat muted gratitude. She felt pushed by me into something that she worried that she may not have the time or talent for. Apparently, keys on a piano can be just as intimidating as keys on a computer! Nevertheless, a few weeks later she booked her first lesson and was finally grateful for me encouraging her.

Nurturing your partner's personal growth requires *empathy*. You need to empathically connect with your partner to know what constitutes personal growth in this point of their life. This is the only way to work out what their needs are. Empathy has two parts. The often overlooked first part is perhaps the more important. To empathise with another, first we have to put aside our own beliefs and judgements. If I thought my wife would be a better singer than a piano player, or my son a better football player than a dancer, when this is not their desire, my ability to empathise evaporates.

We can see now how empathy links directly to love – and how we need to let people into our internal world, warts and all, if we want to be loved.

Is love present?

As you might now appreciate, when we define true love around acceptance, commitment and nurturing, it is not hard to identify. It is not difficult to work out whether it was or is present because these aspects are tangible.

We can ask simple questions such as:

- Do you feel fully accepted by your partner?
- What do they say or do that makes you feel this way?
- Does your partner take the time to really see you and work out what is most important for you to grow?
- Do they take steps to nurture that growth?
- Is nurturing you something that is clearly important to them? Is it something to which they are committed?
- Do they pursue their own personal growth?

If someone truly loves you, you will be able to point out what they have done for you without any difficulty on both small and large scales. It is not about what they say. Declarations of love are nice and endearing, but words are cheap.

If we focus on the actions, there is no risk of us misreading it. Love is a verb, not a noun. Love is as love does. Clichés become so because they contain a kernel of truth. These clichés highlight how love is all about the *doing*. It is about acceptance, commitment and nurturing personal growth. If your partner truly loves you, you will not have any difficulty finding evidence of this.

Handle with care - we are all works in progress

As you have probably realised, true intimacy has very little to do with getting naked and having sex. I am talking about 'in-to-me-see' type intimacy. It is about really seeing our partner as the individual they are and coming to know them well. Indeed, we can have sex with someone without any intimacy at all.

While infatuation is built on a promise, true love is built on intimacy. What you will 'fully accept' in your partner and what you will need to nurture in your partner will be revealed through intimacy.

We have already discussed how intimacy takes time by interacting with our partner as we go through various life experiences. There is another reason why we go slowly: intimacy equals danger. The more someone gets to know you, the more they can hurt you. This is why we all struggle, to varying degrees, with letting people in close. In the Preface to this book I gave Suzanne Wright's definition of love: 'Love is giving someone the power to completely destroy you – and hoping they won't.' That power comes from intimacy.

If you care about a potential partner, work hard to keep them safe as they reveal themselves to you. We are all works in progress – this is the human state. If they tell, or show, you a side to them that they are not proud of, handle with care. We all have our weaknesses, our darker side. The more you handle your partner's vulnerabilities with care, the more likely they are to do the same for you. If you do and they do not, you have a red flag right there.

If you are in a hurry to get to know your partner, or have them get to know you, then pay extra care to respecting and protecting your partner's vulnerabilities as they reveal them to you.

It needs to swing both ways

The final part of the definition of true love is 'nurturing both your personal growth and their own'. While gentle encouragement is good, there is no more powerful way to help another grow than to pursue this yourself. When you nurture your own growth, you awaken in those you care about their desire to do likewise. In the most convincing way, you show that it is okay, and important, to do this for yourself. This is why nurturing one's own growth is such a critical part of loving. After a while, your partner might think, 'That's working well for you. I want some of that too.'

It is true that how much we can love another is a reflection of how much we love ourselves. While it is much easier to love another, compared to loving ourselves, to truly love we have to work out how to love and accept our own self. Nurturing one's own growth addresses this critical component of love. For example, it is often easier to forgive another than to stop beating up on ourselves. Nurturing ourselves requires us to move forward, i.e. to look at what we can learn from our mistakes and how to build a better self from a position of self-forgiveness.

Most importantly, while it is wonderful to have another nurture our personal growth, we must take full responsibility for this. Indeed, another can only nurture our growth once we first clarify what we want for ourselves and then articulate it clearly to the other. On top of this we need to explain clearly what we need next, or what is holding us up, in our personal growth journey. Only fully armed in this way, can a partner really help us to go where we need to grow.

In the same way, a partner cannot meet any of our needs if we have not articulated them clearly. So often in therapy I'm dealing with someone complaining that their partner is not meeting their needs only to find they have not clarified exactly how and when they want their partner to care for them. I find myself saying something like, 'I can't turn to your partner and see if they're prepared to meet your needs as you have not clearly articulated them. Until you do, I have no business with them.'

Children in particular need to see a parent pursuing their own personal growth. Children who only see their parents sacrifice and give, without taking time out for their own personal growth, are given one of two messages. First, you are only good if you are giving to others. This creates adults who feel guilty about doing anything for themselves. They feel they are only 'good' if, like their parents, they are giving to others. While it is not so much the case these days, this has historically been more of an issue for women.

Alternatively, these children can grow up to feel entitled to having those around them 'serve' them, just as their parents did. They can get annoyed when people want to 'abandon' them to spend time doing something for themselves. Neither of these outcomes is great. Our children need to see us taking time for ourselves as we nurture our own personal growth.

And so it is with our partners. From early in the relationship, we need to make it clear that it is important for both of us to take time out to nurture our souls. This can be anything from spending time with our own inner circle of friends to working on a project that is meaningful to us.

How your potential partner responds to you nurturing yourself – after you make it clear that it is important to you – will be an important way of working out whether your partner can truly love you. Indeed, it is a very simple way to evaluate your potential partner's capacity for love. But perhaps the main reason it is so important to pursue our own growth is that in mastering how to do this for ourselves, we will better be able to assist our partner (and children) to do the same.

The world generally is not overly supportive of people taking time out to do something that has a particular meaning just to them. It can be seen as odd or even selfish. It is not a problem if this pursuit does not impact on anyone else. When this is the case we are allowed to 'fill in time' as we please. But try telling friends you cannot make lunch because you want to practise this new meditation you have come across, or because you have been out too much lately, and, at best, they will be confused. At worst, they will think you are lying and have something better to do.

It is only through pursuing our own personal growth that we become better qualified to help a partner (or child) pursue theirs. We will understand that they may be reluctant to fight for their time and will need to be supported as they plant their veggie garden, write those song lyrics or experiment with cooking that new dish.

At a simpler level, if both of you are pursuing your own personal growth, you can do this at the same time, but in different spaces. One person goes off to train for their upcoming event while the other researches their contemplated career change. Few things build a relationship more powerfully than supporting a partner to become more than they were.

Finally, let's consider the key concept of commitment in true love. *Commitment is what carries a decision, made for the right reasons, over time.*

People who are good at life will weigh their values and desires and come to a decision they then commit to. Rather than revisiting and reviewing the basis for this decision on an ongoing basis, the commitment recognises that this work has been done and now we need to follow through. All elite athletes, concert violinists and chessmasters, for example, use a form of this to succeed. Every morning, they don't revisit the basis for their commitment, they know that the work of making a good decision has been done. Now it is just about the follow through.

Commitment remembers and respects that a well-informed decision has been made and now we are in the execution phase. Commitment is the follow through. Without commitment to back it up a good decision is wasted.

When I first heard Nike's 'just do it' slogan. I thought it was silly. Motivation is way more complex. There are intrinsic and extrinsic factors and how they relate to one's values. It took me a while to realise that the slogan was not about motivation as much as it was about commitment to a previously well-informed decision. It is about the personal integrity of sticking to a decision, particularly when the going gets tough. It recognises that we did not make a fair-weather decision that only applies among sunshine and butterflies. Of course, we may revise our commitment at some point, but there needs to be a good reason to do so.

Love has two ends – but only one is reliable

We all want to be truly loved. Connecting through love is a wondrous and special experience. However, we often overlook a critical aspect of this connection: it has two ends.

The fullness of this was taught to me – as has happened with all my great lessons – by a patient. She was a happily married mother of a five-year-old boy and a two-year-old girl. Sadly, she was dying of metastatic melanoma.

She had decided she wanted to record some videos that her children could watch as they grew up. She wanted to record videos for different stages in their life, where they might find it helpful to have some motherly advice. I encouraged her to do this, but she came in to say that her husband was not able to be the cameraman as he found it too upsetting to film his wife talking about life after her death. He was a loving husband and was understandably bereft about watching his wife fading as the aggressive cancer ravaged her 28-year-old body.

I agreed to film her talking to her children five, ten and fifteen years down the track. Even though this was over twenty years ago, I remember it very clearly, with some emotion. It was easier for me than her husband, but watching a loving mother try to capture her love for her children and deliver it to them long after she was gone was an emotional challenge. As so often happens with people who are dying with conscious courage, she led the way for both of us.

We were shooting a segment for her daughter for when she was a teenager, for her to watch if she was feeling down. She said to her future daughter, 'Maybe someone has rejected you. I just want you to remember there is always love. Love will make it better.'

I reached over and turned off the camera. 'I'm a little confused,' I said. 'Isn't the problem that she is not feeling loved? We can't make people give us love when we need it. Even if we have someone around who loves us, they might be busy, preoccupied with their own problems and stressed. They just might not have the energy to give us love.'

What she said next came from a place of wisdom generated by spending months looking death in the face and making your peace with it. It also came from being in a place that was many times more frightening and overwhelming than where her teenage daughter might find herself when faced with rejection by a friend or a boy. Patiently, she explained:

I have had much time to feel alone with my fears and feel rejected, mostly by God. When I looked around for my husband and family to love me, I just felt their pain, as they struggled with losing me. I had to work out how to connect with love when the people who loved me were too overwhelmed to give me that love. I'm not talking about getting love from another. That is unreliable.

What I learned was that when I was feeling low, I could always give love to someone. I quickly realised how it would make me feel better to be part of a loving interaction. It became apparent to me that it did not make much difference if I was receiving love or giving love, both made me feel equally better.

I would start with my husband, my kids, my family, friends, but some days they were all busy, at work or school. Given that I spent so much time at the hospital, I would wander around and look for someone I could have a chat with and give reassurance to, or hold their hand if they were scared. With all the tests and treatment I have had, I know how scary it can be. I might go and see the old lady up the road who lives alone and see what I can do to help.

I realised that what this remarkable human being was describing was that when our brain secretes the love hormone, oxytocin, it feels the same irrespective of how its release in our brain is triggered. It is released, and makes us feel good, through connection. Which end of the connection we are on is unimportant.

By helping another, we also release dopamine, the powerful feel-good hormone that results from achieving something significant or overcoming a challenge. Once released, these neuro-hormones make us feel better – whether they come from receiving love or giving it is irrelevant.

Somewhat in awe, I said, 'Yes, your daughter absolutely needs to hear this,' then reached over and turned the camera back on.

In his inauguration speech as the 35th American President, John F. Kennedy, famously said, 'Ask not what your country can do for you – ask what you can do for your country.' In the world of relationships, it occurs to me that we need to reverse our thinking along the same lines. Do not ask, 'Who will love me?' Ask, 'Who can I love?' Giving love is under our control, receiving love is not. If you want to author your best life, you want to focus on doing what is actually under your control.

While we explore opportunities in looking for a partner, in the meantime, think about who you can develop your lovingness on. Who can you fully accept and commit to nurturing their personal growth?

Relationships are confusing, particularly if we do not understand where we are as they evolve. Let's cut through some of the confusion by breaking this evolution down.

The four phases of a relationship

GBW

I see people my age getting married to people they've known for like a year and a half. A year and a half? Is that enough time to get to know someone and know you want to spend the rest of your life with them? I've had sweaters for a year and a half and I was like, 'What the fuck was I doing with this sweater?'

– Aziz Ansari, Comedian

Most relationships typically go through four identifiable phases and their accompanying emotional or feeling states. This way of thinking about the relationship life cycle may not be entirely familiar to you, but stay with me for a moment as we unpack this.

The Relationship Life Cycle

Feeling states	Curiosity	Infatuation	Power struggle	True love
Relationship phases	Dating	Exclusivity	Cohabitating	Long-term commitment (Parenting)

Take a moment to review this diagram. Note the relative positions of each of the feeling states, when they begin and end, relative to the relationship phases. As you can see, curiosity and infatuation usually predate the phases of dating and exclusivity. On the other hand, cohabitating typically brings on the one negative feeling state of the power struggle. Fortunately, we then end up at the most positive feeling state of all: true love.

Not all couples will go through each state or phase. For example, some people will only cohabitate from the point when they marry. Others will decide to have children and consider marriage later. Then there are the people who meet and marry quickly in the infatuation state. In these cases, the last two relationship phases become one. Nevertheless, it is helpful to understand this progression in the service of us becoming more conscious as we wander down the path that leads to the biggest decision of our lives. More important than appreciating the phases is understanding the emotional drivers, the feeling states, that sit behind them.

As you can see from the diagram, there are four phases that have overlapping feeling states. As you would expect, while we can define the beginning and end of each phase, the transitions between the feeling states are much more variable.

Of course, there is enormous variation in the length of time couples spend in each stage. Nevertheless, a patterned progression can generally be observed. With cohabitating now more frequently happening before marriage, the power struggle has been brought forward in recent years. In terms of the ideal duration of each phase, the evidence would suggest that it is maturity driven. The closer you are to twenty, rather than thirty, the longer you should spend in each phase.

For the last couple of decades, divorce rates have been coming down. Clever mathematical research has found that this is largely because our age at marriage is increasing. We now know that around 80 per cent of the likelihood of divorce can be explained simply by the age of the woman when she marries.[9] A bride of 18 will have twice the divorce rate of a bride only four years older at 22. By their thirties, brides are *four times less likely to divorce*. That is a powerful statistic.

As I highlighted in my TED talk, one of the main reasons why divorce is age related is that it is not until our late twenties and early thirties that our personality settles into something like its final shape. While we continue to evolve, who we are in our late twenties and early thirties has a much higher correlation with who we are when we are fifty than who we were in our early twenties. On top of this, we now know we were wrong in thinking the brain had finished its rapid growth by our late teens. Our brains are still growing quite rapidly, and changing at a physical level, until around age 25.

We can now see what happens to people who marry in their early twenties. These couples literally grow apart. Even if only one partner's personality changes significantly over this decade, it can be a problem for a relationship. Often both partners' personalities undergo a considerable shift – and often not in the same direction.

For this reason, we need to go slower when we are younger. Ideally, and to keep it simple, for those aged 25 and under, we want to spend around a year in the dating/exclusivity phases, another year cohabiting and still another year after we marry before we have children. Whichever way you divide the stages, we would suggest a minimum of three years between meeting and having children.

Around the age of thirty and above, you might halve these times as you are both bringing a more stable and mature personality to the relationship. This allows a minimum of eighteen months between meeting and starting to consider having children. We would suggest that this is an absolute minimum – ideally, it should be longer.

If you think these durations are too long, consider a recent survey from the United Kingdom[10] of 4000 recently married couples. They found that the average couple was in a relationship for 4.9 years before getting married. The total average time living together before marriage was 3.5 years. Divorce rates in the United Kingdom are currently at their lowest in 50 years and this extended courtship is one of the reasons why.

Why we act before we think

Let's take a moment to look at the relationship between thinking and feeling. In simple terms, becoming more conscious is a goal for all of us, but no more so than when it comes to making the biggest decision of our life. Becoming conscious is essentially about becoming self-aware. Self-awareness is about understanding our thoughts and the feelings that drive them.

Remember from our discussion on how the unconscious mind works that, as humans, we feel first and think second. Unfortunately, action typically occurs between the two! I do not need to point out that acting before we think can be a problem. More interestingly, why do we do it?

Picture a caveman enjoying an early morning cup of herbal tea in his favourite clay mug on a misty morning as the night's fire smoulders lazily beside him. He's wondering which of his cousins to make the mother of his future children as a starving sabre-toothed tiger strolls into camp. If our romantic sits there wondering what particular species of sabre-toothed tiger has come visiting, he will not survive long enough to contribute DNA to said children, let alone the human race. When dealing with immediate threats, an intellectual caveman was a dead caveman.

My wife tells the story of how she walked in through our front door and suddenly threw herself backwards against the wall. Confused, it took her a few moments to realise what had happened. The large two metre snake sitting in our hallway had registered with the survival (lizard) part of her brain and her brain had taken action by throwing her body backwards instead of standing on the snake. Snakes usually cannot be bothered to put in the effort to do that snap, recoil and bitey thing, but standing on them typically motivates them well enough.

Those cave folks whose brains were good at acting before thinking this out lived to share their DNA with us. So, while we might like to think that we humans are thinking beings that also feel, the truth is that we are feeling beings first. But most importantly, while we think continuously, it is feeling that makes us act in one direction or another.

Occasionally, people with brain tumours have had operations that leave them unable to access their feelings. They have to rely entirely on their logical mind to make decisions. We might expect them to function like Spock from *Star Trek* – with brutally cold efficiency. Yet the truth is that they cannot function at all. They can take hours to make basic decisions like what to eat for breakfast or what to wear. The feel-react-think process is great for survival, but when it comes to making big decisions, we need to work hard to reverse the 'react' and the 'think'.

Fortunately, as we move down the path towards making the biggest decision of our life, we do not have to make quick decisions. We have time to not just think these things through, but to discuss them with trusted confidants.

Becoming conscious

The point is that we are built to act before we think, and our feelings make this possible. Becoming conscious is about working to overcome this natural tendency to act before fully thinking through the issues that need to be considered. In particular, we need to use our capacity for thought to unpack and understand our greater internal world, particularly our emotions, and why they are pushing us in one direction or another.

For these reasons, in considering the four phases of a relationship it is the feelings on which we need to focus. Becoming conscious is all about becoming aware of your internal emotional weather. Our emotions tell us way more about ourselves and what we are likely to do than do our thoughts. Often our thoughts are just generated after the event by our minds in an insipid attempt to rationalise our feeling-driven actions.

While weather forecasting is hard, noticing changes in the weather is much easier and fortunately that is the job here. Like my wife and the snake, your feelings will give you early warning – which is useful, but without thought they can take us down the wrong path. Feelings can make us leave a relationship we should stay in, and stay in a relationship we should leave. Conscious, self-aware thought is what will save us.

In particular, the problem is our tendency to transition from one relationship phase to the next unconsciously. This occurs when we transition without mindfully stopping and thinking something like, 'I'm getting in deeper here, is this what I really want? Is this relationship good for me?' Getting in 'deeper' is a key point. As we discussed in the 'Sliding versus Deciding' chapter, with each phase we move further into a relationship from which the exit will become increasingly difficult and painful.

Curiosity and dating

The first phase is dating – no surprise there. The emotion that drives it is, ideally, curiosity. I recognise that curiosity may not always be the emotion that drives dating. Loneliness, boredom and a desire for connection could equally drive this phase. For simplicity and because it is the healthiest driver of this phase, I'm going to go with curiosity.

So let's consider curiosity from a particular angle. Curiosity is my favourite emotion because it is the beginning of all great journeys – both inside and outside our minds.

I have alluded to the importance of self-awareness, now let me take it further. I would argue that the secret to authoring a satisfying life of contentment and love begins with self-awareness. And self-awareness begins with curiosity. Indeed, all journeys begin with a version of wonder: I wonder what is there? I wonder what is going on? I wonder what I can discover? I wonder why I did that?

In a relationship, curiosity takes the form of, 'Who's out there that I could make a great match with?' Thus, curiosity kicks off the process, carrying us to that first meeting.

Some might argue that loneliness drives the need to meet someone. It can, but this path is more problematic. Meeting people through loneliness often starts the relationship the wrong way around, as we look to another to fix this problem. The energy around curiosity is so much healthier. This is why we all need to curate our thinking. While loneliness might get you to look online, the challenge is to transform that motivating energy into curiosity when you head out to go on that first date. To move yourself into curious mode think about questions you could ask like: I wonder what makes him tick? I wonder what she really values in a friend? I wonder how open-minded he is? I wonder what experiences led her to her chosen career?

What about attraction? This comes a little later. To a certain extent, we can take attraction for granted. There needs to be some degree of attraction for the relationship to proceed beyond curiosity.

Curiosity also carries us through the dating phase. The core task of the dating phase is getting to know the potential partner in front of you. Keep your curiosity dialled up. You want to work out what makes them want to jump out of bed, what gets them excited about life, who they really are. Curiosity takes us to all the important issues in life. Finally, when it comes to moving into the most helpful mindset, curiosity will take us there. Not only will it get us asking the most useful questions, it makes us a better conversationalist and a better listener.

Everyone should read Dale Carnegie's *How to Win Friends and Influence People*. Published way back in 1936, over fifteen million copies have been sold worldwide, making it one of the best-selling books of all time. Proving its ongoing relevance, in 2011 it was number 19 on *Time* magazine's list of the 100 most influential books. The reason it remains as relevant today is because it speaks to the unchanging nature of the human state.

The chapter I found the most fascinating addressed how to become a great conversationalist. Spoiler alert: being a great conversationalist is not about regaling people with hilarious exploits accrued by travelling to distant, exotic lands or having stand-up-comedian-level jocular insights into the human state. Quite the opposite: people will think you are a great conversationalist because you listen well – because you really 'see' them.

Indeed, we would suggest that there is no way to be a better listener than to come from a place of genuine curiosity. We all know how important good communication is in a relationship.

The truth is that good communication is not about mastery of language and articulate expression; it is about listening well. Of course, curiosity will carry this too.

My father was a great listener – to his own detriment as a busy family doctor. He would often run late in his practice, by up to an hour or more. His regular patients knew to ring ahead to find out how far behind he was. He told me once that he believed everybody had a story worth hearing buried in them and our job was to unearth it. This was clearly why he had such a huge following in his clinical practice. A secretary tells the story of overhearing a new patient complaining about how long the wait was to see my father. A long-time patient (who very probably had rung ahead) leaned over, patted her on the arm and said, 'Just be patient. You will understand when you see him why we're blessed with Blair-West.'

Be a good listener. Be curious before, as well as after, you meet someone.

Infatuation – the honeymoon

If things are moving in the right direction, curiosity evolves into the next emotional state: infatuation. Often with a significant element of sexual attraction involved, this emerging emotion drives the later dating phase. It is during this time that people typically experience 'falling in love'. Actually, it is more about falling in *lust*. From Elizabeth Gilbert's perspective, 'Infatuation is not quite the same thing as love; it's more like love's shady second cousin who's always borrowing money and can't hold down a job.'

Nevertheless, as the infatuation emerges, we certainly do 'fall' further into the relationship. Indeed, by the end of this phase, if both lovers are moving forward they will typically have declared their love for each other. A relationship is no more fun or exciting than it is during this phase. It is a phase of hope and promise. This is where people are on their best behaviour.

Despite its newness, this phase is often characterised by a sense of knowing each other 'like an old friend', with sentiments like, 'I feel like I have known him/her forever.' At the very least, there is a sense of familiarity.

As we remember from Imago theory, what is really happening here is that our unconscious minds are recognising the traits of our caregivers from our formative years in the other person. This is why the other person seems so familiar. This familiarity adds to the sense of connection, the 'falling in love'. Technically, though, we are 'falling into infatuation'.

If the Imago match is high, the feelings in this phase can be quite intense – often 'red hot'. This is when chemistry, aka physical attraction or good old-fashioned lust, reaches its peak. From a purely evolutionary perspective, this phase is designed to result in pregnancy, to ensure the survival of the human race. This in turn, has ensured that the parents of teenagers will, only until the end of time, be driven to distraction trying to prevent teen pregnancies.

How well our relationship fares down the track is of no interest to our DNA. It just wants to see the species replicate. This is fine for your typical cocker spaniel. We humans, however, are now much more interested in how our relationship unfolds for the decades after the kids arrive and leave home.

Sometimes the infatuation phase does not run red hot. Sometimes it is just a warm, growing sense of comfort with the other person. This is the slow burn that Jiveny spoke of in her chapter on Imago theory.

We argue that this is a better way for the relationship to unfold. This is more likely to be the case if we are dating someone who is a six or seven in Imago attraction – that is, located firmly in the Imago sweet spot.

As we have discussed, there needs to be some chemistry. A slow burn is more likely to be the case when we choose a partner because we recognise their mental healthiness, and rate this more highly than physical attractiveness.

While our new lovers will often declare their love for each other during this phase, as we know from the last chapter, it is a long way yet from true love. Indeed, one of the most important things you need to find out about your potential partner is how low they go in an argument. How mean and aggressive can they be? Who are they at their worst?

The problem is that you will not find this out during the infatuation phase. This is because infatuation is defined by a total absence of anger. Each partner is on their best behaviour. This is the time when men discover latent dishwashing skills and women a long-lost interest in football. If the infatuation is powerful enough, men can clean entire kitchens and women can even find cricket, or baseball, utterly enthralling. (Apologies to the men who will happily clean kitchens anyway and women who really do love sports involving bats and balls.) Moreover, people in this phase are incredibly forgiving of each other. Rose-coloured glasses become prescribed eyewear as personal slights and insensitive comments are overlooked and we focus on our partner's positive traits.

Equally, if a partner lets you down or abuses your trust, or you, during the honeymoon phase, you can be fairly confident that things will not improve with time. Indeed, they are very likely going to get worse.

I have often joked with my patients that when infatuation is red hot, you could admit to a partner how you murdered your previous partner with an axe, and your new-found love would say, 'Aah, but that was back then. I can see you are a much better person now.'

There is an interesting upshot from understanding the unadulterated positivity of this phase. This is the time to share your vulnerabilities, shortcomings and embarrassing personal information. During this window, when infatuation is in full swing, it is a spectacularly brilliant time to raise embarrassing issues.

For example, with over ten per cent of the population between the ages of 15 and 49 having genital herpes, this window is the perfect time to raise this issue if it was not raised earlier (preferably before beginning the sexual side of a relationship). Raise it after the window closes and you will be seen as having 'kept a dirty little secret'.

Some people rationalise avoiding sharing their vulnerabilities: 'I will bring these things up down the track when we are more deeply committed' (read: 'harder for them to leave me'). Issues like children from a previous marriage, bankruptcies and criminal offences inevitably have a way of making themselves known over time.

Here's the point. *If your partner will not forgive you for these transgressions in the infatuation phase, they definitely will not forgive you down the track after you have 'hidden' these 'dirty little secrets' from them.* We make them 'dirty little secrets' by not raising them. Raise all your dirty laundry in the middle of this phase and you will be seen as honest and open – the building blocks of trust in a relationship.

The truth is that we all carry shame about certain things. There is always something to talk about, even if it is just the anxieties and fears you have about your future.

Building intimacy through vulnerability

Sharing things we might be ashamed about is not about 'getting away with' hanging out our dirty laundry. It is about so much more. By this point in this book you have probably worked out that sharing our shortcomings and the things we are ashamed of is how we build trust and intimacy with our partner. Indeed, if you do not have any really dirty laundry then pull out something – even if it is only lightly soiled! By sharing your vulnerabilities, you build intimacy. Intimacy and closeness are not built through looking Instagram amazing.

A true connection with another person is developed by letting them see our weaknesses. As we do this, we are saying, 'I feel safe enough to trust you with this sensitive information.' In this way, we deepen our intimacy.

In a social media–driven world, this is more necessary than ever. Social media – especially Instagram – is like wartime propaganda, but the opposite. Wartime propaganda was designed to dehumanise the other side – to make them so bad that killing them seemed to be quite a reasonable option. The moment you see your enemy as a son, a brother, a father, a lover – just like those around you – killing them is much harder.

Social media propaganda is built in the same way: to deliver a singular message. This time the message is, 'I'm AWESOME, you should admire me, because I'm what you want to be.' And then all involved feel bad as they go about busily comparing their backstage with everyone's front stage.

One of my twenty-something patients spoke of the emotional downward spiral that would start when she was feeling down, bored and alone. She would then go on to social media, only to be left feeling even more down, bored and alone as she saw 'everyone' getting out there and having AMAZING fun with their besties. This is the opposite of vulnerability, and it's why being vulnerable is more important now than ever before. We need to balance out the ridiculous level of invulnerability that we project through social media. Instead, with our closer friends, we can admit to situations that cause us anxiety or that leave us feeling insecure. Speaking in public is a common one, not fully understanding a task at work/school/uni is an even more common example.

As we touched on in the last chapter, every one of us has insecurities – it is the human state. To deny them projects a sense of fakeness. To share them simply says, 'I am human ... just like you.'

I do a lot of group therapy, and it has become evident to me over the years that the group really only hits its stride when members share their fears and feelings of insecurity. As they do this, something magical happens: not only do people start to open up, but the group starts to really work cohesively. Other members share their anxieties and concerns, and they then start to come up with really useful ways to reframe each other's pain. New members will tell me later how much better they feel as they come to realise that they are far more normal than they had thought – they are not the damaged, bad people they had previously felt they were.

In group therapy, this has a name: 'universality'. It is where we finally become convinced that so much of our insecurity and doubt is universal and we are not alone. It is just the human state. Equally, the opposing state of 'confidence' is not what it seems.

One thing psychology has come to understand about confidence is that it is state dependent. This means that how confident we feel has more to do with where we are and what we are doing than an underlying state of confidence in ourselves. In my consulting rooms, in my domain, I can look serenely confident practising psychotherapy. Put me in a conference with neuro-pharmacological boffins and get me to carry a conversation with them and I will not feel anything approaching confidence.

So, once the infatuation phase of a relationship arrives, it is a time to build intimacy through sharing our vulnerabilities and our fears. Failure to do this will leave the foundations of our relationship shaky. Sharing our vulnerabilities, concerns and anxieties gives us a rock-like foundation. Keeping them hidden gives us a sand-like foundation.

As Jiveny reminds us in her writing and speaking on 'empowered vulnerability', timing is important. Again, we come back to the window. Sharing too early can make us sound like a victim looking for a saviour, a wound looking for a knife. Too late and our too-cool-for-school façade pushes others away.

Infatuation is enormously variable, lasting anywhere from days to months. As you would suspect, the best way to extend it to its limits – probably somewhere around eighteen months – is to do the opposite of cohabitate. Yes, the less you see of each other, the longer you can stretch out this phase!

This is why affairs are so powerful and seem so much better than the relationship with the cheater's domestic partner. Not only is there much less contact, but it is more intense – not to mention better dressed with makeup on. On top of this, there is its clandestine nature that adds allure and excitement, further supercharging the infatuation period.

Finally, it is worth reminding ourselves what drives infatuation. It is the Imago promise of earlier wounds being healed. Indeed, it is a soul-healing promise: it is the promise and the feeling of being accepted by, and attractive to, another; it is the promise of being loved, despite one's shortcomings; it is the promise of being healed. Those formative events with family and peers that left us feeling ashamed, not good enough or rejected can now be banished ... maybe.

Exclusivity

The next phase after dating is exclusivity. As curiosity rolls into the attraction that blossoms into infatuation, couples typically decide to stop dating others. This is important because if we are not exclusive, the relationship cannot grow. Why? Because we hold back.

We will generally not be too vulnerable around another if we think they are still looking for a better deal, dating others and ready to leave as soon as a preferred option comes along. This is why it is important to openly clarify with each other that you are going to commit to the relationship exclusively. Only this will allow the intimacy to grow.

Some of my patients find this confronting. They are reluctant to raise the issue of exclusivity because of a fear of being embarrassed or rejected. They fear being 'out of step' and misreading the relationship. Yes, there is a risk when you say something like, 'I was thinking of deleting my online dating account. How do you feel about us becoming exclusive partners?' But it is a risk that we need to take.

Another way of approaching this could include simply asking your new flame, 'So, I'm curious ... are you seeing anyone else at the moment?' (It is always best to keep it broad and close any loopholes – much better than, 'Do you have a partner?')

The worst-case scenario would be for them to say, 'Yes.' You can then follow up by asking them, 'How is that going?' At least you will know where you stand. The best-case scenario would be for them to say something along the lines of, 'No. To be honest, I'm not really interested in seeing anyone else at the moment.' And then you can join them with a knowing smile and a 'Me neither.'

As I remind my patients, it is better to be confronted now than to feel hurt and betrayed later. This is all about protecting yourself from unnecessary hurt. Besides, exclusivity *needs to be an agreement*. By definition, you cannot be exclusive if only one of you sees it that way.

So, this phase does not really begin until you both have the pivotal chat and agree to be exclusive.

A big part of a successful relationship is managing each other's expectations *and checking in (often more than once) to clarify that you are both singing from the same song book.* We cannot stress this point enough and it starts from early in a relationship. Moreover, if you feel you cannot raise an issue like this with a potential partner, then you have a flag right there.

If you are both having a red-hot infatuation, then this is an easier conversation to have. If it is more of a slow burn, it can be harder. Find the courage. If your partner responds with some version of, 'What – are you crazy? This is just casual,' you will want to know that too. Yesterday, in fact.

Finally, in agreeing to be exclusive, we are not talking about being together forever. We are just agreeing to not seeing anyone else until further notice. We are stepping things up a notch to see how it works out. Declaring our love for each other, if it arrives at all, typically comes later.

As we step things up a bit, we are now going to get much more information about our potential partner and how they operate in a relationship. In particular, things like their reliability, and how well they follow through, are now going to become more evident.

People who are not so truthful will also become more obvious in this stage, as the increasing intimacy will reveal any inconsistencies between what they tell you and reality.

Before you're exclusive, you're not

What I call 'serial monogamous dating' has become surprisingly common in my practice over the years. While it affects both genders, I see it more in women. This is where the person meets another and immediately stops looking for anyone else. They effectively enter an exclusive relationship from the get-go.

The first problem with this is the time cost. As one of my patients, a thirty-something professional woman put it, 'I take a year to get into a relationship, a year or two in it, another year trying to get out of it and another year before I'm over it and ready to date again.' Yes, if you do the maths that is four or five years she will never get back on a relationship that went nowhere.

As she explained, 'I feel dishonest if I date two people at once. Like I will get found out. It feels wrong.' Despite her intelligence, somewhere along the line her boundaries had become confused. The reality is that we all have the right to date multiple people until we become exclusive.

Sleeping with them does complicate the issue. While less so now, for many people having sex would indicate a degree of greater commitment in a relationship. (Obviously a one-night stand is different, we are talking about having sex in the course of an ongoing dating relationship.) I would suggest that this is another good reason to not have sex too early in a relationship.

The other forces at work here are the discomfort and the uncertainty of dating – most powerfully the fear of rejection.

By only dating one person at a time in the pre-exclusive period, these emotional threats are reduced dramatically. This is perhaps the worst form of settling for too little. It is a fear-based strategy or decision. *Nothing good ever comes from a fear-based decision. Fear should always be factored into what we do, but it should never be the basis for a decision.*

The second and much bigger issue, as I explained to my patient, are the questions that serial monogamous dating leads us to. When you start dating one person you will be asking yourself a version of, 'Should I continue this relationship? Is this relationship good enough?' This can lead to dangerous answers like, 'Well, he doesn't treat me too badly. He's basically a good guy.' What it becomes is a question of, 'Is this relationship bad enough to end it?' Typically, the answer is a form of, 'No … it's not that bad.' Until it is. This is how you end up measuring a relationship, that went nowhere, in years.

This is a great example of how important it is in life to get the question right first.

Let's look at the kind of question that arises from dating a few people at once over time. 'Which of these potential partners brings out the best in me?' Or, 'Which of these people do I have the best match with?' Or maybe, 'Which of them do I think I could build a good life with?'

With serial monogamous dating you are comparing your partner against one that you would leave a relationship for. With normal, non-exclusive dating, you are comparing your potential partner against others. Only in the latter situation do we give ourselves a head-start into a healthy relationship.

So remember, you are not exclusive until you *both agree* you are. Jiveny will pick up how this plays out in dating a little bit later.

Cohabitating: Bring on the power struggle

The start of the power struggle phase is pretty easy to determine as you are waking up in the same house every day. It is a big step. Remember the 'Sliding versus Deciding' chapter in which we spoke about Galena Rhoades' research on how we can unwittingly chain ourselves together? Moving in is a big link in the chain – a strong link that is harder to break down the track.

While infatuation may still be running strong at this point, nothing takes the 'fat' out of infatuation like moving in together. No longer can we be on our best behaviour when we go on a date. No longer will our partner only see us with our public face on. Now our partner will see us in our pyjamas, for example. Pyjamas are generally pretty unforgiving – unless you have expensive designer ones. And PJs mean we have to allow ourselves to be seen *au naturel*.

A worthwhile interim step to consider before living together is travelling together. Taking a holiday together will give you a sense of how you work as a couple and what kind of issues you will have to navigate. Holidays have two big advantages over living together. First, the novelty and the beauty of most destinations put you in a better frame of mind – read 'forgiving'. Second, it is a neutral setting where you get to try out living together. You'll also have to collaborate, make decisions and problem-solve together which can be very insightful. Third, holidays have an end. The time to the end is measured in days and weeks, unlike moving in where we are now looking at months or years.

If you successfully negotiate a holiday, then moving in makes sense. On the other hand, if you cannot make it through two weeks in a holiday setting, then we have a red flag right there.

Cohabitating is pretty much guaranteed to bring infatuation to an end. This is simply because if two intelligent individuals live under the same roof, they will experience conflict. This is simply because we all set up our home life differently. One is in the habit of eating lunch at noon, the other at 1.00 pm or later. Neither will think they need to raise this when they agree to 'have lunch together'. But when one wanders home an hour late and gets hit with, 'you're so inconsiderate', their unwitting, tardy soul has no idea what has happened and why their partner is so annoyed at them. In fact, they thought they were speaking the same language – that 'having lunch' meant the same to their partner as it meant to them.

To take another example, in one family, 'clean the kitchen' means polish it until you can see your face in the sink. In another, it means clear the benches and stack the plates inside the sink to be washed later. You can now return to the dining table and continue an important conversation.

Now, multiply these examples by several dozen. The assumptions that sit around the words we use will prove to be only 'true' for half the relationship. Your partner will typically have completely different meanings for the same words.

And so, the power struggle[11] arrives. In its essence, it is simply a struggle to get our partner to recognise that our version of English, and what our words mean, is the right one. Their version is desperately misguided and needs to be corrected. When the power struggle arrives and our partner starts to annoy us by doing these various versions of leaving the lid off the toothpaste, our rose-coloured glasses slip and our partner's other shortcomings come sharply into focus.

So many couples make the mistake of thinking that when the power struggle phase arrives, their 'love' is ending. It can feel like a 180-degree U-turn in the relationship from the blissful state of infatuation. At this point, many people think that they have just 'fallen out of love'. It can certainly feel that way. But here's the thing: *it is a perfectly normal transition.*

Negotiating this phase is a challenge – so much so that an extended elaboration of how to negotiate the conflict of this phase is beyond the scope of this book. But let me give you a crash course.

Negotiating the power struggle

Gary Chapman's work on languages of love give us another way to understand and negotiate the power struggle. Chapman's ground-breaking contribution to couple therapy is clarifying the critical role of recognising that each of us have different ways of feeling loved. This is an extension of the idea of a couple giving a shared language entirely different meanings. Typically, we humans reliably make the mistake of trying to love our partners in our love language, because it comes naturally, but not in a way that fills their 'love tank' as Chapman calls it. The tragedy is that this loving energy is completely wasted as the love language literally falls on deaf ears.

In essence, languages of love can be divided into three groupings: Give me (acts of service and gifts), Tell me (quality time/discussion and words of affirmation), Touch me (non-sexual touch and sexual touch). Chapman combined the last two into one, which left him with five love languages. In working with couples, however, it is critical to separate non-sexual from sexual physical touch as they have completely different meanings for people. (Visit Chapman's website for a full description of these languages: www.5lovelanguages.com.)

Prior to the power struggle, couples typically use all six love languages from the energy fuelled by infatuation and attraction. (Alternatively, the forgiveness that is the rule in the infatuation phase means they overlook a failure to meet their love needs.) As it takes a lot of energy to use love languages that are not naturally our own, as this phase inevitably comes to an end, we revert to using our own personal love languages. We use the one or two (occasionally three) love languages, that work for us. The problem is they may not work at all for our partner. For example, gifts convey no love to me at all, whereas acts of service do. If my wife wants to show me love, she is wasting her time and money buying me gifts, while cooking my favourite meal will do nicely.

In the power struggle, when demonstrating love does not come as naturally, it is not uncommon to see partners make an effort to reconnect that is entirely wasted as they speak their own love language that is meaningless to their partner. It is so important to know your partner's love languages (Chapman's website has a quiz that helps you to work this out). Once armed with this knowledge, not only will you get it right, but you don't waste energy, and subsequent frustration, by loving in ways that will not be appreciated. Lazy lovers take note! This is how to get 'the most bang for your buck'. When Henry Ford wanted to introduce a new production process to his factory he would ask to the see the laziest man in that section and ask him for feedback on his proposal. The lazy man was highly motivated to ensure the job got done with the least amount of effort.

After getting love languages right, in simple terms there are three other considerations in negotiating the power struggle. The first is to expect this phase and see it as normal. The second is to realise that, despite all the evidence to the contrary, you do not speak the same language. You grew up in different families in different worlds and different sub-cultures, where you learned to interpret languages differently – whether they are words or ways of loving. There is nothing more serious happening here.

Pretty much the only time I do not see this normal transition to the power struggle, especially once people are living together, is when one or both partners do not feel safe enough in the relationship to let their partner know they are feeling annoyed.

Rather than leading to 'peace' (as is usually intended), not raising issues limits true connection. This can feel deeply unsettling as we need to know who we are getting into a relationship with. This can build until someone departs suddenly, with the other saying, 'I did not see it coming at all!' Moreover, when we raise our concerns, while our partner will not always respond positively, in a healthy relationship they will, over time (key words!), try to accommodate our desires.

There is a second, critical reason why we need to speak up. The other force behind the power struggle is that one partner (or both) who has been looking forward to being loved (and healed), now sits back to cash in. Partners will need a 'gentle' reminder that it is a two-way street. While it does not need to match in a tit-for-tat way, both partners need to put the effort in to love their partner in a way that fills their tank.

Third and finally, we need to be patient as we learn our partner's version of what we thought were our shared languages. Patience is indeed a virtue – one of the greatest, and of no greater importance than when the power struggle arrives.

We need the infatuation feeling state to end before the long-term commitment phase. Getting married – or, worse, getting pregnant – during the infatuation feeling state is the most dangerous thing to do in a relationship. Too often, people 'wake up' from their infatuation to find they have chained themselves further into a relationship before they have negotiated the two paramount feeling states: the power struggle and true love.

As annoying as the power struggle phase is, it is an important phase – in fact, it is a critical one. How we negotiate this phase will be the basis for the final phase and the true love that underpins a long-term commitment.

Building true love

The power struggle is a baptism of fire for a relationship. The long-term commitment phase is the phoenix that arises from its ashes. It may or may not mean marriage, but it certainly needs to be a commitment of sorts if we are planning to have children – biological, fostered or adopted. It is interesting to see that, as we mentioned at the beginning of this book, 91 per cent of British couples surveyed in 2017 choose to marry to demonstrate commitment.

If a couple does decide to marry, this typically occurs some months after the partners commit to true love. Marriage is the public declaration of the private commitment on which true love is built. It is because they are both built on commitment that this is the only phase that starts at around the same time as the corresponding feeling state.

Once we commit to be there for our partner and fully accept them, we begin building a love that will, if nurtured, continue to grow – year after year, decade after decade. Equally, it can only be built after the intimacy that comes out of the power struggle, as our partner's shortcomings and their personality conflicts declare themselves (and we declare ours). Remember that true love is built around fully accepting our partner and it does not come into play if we have not actually gone through the process of seeing the parts of our partner that will be harder to accept.

As we have said, this takes time. We have to interact with our partners to discover the parts of them that we need to accept. Most people will not come out and offer up their shortcomings – in fact, most of us do not even accept that we have half of our shortcomings!

The time test for red flags versus rose-coloured flags

There is a difference between the shortcomings we can live with and red flags that are deal-breakers. When we truly love another person and accept them as they are, we are effectively saying, 'I know all of you, and while you are not perfect, like I am not perfect, on balance, I fully accept and commit to you.'

Some flags are bright red and easy to call as a deal-breaker. Often, though, flags can be less red. Our partner may run reliably late, but then we get to know them and realise this is a result of growing up in a family where this was the custom, rather than primarily disrespect for another's time. And while he runs late like clockwork, the fact that he is generally kind and patient outweighs this.

Weighing up what we are prepared to live with and what we are not takes much longer when we're dealing with flags that are more rose-coloured than red – it will take time to work out what weight to give to certain issues your partner might have.

Time is the ultimate test. On top of needing to spend time interacting with each other to get to know what shortcomings we have, intimacy is co-created between a couple by adding time from the point we share vulnerabilities. It is about what we know of the other *and then what we do with that knowing*.

Jan came to see me, very upset. She had shared with her boyfriend several months earlier that she had gone through a phase where she had had several one-night stands after a relationship breakup. She thought he had accepted it, but as the story unfolded, 'We were having an argument over how I didn't feel like having sex after a long day at work. Then he said, "Why can't you get in touch with your inner slut that fucked everything that moved back then?" I was shattered. I couldn't believe that he would throw that up at me like that.'

As it turned out, this was the beginning of a series of breaches of trust that led to the end of this relationship, but it took time to declare itself.

Intimacy takes time: 1300 check-ins

I want to finish this chapter by discussing the subject of intimacy. Even when we get to this final stage, there is more love to build and we do this by deepening out intimacy. I never cease to be amazed at how I can see a couple who have been married for a decade or two who still have very low levels of intimacy. Sharing the same roof, bed and dinner table does not automatically mean that intimacy follows.

As periodic watering and a lot of sunshine are necessary for a flower to blossom, so intimacy needs periodic check-ins and a lot of time dedicated to nurturing intimacy. Let's consider them in order.

Too often, we project our concerns and beliefs onto our partner. This tendency to assume we know what another person is thinking is a unique human quality. If we do not ask what our partner is thinking or feeling, the only other source of information is our view of what we think they are thinking. While it could be considered an attempt at mind-reading, for those of us who do not actually possess this superpower, we end up 'projecting'. While we think we know what our partner is thinking, more often than not, we are pushing our concerns onto them.

Rather than attempting to mind-read, we all need to check in with our partners. Your partner may have been worried about something yesterday, and today they could be more worried, less worried or not worried about it at all. Just saying, 'Hey, how are you feeling about that today?' is a simple but powerful thing to do to connect with a partner – even if you are pretty sure you know where they are at.

The curiosity that, ideally, should drive the beginning of a relationship needs to become a central part of the ongoing relationship. Curiosity leads to connecting. The moment a couple starts to assume they know what their partner is thinking, or will say, connection begins to die. Genuine curiosity means we need to put some effort into our questions. Rather than, 'How was your day?', ask a better, more specific question, like, 'What happened when you gave that presentation?' This phrasing is more likely to get a more meaningful answer than, 'How did your presentation go?'

While I often say there is nothing to life but relationships, this statement is really about connection. ('There is nothing to life but connection' doesn't work as well, as it could equally apply to our devotion to our smartphone.) Connection with others is perhaps the most important thing there is for us as humans. At a tribal level, connection equals safety. Remember, a lone monkey is a dead monkey. Equally, we punish people by removing connection. This is why when being imprisoned is not bad enough, solitary confinement is considered the ultimate punishment. Connections through checking in, out of concern for the other, also shows that you have been listening, which makes them as good as connections get. They show that you really 'see' your partner.

Of course, we have to do this on a regular, ongoing basis. This is not just because our concerns and desires change from day to day; it is also because our memories are imperfect. I have a much greater chance of remembering my wife's concerns and desires if I hear them more than once.

How important is putting aside time to build intimacy? You will recall our discussion about the research by Epstein and others into how we can 'manufacture' love from nothing, by undertaking certain activities with a person to whom we are not overly attracted. In essence, this is all about building intimacy. This research suggests that intimacy alone can create a lasting, loving relationship.

How much time does intimacy require? From when we started living together, until our last child left home around 25 years later, my wife and I had a date night pretty much every Thursday night. That is around 1300 dates.

Over this time, more by trial and error than design, we came up with five guidelines for our date nights to extract the maximum amount of intimacy from them. These are not hard and fast, and we occasionally stepped outside them. They are:

- Check in on all the major, current concerns in our lives.
- No discussion of conflicted subjects that are likely to lead to an argument.
- If we find an argument emerging, we put it on hold until later.
- After dealing with any concerns, talk about the positives in our life, or in our future, that we can look forward to.
- Don't be fancy – just go to a good local, relaxed, casual restaurant!

While this is a book about working out how to choose the best partner through dating, perhaps the most important dates are those you have *after the dating phase comes to an end*.

Before we can build intimacy, though, we have to meet someone we want to spend our life with – and that requires the right approach, more specifically the right *mindset*, which we'll explore in the next chapter.

A meeting mindset: The power of detachment

GBW

> Whether you think you can, or you think you can't –
> you're right.
>
> **– Henry Ford**

Mindset is everything, the saying goes. This is no more so than when we head out to date. The mindset that Jiveny and I want you to adopt will help you to avoid the burnout that often plagues this space.

Finding a partner is a long-distance race, not a sprint. It requires very different mental preparation. In a long-distance race, you prepare to start slowly and pace yourself. You adapt to the conditions along the way. You recognise there are many kilometres to run before you will see the finish line in the distance and you shouldn't go too hard too soon, or peak too early, or you will finish badly.

Henry Ford's quote captures the self-fulfilling nature of our mindset. Get it wrong and we are in trouble even before we begin.

So what is mindset exactly? In psychiatry we make a distinction between traits and states. Our personality traits are relatively stable over time – typically years. In contrast, we move in and out of various states on a daily basis. In essence, our states are emotionally driven. If left unchecked, emotions triggered by all sorts of day-to-day happenings – from joy to deep sadness, and everything in between – will lead us in and out of a variety of states.

The old Persian adage, 'This too shall pass,' speaks to the essence of all emotional states. They are ephemeral, transient. We know that even deep clinical depression will eventually pass, even without treatment.

One of the few certainties of life is that every emotional state will pass; we just need to stick around long enough.

Personality characteristics, such as extroversion and introversion, or whether we respond to a challenge with logic versus intuition, are good examples of time-stable traits. Indeed, we define personality by those traits that we display over many years.

Being drunk is a state. It will pass. How we behave when drunk – how mean we are, or how positive and generous we are – has more to do with our personality traits. (Indeed, getting a potential partner drunk is a simple way to see more of their underlying personality.)

Above, I used the phrase 'if left unchecked' in referring to how emotions lead us in and out of various states. Now we can answer the question. A mindset is when we choose to adopt a particular perspective that is more likely, although not guaranteed, to move ourselves into a particular state. We use our 'mind' to 'set' our state.

We need to do this rather than allowing ourselves to be thrown around like a piece of flotsam on our emotional ocean, which would mean being a victim to our emotions, to an untamed mind.

In consciously setting our perspective to move us towards a particular state, we are equally *taking ourselves out of another, less desirable, state.*

I am choosing my words carefully here as I talk of choosing a particular perspective to move us towards a particular state. The fullness of this is that we cannot fully override powerful emotions such as depression, acute grief or anxiety, by choosing a mindset. Changing these emotions requires us to deal with the underlying driver of the state, on which many books have been written and a therapist may be required.

But outside of the more powerful emotional places we can occupy, when no powerful feeling is in play, we have a greater ability, indeed the responsibility, to curate our thinking, to choose a mindset.

Jiveny and I are all about helping people to author their best life. The opposite of being a victim is not being a perpetrator; it is being an author. Managing our mindset is a key element of how we do this on a day-to-day basis. We need to curate our thinking to take us to the mindset that we want to be in. Don't worry, if you cannot be bothered to manage your mindset, the world will choose your mindset for you. Just jump on social media and allow yourself to react to what you see!

A mindset is made up of a series of statements – like 'soundbites' that summarise an idea – or beliefs that we group together and even give a name to, like 'my dating mindset'. Every elite athlete, often with the help of a good coach, has built the mindset that they know works best for them as they head out to meet their competition.

As you read this book think about what will be part of your particular dating mindset.

Here is a simple example to start with: be open to meeting people 24/7. While we have been talking about meeting people as 'something you go out to do', when it comes to meeting potential partners it is more a way of life. We need to be open to meeting people as we go about our day-to-day life. The universe is running 24/7, so be open to meeting someone anytime, anywhere. Jiveny will talk about this more when she looks at dating in the offline world.

Choosing to be happier (and more attractive)

To maximise our chances of finding a great match, we want to put ourselves into a mindset that makes us happier. We do not need to tell you that the happier you are, the more attractive you are.

Most people have had the experience of being in a relationship drought. When it breaks, it doesn't just rain, it pours. You will go through a dry spell where no one seems to be taking an interest in you and then you find someone who does, and maybe you go on a date. Suddenly, another, and maybe even another, person shows interest in you. What is going on?

What happens is that the first person breaking the drought leaves us feeling more attractive, more confident about our desirability. This in turn makes us much more attractive to others. It is a subtle shift. Often, we cannot put a finger on how we are different, but we have become more attractive by operating with higher spirits, from a more relaxed, detached place. Feeling desired has shifted our mindset and made us more desirable. I call this phenomenon the 'draw of desirability'.

In a similar way, we are also more attractive when people see that we have a partner. In essence, someone is 'vouching' for us. It is as form of social proof in that if someone is already with us, we are that much less likely to be a serial killer.

So, how can we engineer this attractiveness when we are not in a relationship, not being hit on by a bunch of people? One mindset that has been well researched is that of gratitude. Few of us are born or bred into automatically being grateful for what we have. We need to make this shift into this mindset ourselves.

Psychologists Robert Emmons and Michael McCullough used writing as a way to move people into this state. They got one group of participants to write about things for which they were grateful, while a second group wrote of their daily irritations or things that had displeased them. A control group just wrote about things that affected them, both positive and negative. After ten weeks, those in the first group were more optimistic and felt better about their lives than those in the other two. More unexpectedly, they were exercising more and were less likely to need to see a doctor.

Famed optimism researcher and author of the must-read book for any parent, *The Optimistic Child*, Martin Seligman, asked over 400 people to personally deliver a letter of gratitude to someone who had been kind to them. Participants reported a significant increase in happiness scores, with benefits lasting for up to a month.

The astute reader will see that this is the research that sits behind what we spoke about in the chapter on defining true love. Showing gratitude to others is a form of loving them. As we discussed, this releases the neuro-hormones oxytocin and dopamine. Interestingly, these hormones do not discriminate between whether we are receiving love or giving it. The result is the same: we feel better.

The big opportunity here is to look around us and find people to help out, or show gratitude to, so we can generate a similar state to people finding us attractive. We can voluntarily create the draw of desirability. The mindset 'soundbite' would be something like: I want to be a person who looks for opportunities to help or show gratitude to those around me.

This is worth forming as a habit for down the track when you are in a relationship. A study of couples found that when they took time to express gratitude to their partner, they not only felt more positive *towards* their partner from giving this feedback, but importantly, they were more comfortable about expressing concerns about their relationship. This is critical, because couples need to feel safe enough in the relationship – to believe that there is enough 'containment' – to raise concerns. Building containment leaves both partners feeling safer in the relationship so that crucial concerns are aired and processed, rather than being left to fester and undermine the relationship over time.

An attitude of gratitude: What a four-year-old can teach us all

If you are wondering what an attitude of gratitude looks like, search YouTube for 'Jessica's Daily Affirmation'. There is a good reason why it has over 20 million views at the time of writing. Even just watching four-year-old Jessica do her thing for 49 seconds is uplifting. Note that it is just Jessica and a mirror. No other human beings required.

Just thinking about what is going well in our lives, what we can be grateful about, without interacting with anyone else, lifts our spirits. Try it. Write out a list of all the things for which you can be grateful. It is often good to do this when we are not too down, as it can be hard to reach for these thoughts in difficult times. Put it in your smartphone so it isn't hard to find. If you need inspiration, listen to four-year-old Jessica rattle off the things for which she is grateful.

When you are heading out to meet a new potential partner, just revisit the things for which you are grateful. Even better, first, find someone to share it with. Be careful not to do this with someone who is in a particularly negative state, as they may well drag you into their world. It is better to tell the other person first, why you are doing what you are about to do. Best of all, find someone who is generally positive about life.

The dating mindset

I have spoken about a mindset of gratitude that makes us generally more attractive. What about the specific mindset we want to bring to meeting a potential partner?

Two words spring to mind here: curiosity and detachment. We have spent some time with curiosity in the chapter about the relationship life cycle. It is the feeling state that we want to sit underneath dating. The beauty of curiosity is that while it is an emotional state, by its very nature it is one of the few emotions that we can more readily move into by thinking in a particular way: by questioning.

In therapy, genuine curiosity is one of my simplest but most powerful techniques. A patient will come in upset, anxious, sad or experiencing one of many problematic emotional states. Obviously, I will ask them why they are feeling this way, and then we move into the space of their underlying emotional drivers or concerns.

At other times, particularly if I have a good understanding of why they are feeling this way, I take a different tack. I will ask them just to step back a little and wonder what it is that gives that emotion so much power over them. I might ask them to tell me where in their body they most notice this feeling. Here, I am simply using the power of curiosity to shift their emotional state. (Even giving away this secret will not decrease its power. Indeed, I teach it to my patients to help them to manage their own emotions.)

As we head out to meet a new person, curiosity is not a difficult emotion to reach for. On the way to meeting them, think about the following questions:

- What kind of person are they?
- What are they interested in?
- What gets them excited about life?
- What interesting experiences have they had in their life?
- What do they know about a part of life I know little about?

The list of questions that can take us into the mindset of curiosity is endless. The 'soundbite' here is something like: I am really curious about this person.

The power of detaching

As well as stimulating curiosity, we also need to detach. When we are powerfully attached to a particular outcome, things tend to go badly. Ask any guy who has tried to come up with a killer pickup line after finally finding the courage to walk over to that woman he finds incredibly attractive.

What I like to call the 'law of attachment' dictates that the more we want to impress, the more idiotic the things that come out of our mouth are likely to be. Conversely, when we are with people we do not need to impress, we will say the cleverest, wittiest things imaginable. The law of attachment can be defined thusly: *the more intensely we are attached to a desired outcome, the less likely we are to achieve it.*

I was first introduced to the concept of detachment as a central life skill by the speaker and author Andrew Matthews. I was fortunate to meet Andrew at a typical 2007 personal growth seminar we were both attending. I later learned that one in twenty homes in Australia had a copy of his book *Being Happy!*[12] and sure enough when I got home my wife pulled out a copy she had bought years ago.

Andrew kindly invited my wife and I to visit him and his wife, co-author and publisher Julie, in North Queensland. Before breakfast one morning, I picked up Andrew's million-selling *Follow Your Heart*[13] and read with fascination about determination and detachment.

We all get determination. Many writers since Jesus, and quite a few before, have spoken of the power of persistence in achieving our goals. But detachment is a much more elusive animal. Moreover, I would suggest it is the foremost of the two.

So, after reading this section, I looked forward to discussing it with Andrew over breakfast. I said, 'Mate, I have just read what you wrote about determination and detachment and I found it absolutely fascinating. Tell me more.'

Andrew gave me my first lesson in detachment by responding, 'Mmmm, I don't recall writing about that – which book was it in?' Andrew is spectacularly unattached to the outcome he desires! He explained how his greatest successes came from detachment about the outcome and his greatest failures came from being too attached to it.

I could see parallels in my own life. As we reviewed our greatest successes next to our greatest failures, there was one common thread: the intensity of attachment to a particular outcome.

I have come to understand that when we are too intensely attached to a particular outcome, we move our mind into a less creative, less inspired mode. We simply do not do our best work. Playfulness is key, as is being excited about what we are doing along the way, with less of a focus on the outcome. Time flies when you're having fun. ('Flow' is the scientific term for it as described by Mihály Csíkszentmihályi back in 1975, but I think 'fun' captures it nicely.)

Imagine what would happen to a young child's creative expression if you said, 'You must have that Lego city completed by close of business today!' Or, 'You need to have Ken and Barbie dating, married and divorced before your bath!' In short, detachment is about letting go of the outcome – particularly the 'how' and the 'when' of the outcome.

My patients who apply this best to the dating world let go of how they will meet their partner and when it will happen. Too often in life we think we are ready for what we want only because we want it now, when in reality we are nowhere near ready. We need the universe to step in and slow things down. The worst thing that could happen is for you to meet someone with whom you could happily spend the rest of your life when you are not in a good place, and unable to bring your best self to the interaction.

The most common example is when people are on the rebound from another relationship. They are still hurting from, and grieving, their last relationship. There are a number of problems that follow from this, but a big one is that we cannot help but compare our new partner with the best, most missed parts of our last partner.

A second issue is that we will take the things we are most angry at our last partner for and expect (quite unfairly) our new partner to wrong us in the same way. Our mind does this as a simple protection mechanism. If you have ever been on the receiving end of this, you will know how destructive it is and how it pushes you away at a rapid speed. It really rankles when our partner expects us to behave badly because of how others have treated them. We then withdraw from them and they see it as proof that they were right.

This is the ultimate self-fulfilling prophecy, and is all too common – particularly for those on the rebound. In many ways, you will know you are not in a good place to meet someone if you are struggling to detach from the outcome.

When we let go of the outcome and the need for it to happen in a certain way or within a certain timeframe, we adopt the mindset of detachment. This applies equally after you have just met someone who appears promising. Indeed, staying detached after we meet someone until mutual infatuation kicks in is critical. I see many people screw up their potential relationship within just a few dates by attaching too quickly. The other person can find this suffocating.

The journey is the destination

Detachment from focusing on the outcome forces us to focus on the process. The old adage that the journey is more important than the destination is more relevant to dating than most things. It sounds obvious, but so many people carry a version in their heads of what their ideal partner will look like. This is problematic on two levels. First, it means you are measuring a potential partner against an ideal that they will inevitably fail to meet. Second, you are missing the opportunity to be genuinely open to meeting a new kind of soul. A person may have parts to them that you do not have in your 'ideal partner' because you have never come across these aspects before.

This nicely loops back to curiosity. Those who adopt the mindset of curiosity to meet new people who may or may not become a partner, who may or may not become a friend, who they may or may not ever see again, but who may enrich their life in some small way, will succeed. With this mindset, you will be able to date for long enough to find your perfect match.

At a psychological level, this might require us to have a stern talk with ourselves and to be less needy and more relaxed, more philosophical about allowing life to unfold as it will. Yes, you may feel lonely, but please accept that nothing good will come from allowing that neediness to influence or drive your dating and your selection of a partner. A great relationship cannot be built on neediness; however, plenty of divorces are.

In short, watch your thinking and your behaviour as you remind yourself that while it is okay to be determined, it has to be matched by a healthy, equal dose of detachment.

It's about making a match, not rejection

Rejection is perhaps the hardest thing about getting out among it and meeting people. The people who can carry on long enough to meet their best match have a very particular form of the detachment mindset. They detach from seeing a relationship that does not proceed, for whatever reason, as rejection. *More specifically, they detach from seeing rejection as something wrong with them.* This is critical.

If you see a relationship not working out as evidence that there is something wrong with you every time, it will feel like a failure. Worse still it will leave *you* feeling like a failure. Most normal people can only take so much of this.

So, what is the mindset of people who are able to shake off a relationship not proceeding, without taking it personally? What is the mindset that allows you to date repeatedly until you find a good match?

The word 'match' is the key. The best possible mindset is built around recognising that you are looking for a good match. If it does not work out, it is simply because that particular pairing of you and that person is not a good match.

Bonnie and Clyde were an American criminal couple who murdered at least nine police officers and four civilians in the early 1930s as they went on a bank-robbing spree throughout the Midwest. They were glamorised in the 1967 movie starring Warren Beatty and Faye Dunaway, but treated more soberly in 2019 in *The Highwaymen*, which showed the Texas Rangers (played by Kevin Costner and Woody Harrelson) successfully hunting and killing the pair in a hail of bullets.

Bonnie and Clyde appear to have been a good match: they were *both* psychopathic killers. Hopefully if you or I were paired with Bonnie or Clyde, we would not have made a good match. Imagine the girl dating Clyde before he met Bonnie. When it didn't work out, there's a good chance she felt there was something wrong with her!

You don't have enough information to blame yourself

When we blunder or drop the ball in life, we need to wonder why. Indeed, being prepared to take on what I call 'healthy self-blame' – that is, take responsibility for our mistakes and screw-ups – is a good thing if you want to grow and become the author of your life. Looking at what we can learn from our mistakes is an important exercise for anyone wanting to become more conscious. When we do this, it is very different from just beating ourselves up. Self-talk like, 'I'm such an idiot ... I always screw up ... I'm such a loser ... why would anyone like me?' is not 'healthy self-blame'.

The self-talk of healthy self-blame is more like, 'Well I screwed that up, but then I am human and that is the human state. What could I do differently next time?' Because it is uncomfortable to hold painful feelings about making mistakes, we need to be gentle with ourselves at these times. In this way, we can examine what we did and work out how to do it better.

Paradoxically, the harsher we are with ourselves, the less we can hold the discomfort to learn from it.

NOTE WELL: Healthy self-blame does NOT apply when a relationship does not work out.

Beating yourself up when a new relationship does not work out is an exercise in self-destruction! After only a handful of dates, *no one has enough information to meaningfully learn anything*!

I have had patients come in convinced that a relationship ended because of something they did, only to find out later they were not just off the mark, but the real reason was in fact something completely different. When I'm working with couples, I can easily see how very wrong we can get this. She will say, 'He clearly does not find me attractive anymore. He has totally lost interest in sex.' He will tell me, 'Ever since I had trouble getting an erection, I have been really anxious about having sex in case it happens again, even though I still find Sarah really attractive.' Rarely do people guess correctly what appeared to be the cause of a relationship problem. This is true even with couples who have been together for many years. As I have said, unsurprisingly we humans are rubbish at mind-reading. It is why it is so important for even long-married couples to communicate where they are at with each other and why.

After a handful of dates, there is almost zero chance that you will know the other person well enough to accurately guess why they do not want to continue the relationship. Even when the other person has explained what brought the relationship to an end for them, it still may not be the real issue.

When my patients ask me for advice on what to say to the other person when they want to break it off, I give the following advice. Learning from Julie, our professional matchmaker, don't tell them about something they couldn't have changed. That is too hurtful, not to mention pointless. To tell someone that they are not smart enough, tall enough, funny enough or extroverted enough is cruel.

Equally, I will suggest that if it is something the other person could have changed, you may want to let them know, but even then only if you are confident that it would make them a better person. You shouldn't raise an issue that would just make them a better match for you. It would be okay to say, 'I'm ending it because you are just not reliable enough. You keep on flaking on me, even though I have raised it with you several times.'

It is not okay to say to an introvert, 'I'm ending it because you're too happy to stay home and don't want to go out with me.' Indeed, extroverts need introverts to slow them down and not burn the candle at both ends. Often my patients find it simplest to say something like, 'I'm sorry, but I just don't think we are a good enough match.' And yes, this does leave the other person with too little information to be clear about where the issues with them lay. This is why you do not want to try playing this most pointless of guessing games if you are on the receiving end of someone ending a relationship.

It still hurts

Finally, let's acknowledge that it can be heart-wrenching when yet another relationship doesn't work out. In his book *The Last Lecture*, Randy Pausch gives us a powerful perspective on how to see things when they do not work out: 'Experience is what you get when you didn't get what you wanted. And experience is often the most valuable thing you have to offer.'[14] I would add that wisdom is built on experience, which means we only gain more wisdom from things not working out for us. Remind yourself of this at these times, and think about what you can take away from this that makes you a little wiser. If you are up for it, next time things are not working out for you, see whether you can make the mindset shift to actually thanking the universe for giving you more wisdom. I find it helps.

At the very least, we can get better and more experienced at being philosophical about things not working out. We need to perfect healthy ways of moving on and not beating ourselves up. (Sometimes, less healthy ways involving some alcohol and commiserating with a close friend or two are okay too.) When it comes to making a match, you are not right or wrong, or a good or bad person. A match simply is or it is not. Remember, Bonnie and Clyde were a perfect match – they even had the good fortune to both die at precisely the same time.

When the pain from a past relationship has eased, it is time to enter the dating fray again, but first we need a quick self-check on how we see dating.

Dating sucks! Or does it? Why we date

JBW

> So much of dating involves this interplay of empathy
> and narcissism: you weave an entire narrative out of a
> tiny amount of information, and then, having created
> a compelling story about someone, you fall in love with
> what you've created.
>
> – Kristen Roupenian[15]

Dating has evolved so much over the last 20 years that it has left many people with mixed feelings about the whole process. I often hear the sentiment, 'I hate dating!' from my single clients. It is as if they want to jump from the introduction phase directly to the exclusive phase, and skip dating altogether. Yet dating has its purpose. It is the opportunity to 'try before we buy', which can help to save us from enormous hurt and pain down the track. Trying to avoid or rush it is precisely why so many people fail to find lasting love.

Moreover, dating is meant to be fun – and it should be. The excitement of meeting someone new, the charge of sitting across from a fresh face who may want to really know, hear and see us. There are few things that are more refreshing than having a genuine laugh with someone we have just met as we experience a coming together of minds. Discovering a like-minded soul is like scratching a winning lottery ticket. These times sparkle with the wonder and promise of what relationship happiness could be coming our way.

The problem is that, for many people, dating is not seen as fun at all. It is scary, or at the very least threatening in some way. It can be yet another opportunity to be rejected and another way the world can leave us feeling we are not good enough.

Most people think the challenge is to capitalise on the promise of finding a lifelong partner – to find new love and make it come true. In this book, however, we suggest that the goal is very different. In our view, dating is not first and foremost about finding a partner who will make you happy. Instead, it is about mastery – mastering the skill of assessing and choosing wisely – and this is the very essence of dating. Most importantly, it is about having fun and enjoying ourselves along the way.

Why do people have such a problem with dating?

At first glance, it seems that we do not like dating because it may lead to one of the most painful forms of failure: rejection. And more dating experiences tend to put us at more risk of rejection. There is also another significant issue that sits behind this: *uncertainty*.

Many people rush this critical phase because they do not understand the importance of dating – how it works or how to manage it. It is confronting, so we seek to avoid it. Yet the short-term gain of avoiding the discomfort of dating often comes with a huge long-term cost.

The human mind has a major problem with uncertainty. The less we know about the future, the more the human mind tends to fill in the gaps to make it more certain. This can work in both a positive direction (assuming the best and ignoring warning signs) or a negative direction of assuming the worst. Both directions can work against you. For example, have you ever caught your mind straying in the direction of thoughts like, 'I'm going to end up alone' or, 'At this rate all the good ones will be taken'?

As our mind becomes fixated on the worst-case scenarios, settling early on a potential partner becomes dangerously more attractive. Once we find someone with potential, our mind goes, 'Great, I can relax now. My problems are solved.' Chances are they are just beginning.

Similarly, it is important to recognise that we shouldn't fall in love with potential. As discussed earlier, the infatuation phase of the relationship is often when a potential partner is going to put the most effort into being the person we want them to be. While they might show potential, if they are not taking action towards fulfilling their potential (of their own accord), it is unlikely that they will fulfil it in the future. This is why we can't live on the hope and dream that we will inspire another person into changing. They need to decide that on their own terms. Potential is an alluring quality in a partner, but realistically useless until fulfilled.

Nothing will sabotage our hopes of a successful relationship as much as settling too early and *not* taking the time to evaluate someone and our relationship with them fully (based on real evidence which takes time to collect). We need to make our peace with uncertainty playing a constant role in our dating life, and rather find ways to ensure our fears and fantasies don't ruin our chances. Detaching from our need for certainty is a particular focus of the detachment mindset we discussed in the previous chapter.

Mostly, we need to keep a close eye on that part of us that wants us to settle to avoid uncertainty, rather than because we have made a good match. Our normal human discomfort with uncertainty is further aggravated by our genetics. We are neurobiologically programmed to be in a relationship.

To minimise the chances of making the biggest mistake of our life, we therefore need to resist the urge to commit ourselves too early in the dating process. After all, dating is where we perfect a vital life lesson: how to choose well. For this reason, we do not want to rush this phase – instead, we want to master it.

You may have to kiss a hundred frogs

At the end of the day, when it comes to evaluating our options effectively, experience goes a long way. The main benefit of experience is that we learn what is important to us in a relationship as well as who we need to grow into in order to get the love we want. Ideally, dating is just as much an experimental period for us to explore ourselves and our options.

For this reason, dating is largely a numbers game. As the saying goes, we may have to kiss a hundred frogs – maybe even a few toads – before we find our Prince (or Princess) Charming. Unfortunately, there is no way to tell the difference from a distance – we need to get a little closer. Chances are that the first (or second or third) frog we kiss will not prove to be a partner who is a good long-term match for us. In that case, we'd better get kissing!

In many ways, the art of dating is about getting comfortable with saying 'no' to unsuitable partners more often than saying 'yes'. In the end, you only need to say 'yes' once, but you may to have to say 'no' twenty times to get there. It is also more about getting into and out of relationships and learning from those experiences than it is about finding our perfect match. If we master this phase, choosing a partner who is a better match for us is almost inevitable.

But where do we find all these frogs? One solution is online dating. With online dating, we are no longer restricted to the frogs in our own backyard – we've got the whole world at our fingertips. Yet sometimes this can get overwhelming. The trick is to use this tool well.

Online dating: More choice, more challenge

JBW

Today, if you own a smartphone, you're carrying a
24/7 singles bar in your pocket.

— Aziz Ansari, Comedian

For the millennial generation, online dating seems to be both
a gift and a curse. In many ways, it is just one big social
experiment riddled with pros and cons. On the one hand, we
have more access to people than ever before (which is the main
benefit — and it is a big one). On the other, this unnatural way
of connecting has produced a lot of uncomfortable symptoms
that ironically tend to create more barriers to connection than
ever before.

   We see this with the rise of dick pics and new dating
vernacular like ghosting,[16] catfishing,[17] breadcrumbing[18] and
simmering.[19] Other troubling symptoms include app addiction,
tedious digital small-talk messaging, flaky (unreliable) people
and disappointing dates coupled with an overarching sense
of overwhelm. Add to this the rise of 'the hook-up culture',[20]
with many millennials complaining that they can't seem to

find anyone who takes dating seriously enough. Part of the problem is that online dating requires us to essentially reduce our beautiful, complex three-dimensional self into a two-dimensional, symbolic representation.

Then there is the way the apps commoditise humans, reducing us to products that are literally compared side by side. This is all fine if we are buying a new smartphone, but not so much if we are looking for a lifelong relationship. A commoditised approach shifts our mind into the two-dimensional world of online shopping – not the mindset we need for finding a good life-partner. The problem is that we lose a lot of our humanness in the process. It is hard to make a real connection with just photos and text on a screen.

Moreover, the gamification of dating apps takes us down the rabbit hole of seeking likes and matches rather than actual dates. Sometimes online dating can feel like a game of 'collect them all' designed to boost our egos rather than actually improve our dating life. This is not a helpful strategy for finding the love of our life. Thinking in this way makes it easier for people to cancel plans, ignore messages and send dismissive, rude and offensive texts. After all, you're no longer a real person – just a digital representation.

This often results in what I call 'online dating burnout' – that moment when you reach your limits of demoralising outcomes and swear to delete the apps and take a break from dating. Still, it's not all doom and gloom, and this kind of reaction is a sign that we are not using dating apps in a healthy way. For this reason, if you are finding online dating a drag, we would suggest you put it on hold until you finish this book. Online dating from the wrong mindset can be incredibly demoralising.

I believe in using online dating apps as a tool to practise new skills and meet new people, but we shouldn't rely solely on them as the be-all and end-all of dating. Offline dating is still incredibly important, and in some ways even more effective than finding love on dating apps. The key is to make the most of the opportunities the online world offers us, without getting caught up in the virtual vortex.

Get out of the game and into real dating

We first need to manage our expectations. While around one in four long-term couples do meet their long-term partners online, three in four of us still do not.[21] That was, at least before COVID-19. Granted, when pursuing love under lockdown, online introductions certainly became the easiest option. However, knowing that this too will eventually pass, it's important that we don't lose touch with our offline dating skills (more on that in the next chapter).

Overall, I recommend approaching online dating lightly, with one main objective in mind: to practise our dating skills. By using the apps to set up dates – even *virtual* dates – we can practise flirting, screening, building connections, asserting boundaries and dating different kinds of people while we learn about ourselves in the process.

However, it is crucially important not to spend hours (or even too many minutes) speaking to strangers online, as this is more often a time waster than an actual dating experience. This is why I recommend moving things off the apps as soon as possible. Online dating apps can be a good way to meet someone new, but until we meet them in the flesh, it's very difficult to gauge the most important aspects of a romantic connection, and easy to become over-excited and blinded by fantasy.

Technically, what we tend to do is 'project' our hopes onto our new-found potential date. The less 'real' information we have about them, the more we can project onto their empty canvas. Speaking on the phone, scheduling a video call or better still actually meeting in person, colours their canvas much faster. This leaves us much less space to fill with our misleading paintbrush of hope. By moving things offline quickly, we can avoid wasting hours on unrealistic connections and start getting to know the real person on the other side of the profile pic.

A key to making the most of online dating apps is to manage our time effectively. As I mentioned earlier, one of the more addictive aspects of online dating apps is the gamified ego-rush that comes with getting matches. Sure, it feels good to know that someone finds us attractive enough to swipe right; however, we must not get seduced by this gamification.

Another complexity to online dating is that it has introduced us to more choice than ever before. This can leave many of us wondering when to stop and invest and *what if there is something better just a few more swipes away?*

This is particularly troublesome for people who have anxiety around intimacy as often their mind will encourage them to keep on looking rather than giving a good potential relationship a real go.

In 2008, online dating users were already spending an average of twelve hours a week on online dating apps and websites.[22] Twelve hours! That's almost a month of non-stop swiping and clicking per year – and that doesn't even include the time we spend out on dates, it is *only* the time we spend online.

So, remember that true dating skills are *offline* dating skills and can only be acquired through real-world experience. Moving dates offline as soon as possible (or at least having a phone call or a virtual date early on) can save us time and help us to screen out people who are not a good match or are just looking to hook up. The reality is that, whether you first meet online or not, there is a lot more to building a connection than pictures and messages. It is actually our offline dating skills that allow us to create a sustainable connection, so we may as well be realistic and focus on building the offline connection sooner rather than later. That said, a good dating profile certainly helps to get your foot in the door. If you want to learn how to maximise your online dating profile, you can download my free guide here: www.jiveny.com/maximise.

Start with a phone call

Given that time is our most valuable asset, you don't want to waste a whole hour on a date that you realise you're not interested in within the first five minutes. That's why I always suggest starting with a phone call. So much critical contextual information is lost in online communication. We can tell so much more about a person from their tone of voice, cadence and ability to converse in the moment.

I learned this from a guy I met online. Just as I was starting to feel the online dating burnout creep in, he popped up and asked whether we could talk on the phone. That was a fresh approach to me among the countless mundane messages I had been exchanging with my other matches. I liked this guy's initiative.

We talked for about ten minutes before agreeing to meet up in person at the farmers' markets that weekend. And when we did meet up in person, things already felt much more natural between us. We had both planted seeds during the phone call that gave us an idea of topics in which we were both interested, which we could talk about on our date. I also noticed that I felt less anxious about meeting a virtual stranger in real life because I knew the man behind the profile had a kind and intriguing voice.

If you're cringing at the thought of having a phone call with a stranger, allow me to make the transition easier for you. It's possible to be flirty about this – after exchanging a couple of messages online, we might say, 'You seem fun, I wonder what your voice sounds like … Up for a phone call?' Or for a more direct approach, 'You seem cool, but I've got to be honest with you, I find the messaging side of these apps a little tedious … Would you be up for having a chat on the phone with me?'

The beauty of having a five- to ten-minute phone call before committing yourself to a date is that you also get to make a real connection. And once a real connection is made, it's harder for people to flake on you.

Warning: I wouldn't recommend talking for much longer than fifteen minutes before your initial date. Fifteen minutes is honestly enough to decide whether you are interested in meeting with them. And if you do decide to meet with them, a fundamental dating tip is to save some secrets for later. Have the phone call and if you still like them, send a follow-up text after along the lines of 'Hi (name), I enjoyed talking with you earlier. We should grab a coffee sometime. ☺'

Starting with a phone call before setting up a casual coffee, cupcake, drinks or gelato date will save you from boring dates with an online babe who is actually a total mismatch.

Breaking the wheel: Begin as you wish to continue

I often hear people complaining about the state of the online dating scene. They seem to think the rules have been written and they just have to follow them. This complacency is one way to get overlooked and be taken advantage of. Instead, we need to recognise our individual power in setting our own dating standards. When we stand up for ourselves, we stand out – in a good way. It's good to be different! Different is interesting, and interesting is often the basis of attraction.

In the early stages of dating, we are essentially teaching others how to treat us. What we tolerate now is what we will have to tolerate in the future. When it comes to relationships, we must begin as we wish to continue. Things don't get any better than in the beginning when you are both aiming to make a good impression. For example, if your date is regularly late and hard to reach, this is a behaviour that is likely to continue into the future. Ask yourself whether this is the kind of standard you want from a future partner.

Part of teaching others how to treat us is about asserting our standards and boundaries – not in an aggressive way, but in an assertive way. Staying true to our standards and respecting our boundaries is an important step when it comes to filtering out inappropriate dates.

One mistake I see people make online is that they can be very quick to get snarky and aggressive, which often unnecessarily burns the bridge of opportunity between two people. Instead, we want to use playfulness and flirting to challenge a potential partner to step up their game.

I remember one of my clients telling me about how she had been talking to a guy online and they had made plans to go out for dinner. On the day of the date, he texted her saying, 'Hey, I'm really sorry but I think I'm coming down with the flu. Can we please reschedule?' She wrote back a very quick and aggressive response: 'The flu? Or just found something better to do? Don't bother rescheduling. Goodbye.'

Bridge burned!

Instead, I would have suggested she write a more sensitive response along the lines of: 'What a bummer! Happy to reschedule as long as this doesn't become a pattern. I hope you're feeling better soon. ☺'

Here, a little empathy goes a long way. Even if he was using the flu as an excuse, it does not necessarily mean he was a bad guy. Meeting strangers through online dating comes with its own anxieties and can turn even the most genuine people into flakes. For this reason, it's not worth burning a bridge unless such behaviour becomes a pattern. As our matchmaker discussed in an earlier chapter, men are particularly looking for a partner who can provide them with a 'soft landing' (translation: warm, kind and caring) and this sort of scenario is a prime opportunity to communicate these sorts of qualities. In this alternative response, we can express ourselves as a person who is caring, direct around our expectations and also willing to give the benefit of the doubt. The key is not to get sucked in by a repeat offender.

Certainly, one of the downsides of online dating is the lack of respect people often demonstrate in relating to each other. From disappearing completely to rudeness and unwanted pics, online dating seems to bring out the worst in many people. This lack of respect and the trend of people wanting to 'keep their options open' when it comes to making offline plans makes sense on one level. The truth is that an online date comes at little cost – essentially nothing in fact.

In the 'olden days', a lot of work and money went into going out and procuring a date. There were outfits to buy, bars or clubs to gain entrance to and the cost of overpriced, watered-down drinks to consider – even before you met someone. Because of this initial investment, when you finally met the person of your dreams and organised a date for the following Saturday, you did not flake on it! These days, though, cancelling a date after a few swipes and a couple of messages does not feel like a crime to most people.

The point is not to take it personally. It's a thing. It is not about you. As frustrating as this can be, it also presents us with an opportunity to show others how we expect to be treated. Too many people miss this opportunity. They either get aggressive and cut ties at the first sign of disappointment, or they turn a blind eye, silently hoping that this person's behaviour will magically change overnight. Neither strategy is ideal. Instead, we need to assert our standards by gently letting people know when they are letting us down.

Unfortunately, our inner people-pleaser often gets in the way of this. Particularly when we find a profile that speaks to the image of our ideal partner, we can find ourselves more willing to compromise our standards and boundaries in an effort to meet this unicorn of a match. The problem is, the more we compromise and make ourselves available for this person, the more desperate we appear to be and the less attractive we become. This is why it is important to stay true to our personal standards, even if it means missing out on meeting that one guy you found yourself projecting a whole future and two and a half children onto.

If someone seems to be leading us on without making any concrete plans, we can tell them, in a playful way, 'My weekend is getting busy – you'd better make plans now or forever hold your peace. ;-)' Bringing a clear sense of playfulness and cheek is very useful when setting your standards, as tone and intention can easily be misread in text formats. (Emojis can help as long as we don't go overboard.)

This isn't about giving ultimatums or trying to manipulate someone into dating you (that is a sure way to scare someone away). It just means being clear and not allowing yourself to be treated like a last-minute back-up plan. Organising and showing up for a date on time is a clear indicator of respect, and healthy relationships are built on respect.

At the end of the day, dating is an evaluation process, and bad behaviour is a good reason to move on. After all, the more we say no to what we don't want, the sooner we will get to say yes to what we do want.

Staying safe while dating online

In October 2020, the Australian investigative journalism program *Four Corners* launched an exposé into the dark side of Tinder. In this disturbing account several women came forward to tell their story of how some opportunistic sexual predators have been taking advantage of such apps to access innocent women – and assault them.

In many of these stories the women trusted these men based on attributes in their profile like, 'He's a firefighter, he must be a good guy.' Or, 'He lives with his grandmother to take care of her, he sounds like a sweetheart.'

Making assumptions like this is totally normal; we all do this to some extent. Our minds learn to filter through the millions of bits of information coming at us at any moment by taking these mental shortcuts. It's how we've learned to function in such an overwhelming world. Yet by making assumptions like in the examples above, we can be lured into a false sense of security where we trust a stranger more than we should. Later, these assumptions can lead us to overlook warning signs that might appear down the track.

When you're faced with 100 online dating profiles and encouraged to swipe left or right based on very superficial information such as looks, a short description and occupation, of course we're going to make some mistakes. Especially when people are curating their profile to make themselves look as good as possible.

Now, in writing this I don't mean to scare you off online dating altogether. For every account of abuse there are, of course, countless people who have used these apps safely, and some have even legitimately found love. Like with all tools, the outcome lies in the care we bring to using it.

So how can we make dating safer for ourselves? Below are my top tips for keeping yourself safe while dating online.

For women

- Beware of anyone you notice showing up in your feed with different names, details or photos, but who are obviously the same person – this could mean that they are hiding something or inventing a fake persona to cover their tracks.
- If a guy makes you feel uncomfortable by making sexual advances online – particularly before you have even met – cut him loose. Even if you state your boundaries and he backs off, don't assume he's no longer only interested in sex. As one of the women in the *Four Corners* story shared, this is what happened to her. After rejecting his early sexual advances online, the buff firefighter assured her through their subsequent messages that they didn't have to do anything sexual before she felt comfortable with it. He then went on to rape her on their first 'date'.
- Schedule your first three to four dates during the day in public places that you feel comfortable going to. Often the night can come with a heavier weight of expectation to go home together or whatever else.
- Don't go to an online date's house at least for the first three dates. Current statistics suggest that the

majority of dating app–related sexual assaults occur on the first date. With that in mind, don't be afraid to pick the place you meet. If an online date suggests a venue that you are not sure about, give him a counter-offer. (The majority of these assaults also took place at the perpetrator's house or at a location the perpetrator suggested.)

- Avoid letting someone pick you up or drive you anywhere until you feel absolutely comfortable around them. Until then, meet them somewhere public with your own transport so that you can leave at any time.
- Trust your instincts. If you feel uncomfortable or unsafe at any point during a date, don't worry about hurting the other person's feelings – take your leave! If this feels tricky, have a simple code word you can text to a trusted friend to call you about an 'emergency' to get you out of there.
- Finally, while it's tempting to think 'that will never happen to me', just in case it does, keep some sort of record of the people you're meeting online. At a bare minimum, save their name, phone number and a screenshot of one of their profile photos.

In many accounts of those abused the most frustrating thing was that they had no ability to hold their abusers accountable. This was because once the perpetrator unmatched on the app, all their text history and access to the perpetrator's profile details were revoked. This made it difficult to report their assault to the police as they had nothing to point to as evidence of who had assaulted them. While this feature was originally designed to protect users from unwanted attention, it was instead being used by perpetrators to effectively disappear off the face of the earth.

This is another reason why I encourage people to *move interactions off the app as soon as possible*, even if you just transition to texting, or better yet, a phone call. Some women are worried about sharing their number with a stranger but keep in mind that you can always block someone you don't want to interact with anymore. By moving the conversation off the app and into your text inbox you retain ownership of your written interactions, along with the insurance of having the person's phone number. While most people you date online won't turn out to be such horrible humans, if things do go wrong you have control over any evidence that could help your case. Furthermore, perpetrators will be put off if they know that you have their phone number and/or email address which police might be able to use to further identify them after an assault.

For men
Men are not immune from having their trust abused on dating apps either, although more commonly the danger lies in being scammed out of money by a catfish. Indeed, this is a risk for women too, and the other loss after the money is trust, leaving people jaded, bitter and overly cautious. This, in turn, can make it harder to find true love.

According to Delia Rickard, Deputy Chair of the Australian Competition and Consumer Commission, 'Scammers go to great lengths to gain your trust, spending months and even years building a relationship with you. Once your defences are lowered, they spin an elaborate tale about how they need your financial help with a crisis, such as being ill or stranded, and ask for money.'

With this in mind, it is important to watch out for people who try to build an emotionally invested long-distance relationship with you. This is yet another reason why I encourage meeting in person within the first two weeks of contact.

One warning sign is if a person tries to keep the conversation focused on you; when they ask many questions to engage you, yet barely share about themselves. Other warning signs include an ongoing reluctance to meet in real life, weeks or even months into the connection. Some might even say they are stranded overseas or travelling for work. The real clincher is when they start asking you for money.

If you feel suspicious that you might be dealing with a catfish, you can always google 'reverse image search' and upload a screenshot of the images they provide on their profiles. These services can then tell you where else the image shows up on the internet.

The measures I have discussed here should be like putting on a seatbelt. While driving can be risky, we don't stop driving cars. By taking these simple precautions you can make online dating a much safer way to meet and connect with new people.

Maximising your first date

When it comes to organising your first date, you don't want to bite off more than you can chew. In the realm of first dates, there is nothing worse than meeting someone new, ordering food and *then* realising that the person in front of you is an obvious mismatch. Yet you still have to make small talk while you wait for your meals to arrive – and then get through eating them! At least if you've had a phone call or virtual date first this is less likely to happen.

Even so, it is for this reason that I encourage people to keep the first date brief (about an hour or so) with a secret option to 'spontaneously' add on a fun activity if you really hit it off. If anything, you want to leave them wanting more.

With a heavier reliance on meeting online, dating in the time of COVID also saw us doing first dates differently. With bars and restaurants closed, lockdown laws meant that the first date was a walk through a park or by the water. Some even turned grocery shopping into a fun date scenario.

As many people have since discovered, the laid-back activities that get people connecting side by side (rather than sitting across from each other in a noisy café with nosy waiters hanging around) can often lead to a much more relaxed and informative interaction.

Taking this on board, if you do decide to go out for drinks, cupcakes, coffee, gelato (or whatever else floats your boat), try to sit side by side or at a ninety-degree angle where possible. And if you can, go for some sort of walk together. This can help to calm your nerves and ease each other into the date as you are in a less confronting position. Symbolically, and in reality, connecting side by side is about a team taking on a challenge and meeting life together. Plus as the environment around you changes you can point out things you see to spark new tangents of conversation.

Another tip when it comes to the first date – aim to do something mid-week where possible. It is generally better to save weekends for friends and family. Too many people offer up their weekends, giving away prime social time to spend with our loved ones. The fact is, whoever is on the other end of the dating app has not yet qualified as a part of our inner circle, so giving them an all-access pass to your weekend is unearned. If your mid-week first date goes really well, then maybe arrange to follow up over the weekend.

When it comes to creating sustainable attraction, people need to eventually feel that they have earned their place in your life by taking respectful action and being reliable. In the meantime, if you haven't got much of a social life to speak of, use your weekends to work on that. Explore different workshops, events, meetups (meetup.com is a great resource) and focus your energy on making new friends. You never know – you could meet someone special this way too.

The first date is really about finding out whether there is going to be a second date. As our professional matchmaker, Julie, taught us, go on at least a second date (and maybe a third) unless there is zero attraction on the first date. So often people only reveal their true (more interesting) selves when they relax on the second and subsequent dates – as you will, too. Remember, you're not exclusive at this point, so you can do this with a few people at the same time. Don't worry about where you see the connection 'going' beyond that. Just keep it light-hearted and fun.

Remember, dating is a numbers game, keep showing up and you'll keep getting closer.

Offline dating in an online world

JBW

> Your task is not to seek for love, but merely to seek and find all the barriers within yourself that you have built against it.
>
> **– Rumi**

It was a cool, clear Melbourne night and Joe had only missed his tram by seconds. 'Dammit!' he said to his friend, frustrated that they would have to wait out in the cold for another ten minutes. Meanwhile, I was on the next tram, making my way home after a Cat Power concert. There I sat, towards the back of the carriage, listening to more Cat Power on my phone as I looked out upon the city I had just moved to. Melbourne was dazzling at night. So big, so full of opportunity!

As the tram slowed to make another stop, I looked up to watch new passengers hop on. That's when I saw him. Tousled ringlets, hazel eyes and a chiselled jawline, rocking a brown leather jacket and jeans. 'He's cute,' I thought as he found his place at the other end of the carriage.

But then I saw that he was carrying a guitar. *Oh no, not another musician.*

Still, I let my gaze linger on him a while longer. When he caught me looking, I playfully looked away and then back again. Our eyes met again and we both smiled. It only took a few more glances before he started making his way towards me and planted himself in the seat behind me.

I took my earbuds out and turned around to greet him with a warm 'Hello.'

'Hey, nice to meet you, I'm Joe,' he said to me.

This is how I met my husband.

To be honest, it wasn't the first time I'd met someone special offline and out of the blue. Having spent years travelling the world on my own, I had to learn how to break the ice and make friends with strangers in public places. Many of those encounters turned into dates and some of them turned into boyfriends.

In 2018, I started offering a monthly workshop entitled 'Offline Dating in an Online World' and every workshop sold out. The message was clear: many people are growing tired of online dating and are longing for more organic ways of meeting. The problem is that we seem to be out of practice when it comes to meeting people the old-fashioned way.

Most people are now so glued to their phones that they just don't see the opportunities to which they are incidentally exposed every day. Even if we do notice the opportunity to meet someone new, our lack of experience can often paralyse us with fear. Instead of rising to the challenge of a new connection, it often feels much easier to reach for a virtual distraction.

In many ways, our phones have become our security blankets, allowing us to maintain some illusion of dating effort while sheltering us from the risk of real-world rejection. As with anything in life, though, we have to take risks in order to get results. The good news, as you can see from my own story, is that making the most of offline dating opportunities is actually quite simple. We just have to find a little courage to put ourselves out there and it can be a lot more subtle than many people think.

Keep your heart, mind and eyes open

The first step in offline dating is to remain open to possibilities. This means consciously recognising that every time you leave the house, whether it's to commute to work, exercise or buy groceries, there will be opportunities to meet someone – so keep your heart, mind and eyes open.

Of course, if we want to meet more people in our day-to-day lives, we also need to communicate that we are ready for it. Sometimes we might have the passing thought that 'today might just be the day I meet someone special', yet once we are out and about, fear takes over. With our shoulders hunched and eyes averted, we are not really communicating that we are open to connection, which is why we need to make the effort to *stay* open.

Instead of scrolling through social media while we are on public transport, we need to keep our eyes up and be curious about the people around us. And when we see someone who piques our interest, the simplest way to get their attention is often just to make eye contact and smile (a few times). This is what I call 'signalling'. Yet so often we do the opposite: when we see someone we like, we pretend to ignore them. I used to do this too, flaunting my poker face, hoping in vain that I could attract someone by being aloof and 'mysterious'. In hindsight, I can see that as a young woman I used this misguided strategy to hide. I tended to play things very cool and coy because it was safe – because it meant that I didn't have to face my fear of rejection or of coming on too strong. And this strategy was costing me so many opportunities to meet men who I was actually attracted to.

Of course, this doesn't mean I want you to run up to the next person you find attractive and give them your number. Trust me, that strategy doesn't work so well either! I'm talking about the art of flirting. So many people see flirting as a dirty word, yet it is a critical skill we need to master. Not only is it the way we communicate that we are open to interaction, but it is also how we avoid the humiliation of making an advance and getting rejected.

The thing about playing hard to get is that it doesn't work until we have made some kind of connection from which to pull back. In order to make a connection, we need to bring some warmth – which can be expressed as eye contact, smiling and making small talk. After all, what man in his right mind is going to want to approach a woman who is showing him absolutely no sign of being open to interaction?

A Mona Lisa smile

Many men agree that women can be intimidating to approach, so we shouldn't forget that they also share the very human fear of rejection. Furthermore, we women can often fall into the habit of going through our day-to-day life with a 'resting bitch face'. I get it – we've developed this skill for a reason. As women, there are times when we *do* want to non-verbally signal to men 'don't bother me'. This is when the resting bitch face comes in handy. The problem is when it becomes our default face and we don't even realise it.

See for yourself – get your phone and take a selfie. Before you look at the screen, feel what you think is your neutral, resting, everyday expression. The kind of face you walk down the street with. Then take the photo and have a look. Do you seem approachable? If not, then what can you do to open yourself up a bit? This is the next challenge for us all: we need to learn how and when to turn that resting bitch face off and on consciously.

Be warned, though: this doesn't mean going through life with a permanent smile on your face. The problem with a permasmile is that you have nowhere to go when you want to express a truly happy emotion. And if the smile fades when you start talking to someone, it can make them feel discouraged. At the end of the day, we just want to look approachable and genuine.

Research into this has suggested that the most approachable expression we can have on our face is the 'just about to smile' look – think Mona Lisa. If you look closely at the *Mona Lisa* you might notice a subtle glint in her eyes and a very slight upturn of her lips that is mostly carried by a lift in her cheeks.

You can use this reference as inspiration when you are out and about and willing to connect. Think of the key words 'pleasant and approachable' as if you are just about to smile. You may also want to practise it in the mirror, particularly focusing on how it feels on your face. Although don't overthink it – often the intention to appear approachable is enough to direct our body language and expression.

If you're a man, the advice is much the same. Think about what you are projecting when you are out and about. How can you appear more approachable?

And for both sexes, remember to look up from your device as you go through your day. Look around and into people's faces. Look for connection – you never know who might be looking back.

The power of signalling

Next, if we want to make more connections offline, we need to take our 'signalling' to the next level by directing it towards a particular person. The simplest way to do this is to hold eye contact for a moment longer than usual and then smile at them. (Again, note the difference between walking around with a permasmile plastered on your face and actually letting someone see you change your expression to smile at them.)

The beauty of signalling is that it allows us to start slow and observe for feedback. How do they respond to us when they see us looking at them? Do they seem interested? What if we smile at them? Do they return it with warmth, or does it seem forced and awkward? The latter is okay too – it might just mean that they are in a relationship or, for whatever reason, don't feel comfortable engaging with you, or best of all, they are just plain old nervous … but interested. Feedback is everything and if the feedback is positive we can either wait and see if this person decides to approach us, or we can go over and say 'hi' to them ourselves.

Seriously, don't under-estimate the power of a simple 'hi'. So many people do. They waste the moment obsessing over the wittiest, smartest line they wish they could lead with and before they know it, the moment has passed. The important thing to remember is that when we have an opportunity to start a conversation, it doesn't really matter *what* we say. All that matters is that we say *something* to break the ice and get the ball rolling. Often small talk will flow from there and if we stumble and embarrass ourselves that is okay too. It can be helpful to know that our imperfections and vulnerabilities (like being too nervous to get our words out right) are endearing. These moments make us human and relatable, and connections are built on relatability.

Perhaps the most misguided notion of modern dating is that we need to be 'perfect' to be loved. Perfect is not relatable (remember our earlier discussion on being vulnerable). In fact, perfect can be a barrier to intimacy, a shield to real love, because it prevents us from letting people into our inner world. Instead, we need to embrace our imperfections as opportunities and let people see us without the mask. You're imperfect, I'm imperfect, the person you are most attracted to is also going to be imperfect. So, let's not start out by being inauthentic and pretending we are approaching perfection when none of us are.

Breaking out of small talk

One way to maximise the dating opportunities in our day-to-day lives is to bring positive energy wherever we go. This means interacting warmly with others, including the gym receptionist or the cashier at the local grocery store. These are excellent people on whom to practise our offline dating skills, whether we are attracted to them or not.

Look, smile, make small talk and share a small titbit about yourself. This communicates to the people around you that you are open to connect – not necessarily to go on a date (that's up to you to decide later), but at least to connect.

You might not be a huge fan of small talk. Not everyone is. Yet small talk is still an important stepping stone to making a connection. It is a tool that can lead us smoothly towards the deeper conversations where we can really bond. The trick is not to get stuck in boring small talk. Use it as an opportunity to break the ice and then transition into something more interesting.

The truth is that it is our responsibility to initiate more interesting conversations with people. As British dating coach Matthew Hussey says, 'Boring questions do not require boring answers.' If we want to become better conversationalists, we need to take it upon ourselves to direct our conversations down more interesting avenues.

It can help to come prepared by having some conversation topics up our sleeves that we can share with anyone at any time – like an experience we have had lately or a book we have been reading. When someone asks, 'How are you?' or 'What have you been up to?', take it as a cue to share something a little more specific.

For example, when someone asks me how I am, I might say, 'I'm great, thanks. I've just been listening to this great podcast about X, Y, Z – have you heard about it?' and the conversation will transition from there. In this moment, not only have I taken the connection slightly deeper, I'm also revealing a little about my interests and how I spend my time.

That question at the end, 'Have you heard about it?', is an important piece of this puzzle as it invites the other to engage with you. If they have heard about the podcast, article, book or documentary, you can both share your thoughts on it. If they haven't, you can introduce them to something new and tell them why you would recommend it.

Having these brief social interactions – even if they only last a minute or two – is an important step in building our social confidence. The more we practise connecting with strangers while the stakes are low, the easier it is to naturally connect with someone we find attractive when the opportunity arises.

Practising these skills of signalling and transitioning out of small talk opens new doors for us as it widens our range of dating possibilities. It also makes it more likely that when we meet someone in whom we are interested, we'll be able to get their attention and make a lasting impression. Now you're not just Suzi who he sees at yoga from time to time – you're Suzi who has a passion for permaculture and told a fascinating story about how a guy turned a desert into a food forest. Before you know it, you've gone from meeting someone on a tram to 'offline dating' and from there ... who knows?

'But I'm too busy to date!' Making love a priority

Many people who choose to sacrifice their social life for their careers regret making that decision down the line – even when it was a conscious choice. Unfortunately, the older we get, the more effort we will need to put into finding a mate, simply because there is less access to the singles scene.

For this reason, in addition to making the most of offline dating opportunities in your day-to-day life, you may also want to consider what extracurricular activities you can involve yourself in to meet more dates. In this age of 'busy', this often requires a bit of forethought. I recommend setting aside time at the beginning of each month to google upcoming events and research workshops in your area. Even better, enrol yourself in a six-week course to learn a new skill. Partner dancing (like salsa, swing or tango), acting classes and mixed sporting teams are great for this. Tailor your choices to the kind of person you think you might like to meet – where would they hang out?

The beauty of taking on a regular class or course of lessons is that it means you get to socialise with a new group of people for a set number of weeks. This naturally helps to facilitate new relationships as you get to know each other session by session. Even if you don't directly meet someone you would like to date, these activities can also help you to make friends with other single people – and you never know who they might introduce you to.

While we're at it, another key to finding love for the busy single person is to make friends with people who are also single and share a similar lifestyle. This is about finding a 'wingman' or 'wingwoman' who can accompany you to different events. Note that when wanting to meet new people, small groups of two or three are much more approachable than large ones.

In some cases, it may even be worth considering a location or career change in order to support your quest for love. Dating is a numbers game and sometimes our location or career can severely limit our options. Honestly, this is one of the main reasons why I decided to move to Melbourne – a bigger city with more events and brand-new prospects. As an introvert, I also found that moving to a new city gave me the monumental push I needed to put myself out there and be more social.

Then there are the limitations enforced by our career. Before the invention of dating apps, meeting a potential partner through work was not uncommon. Today it still accounts for around 15 per cent of relationships, although tread carefully – dating a close co-worker is ill-advised. Ideally your career can connect you with eligible singles who work in different sectors – maybe in the same building, but not necessarily the same office.

One other concern about how our careers can impact our dating life is the hours we work. Shift workers can have a harder time meeting new people as they are often unable to participate in regular social activities. If this is you, we suggest showing up and going out whenever you can, even if it means going to a party for only an hour before you start your shift.

The key for all of us who work hard is to put in that extra effort to 'play harder' by showing up even when we don't feel like it and making the most of the moments when we do get to socialise.

Become an initiator

Another great way to expand our options is to become an initiator and start hosting our own events. This could be a monthly picnic in the park or a fortnightly games night (my personal favourite), a weekly after-work gathering with colleagues at a local bar or anything else that excites you. Invite your friends and new acquaintances (from all the activities you've been involving yourself in) and tell them to bring a friend. Whatever you choose, I recommend keeping it low key and fuss free so that all you really have to do is set the date, invite people and show up. If you are hosting something at your own home, don't be shy about asking people to bring a plate of food to share.

This is a powerful strategy because so often we meet people while out and about but feel too anxious to ask them to hang out one-on-one and so we never follow up. When you get into the habit of hosting a regular event like this, you instantly have something you can invite new acquaintances to in a casual way. Games nights are particularly great because they serve as a natural ice-breaker and get people engaging with each other and having fun. Board games like Catan (for smaller groups of four to six people), Codenames and Articulate are some of my favourites to get the party started.

Face it until you make it

Perhaps the greatest force that gets in the way of offline dating is simply inexperience. This, in turn, augments our fear of rejection. If we haven't allowed ourselves to gather much relationship experience during our early adult years, we may experience more anxiety about putting ourselves out there.

Regrettably, there is no other way to overcome this than through immersing ourselves in the experience and being willing to learn from our mistakes. Sadly, relationship experience cannot be faked (at least not in the long term) and theoretical knowledge can only take us so far. In order to overcome this anxiety, we need to face our fears, put ourselves out there and experiment with what we have learned as we develop our own relationship skills.

Having said that, something that does seem to help with this journey is developing deep and meaningful friendships with the opposite sex (particularly if you are looking for a heterosexual relationship). Especially if we find ourselves feeling intimidated by the opposite sex, building such friendships can help us to develop the understanding we need to relax and connect. Perhaps we will even realise that we are not so different after all.

In John T. Molloy's book entitled *Why Men Marry Some Women and Not Others*,[23] he found that the women who got follow-up dates were more likely to have long-term friendships with men, or brothers. This gave them a better understanding of how to relate to men. These women were also less focused on impressing their dates and more focused on enjoying the experience, which consequently made for better company. They also rarely had sex on the first date and while they often went along with a man's plans, they were also willing to openly object to things they were not happy with.

I would argue that this insight is just as applicable to men – that the more friendships men have with women, the better insight they have and the less likely they are to become concerned with impressing their dates too (an absolute attraction killer). Many of the women with whom I work also talk about how they want a partner who is confident enough to be upfront about what they do and don't like (without being overbearing), and willing to take the lead sometimes.

Overall, offline dating is about becoming more social. You may have come across the saying 'You'll meet someone when you least expect it.' The problem with this advice is when people use this as an excuse to stop trying at all. Instead of going out, they stay home and watch Netflix, waiting for Mr or Ms 'Right' to beat down their door. Unless you're looking to date the pizza delivery person, it's a terrible strategy.

Rather, this advice rings true when people get into the habit of being social and learn to enjoy themselves along the way. If we can focus on enjoying ourselves in the world regardless of whether something romantic might happen, we naturally become much more attractive to the people around us. Finding a partner is no longer our sole focus; we are simply open, curious and ready to connect with others. It is this healthy attitude of detachment (as we discussed in an earlier chapter) that is often the key to finding the ultimate attachment.

With our newly detached and opened minds, this might be the time to look at our 'perfect match' in a whole new light.

Being opposite, the same and complementary

GBW

> It is the things in common that make relationships enjoyable,
> but it is the differences that make them interesting.
>
> – Todd Ruthman

A recurrent problem I see with dating sites is their over-reliance on matching partners based on similarities in personalities and interests. I am going to suggest, and review the research that confirms, that when it comes to our personalities and interests, Paula Abdul got it right. Sure, there needs to be some alignment or similarities between partners, but only in very particular areas. And there also needs to be some approximations between partners.

We have already looked at the psychology of attraction and the key role of Imago theory. Now we need to add another layer of complexity when it comes to understanding how attraction and partner pairing works.

So who is Paula Abdul and what did she get right? More recently, she's been best known as a judge on the first seven seasons of *American Idol*. She was originally a cheerleader who became the head choreographer for the Los Angeles Lakers when she was discovered by The Jacksons. Her dance choreography skills suddenly became highly sought after as she found herself on the wave of the emerging music video era in the 1980s. Then she had a go herself – and had four number one singles off her debut album, a world first.

Your homework, dear reader, is to stop reading and go and watch Paula Abdul's YouTube video of 'Opposites Attract' – one of those four number one hits. With 18 million views at the time of writing, you should not be disappointed. This video garnered several firsts. It was the first number one hit in America to feature rap verse performed by an African American (actually a duo, The Wild Pair). Then the video won a Grammy for its dance choreography. Not only was her dancing cool; it was her dancing partner that really made the video. She dances with MC Skat Kat – a cartoon figure created with Disney's help (she choreographed him too, of course) – who went on to have his own career.

The song, written and produced by Oliver Leiber, is all about how opposites attracting is the way of nature. I don't normally build a psychological thesis upon a pop song, but these lyrics just hit the nail on the head when it comes to the science – about how love is a 'natural fact' and 'we come together, cuz opposites attract'. There are good reasons why we want a partner who is very different from us genetically. Surprisingly, smell is one of the better ways to establish just how different a potential partner is from ourselves.

Smellovision

Almost for as long as humans have been farming, we've known that inbreeding weakens the species. It is well known that purebred dogs are more susceptible to certain illnesses than cross-breeds. Labradors, for example, are particularly prone to hip dysplasia and progressive retinal atrophy that causes blindness. Pure-bred dogs have a 2.5 times greater risk of inherited diseases than mixed-breed dogs.[24]

And so it is with humans. The less inbred we are, the greater our genetic diversity and the more disease resistant we are. This is why it's not a good idea to procreate with close relatives who share our genes. But how do we work this out? Generally, it is not too hard to identify our own immediate family of parents and siblings and not marry them. Cousins, aunts and uncles are also reasonably readily identified. Beyond that, it can get a little trickier. So, nature to the rescue.

Studies have shown that smell plays a significant role in attraction. Women – who are generally better at smelling than men – were found to be attracted, sight unseen (by smelling their t-shirts, for example), to men who were more genetically different from them. This triggered further research into the link between smell and our genetic makeup. In turn, it led us to Major Histocompatibility Complex (MHC) – the genes that determine key aspects of our immunity. What women are smelling corresponds to different kinds of MHC. We now have decades of research on mammals, birds, fish and reptiles, which support a female preference for MHC-different males. And it turns out that males can do it too.

In essence, being able to recognise MHC is a kin-recognition warning system. 'Do not make babies with this person' is the warning message if the smell is wrong. MHC similarity is problematic for the offspring of such a relationship. For example, multiple sclerosis has been found to be more common in children of parents with greater MHC similarity.[25]

While I have skipped over the research behind these points, I want to look at one recent study that brings it all together. In 2019, the Royal Society published 'Genomic evidence for MHC disassortative mating in humans'.[26] They studied 880 couples across seven countries – Belgium, Germany, Ireland, the Netherlands, the United Kingdom, Spain and Israel. The findings showed that we pair up with partners who have more dissimilar DNA.

The greatest factor that impacted this significant finding was the culture within which one chose their partner. At one end of the spectrum was the Netherlands, where the greatest genetic difference between partners was found. At the other end was Israel, with the least. Jewish people were found to have the greatest social pressure placed on them about who they married. The Dutch were the least influenced by socio-cultural constraints, so their partner selection was most true to MHC-driven, natural selection processes.

How does this play out in real life? Well, smell is an element of how women in particular select partners. If someone has the wrong smell, you don't make it much past the first kiss. This becomes an argument for why getting to the first kiss sooner, rather than later, is a good thing – we need to tick the up-close smell box.

Giving children the best head start

As well as our smellovision, we also have other ways of identifying a partner who is genetically different from us. The research shows that while friends tend to have greater similarities, we tend to look for partners who have different personalities and interests from our own. This has been found across cultures and is often driven by the women.[27] Not only is someone who is different from us more attractive to our DNA and more likely to contribute to the survival of our species, but there are more immediate benefits.

When George Clooney's and Brad Pitt's characters put together their first *Ocean's Eleven* team, what defined the choice of each member of the team was their differences, not their similarities. A successful casino robbery needs an electronics expert, an explosives expert, a talented pickpocket and so on. We can guess how successful the robbery would have been if everybody on the team was the same as George Clooney. Devastating good looks doesn't get a robbery done.

The typical couple of today has a different job to do, but the principle is the same: we need to deal with a range of life challenges, not to mention raising children.

This evolutionary reason for why opposites attract was nicely summarised by Dale Carnegie, who said, 'When two partners always agree, one of them is not necessary. If there is some point you haven't thought about, be thankful if it is brought to your attention.'

Children particularly benefit from two parents who are very different to guide them through the challenges of life. Children watch very carefully as each of their parents (if they are lucky enough to have two around) apply their different strategies to the various life challenges thrown at both the children and their parents. They learn from both parents and develop a much wider repertoire of responses to whatever life throws at them. Two very similar parents will only have half as much to offer their children.

Not at all surprisingly, research has shown that dominant personalities are more likely to pair up with submissive personalities. We can readily appreciate how two dominant personalities would quickly end up in a huge power struggle, while two submissive people could be somewhat directionless.

The most recognised difference in how partners pair is between introverts and extroverts, who are more likely to marry their opposite than not. It is not hard to see why. If you put two introverts together, they are both happy to stay at home, sit on a device or watch TV – little social interaction happens. Alternatively, put two extroverts together and they are competing with each other for stage space. They always want to go out and socialise. There is no one to hold them back from burning the candle at both ends. Research has also found that people who see themselves as witty, and good at being humorous, tend to pair with people who are not, but are appreciative – that is, they are a good audience. As we consider these pairings you can see that it is about more than just being opposites.

It's really about being complementary

We can see that it is about something a little more than simply choosing an opposite to get the best DNA mix. To dance in a powerful, intimate way requires one person to go forward while the other does the opposite. Which brings us to the word 'complementary' – perhaps a more useful word than 'opposite'.

Oxford Languages online defines it very nicely as 'combining in such a way as to enhance or emphasise the qualities of each other'. This is why Jerry Maguire's heartfelt words, 'You complete me' bounced around the world for so long. (Never mind that they were apparently completely lost on Dorothy, who responded with the almost equally immortal, 'Shut up. You had me at "Hello".') What Tom Cruise and Renée Zellweger's characters are capitalising on here is the fullness of complementarity. (Search 'Jerry Maguire You complete me' for the full scene on YouTube.)

Of course, it is very difficult for a matchmaking site to match potential partners on the basis of complementarity. Oppositeness would be easier. But the opposite of someone who is witty is someone who is not, whereas what we need is someone who appreciates humour – which is different again. It would take a complex computer algorithm to do that. For this reason alone, I discourage people from using dating sites that match people based on their similar personalities and interests.

There is another bonus to being with someone who is dissimilar to you: you have more fun. This is simply because a partner who is different from us makes our life richer in many ways. They take us into their world that is different from ours. Novelty is a key ingredient of fun and we are encouraged to experience and appreciate things that, left to our own devices, we would simply never encounter.

I would never have enjoyed bushwalking at all, let alone bushwalks in different countries, if my wife was not so mad keen to find every waterfall on the planet. Equally, she would not enjoy sailing to remote, palm tree–lined beaches or driving in fast cars if she had not married me. Okay, she still doesn't enjoy driving in fast cars ... which brings us to the next issue and the next chapter. There are some problems that follow from our attraction to those who complement us.

While opposites attract, there will be problems

GBW

> A great marriage is not when the 'perfect couple' comes together. It is when an imperfect couple learns to enjoy their differences.
>
> – Dave Meurer

In the last chapter, we looked at how we are drawn to, and why we benefit from, partnering with people who have different personalities and interests from us. As we saw earlier, given the way our Imago works, our mind may also draw us into relationships in order to have certain healing experiences. This unconscious agenda can cause us significant problems down the track. This also applies to our attraction to difference.

The good news is that these factors can be happily managed as long as we understand what is going on. Many relationships fail, leaving both parties hurt and confused, because these forces wreak havoc if they are allowed to roam free and unchecked. We all need to have a good understanding of how attraction sets us up for conflict and how *this is perfectly normal*. Not understanding the principles that I talk about in this chapter have brought many, many relationships undone.

Tom and Sue[28] came to see me for marital therapy. While they were grappling with a number of issues, I want to cover a particular one here. Sue was unhappy with Tom because he wanted to go out all the time or have friends over.

'He just wants to go out and party all the time,' Sue bemoaned.

'She just wants to stay home and hibernate,' Tom responded. 'I want to catch up with our friends. And not just my friends, other couples who Sue likes just as much. If only I had a partner like me,' he added.

I let his last comment stand, deciding to come back to it later. I asked the question I generally find quite revealing: 'Sue tell me what attracted you to Tom in the first place? Maybe go back to when you first met.'

After thinking about this for a while, she said, 'Well, I guess I was drawn to his animation and storytelling. He had an energy. I remember when I first met him, he was standing with a couple of mates telling a story and I could see that they were all laughing. I guess I wanted to have some of the fun they were having.'

In a nutshell, Sue had captured the difference between them. Tom was gregarious and entertaining; she was more of an introvert, who at one level – like most introverts – wanted more (but not too much) social interaction, but found it hard work to engage. Tom held the promise of taking her places socially to which she would not naturally take herself. On the other hand, Sue needed to be on her own to recharge her batteries. Like most extroverts, Tom did this by catching up with friends.

When I asked Tom a similar question, he said, 'Sue, was different. I could see she was a thinker. She also had a lovely laugh. I was drawn to her depth. Her calmness. She was different from the dizzy girls who laughed at my jokes whether they were good or not. She really appreciated the good ones. She would also challenge me by asking me why I thought so and so. She didn't let me get away with saying anything that came into my mind. She made me think more deeply about things. I also liked going to her place. She had spent a lot of time making it feel like a home.'

Once I painted a picture for this couple as to how they were actually together because of the personality traits that now annoyed them so much, they began to relax with each other.

I asked Tom, 'Have you ever had a girlfriend who was more like you and liked to socialise?'

'Sure, there was this girl I dated at college. We were friends first. She was in the same group that would hang out in the local bar. She loved to party. One night after we had both drunk too much we went home together, and it went from there.'

'And how did that work for you?'

'Actually, it was pretty crazy. We didn't get much sleep. We both drank too much. I almost failed that semester.'

'Did you ever think of marrying her?'

'Don't be silly,' he laughed. 'That would have been crazy. She would have killed me.'

'And Sue, did you ever have a boyfriend more like you, who was happy to stay home?'

'Sure. At college I dated this guy for a few months after we had studied together for a while.'

'What happened?'

'Well it was good during semester, but in the summer holidays he wanted to stay home and build his models and I wanted to get out and do some things.'

'Would I be right in guessing that you did well at college while you were with him?'

'Sure.'

'And did you think of marrying him?'

'Nah. He was too boring.'

I didn't need to go too much further before Tom and Sue saw what they were up against. As we explored how their very differences were part of the basis of their relationship, they realised they had been attracted to aspects of each other's personality that were coins with two sides. They could not have one without the other. In therapy, they came to rebuild their respect for the other as they remembered and embraced the key ways in which their partner's differences enriched their own lives. Their differences offered the complementarity that they knew, from their previous relationships, was a better match for them.

There were the expected Imago factors at play as well. Sue's father had been a gregarious executive who was often away on business. He had had an affair and Sue's deeper concern was that Tom might end up going out and having a fling. Tom had been closer to his father, who was an introvert, and who spent a lot of time pottering around the house and teaching his son all sorts of handyman skills. Like Sue, his father was smart and would encourage Tom to think more deeply about issues.

Tom and Sue's story highlights something else. Our friends are more likely to share similar personalities and interests. Think about friends you made at school, or university, or playing a sport, or in the computer club. The shared interests provide an immediate glue, then the reasons why you are both drawn to the same interest provide further glue.

Here you see both Tom and Sue talking about dating ex-partners with similar interests. These are typical examples of the problems that arise from dating people who are similar to us. This brings us to a key point. The research shows that while we look for a partner who complements us, *we have more conflict with them.*

Luo and Klohnen, researchers from the University of Iowa, studied 291 newlyweds to look at who they paired with and the subsequent quality of their marriages.[29] As an aside, they again found that extroverts marry introverts. Overall, they confirmed that people married partners with personalities that were different from rather than similar to their own. They then looked at how happy these couples were after they married.

As they pointed out, the relationship between similarity of personalities and marital satisfaction is not cut and dried. Other studies have been contradictory in their findings on this interrelationship. Nevertheless, they found that the more similar the personalities, the better the marital satisfaction. So, as you can see, we have a complexity. We are drawn to opposites, which enriches our relationship – but this leads us to some issues, which means it may not be all butterflies and rainbows down the track.

I remember working with one couple where the guy was a tragic when it came to managing his finances. She was really good with money and had bought her own home. He was still renting and paying off his car. This complementarity would have been fine if he had respected her ability and handed over the management of the bulk of their money. As they approached marriage, from a misguided sense of 'manliness', he insisted he would be controlling the family finances. She, not unreasonably, pulled the pin a week before the marriage. You did not need to be Freud to work out that this couple would have issues down the track.

Here lies the paradox. We are attracted to people who have different personalities and then this pisses us off! But, we are attracted to them because they make our life richer, more fun. But then, they annoy us – and so it goes around. The logic that follows from this is that if a couple is not particularly good at working through conflict, the partners are better off if they have more similar personalities and interests. Life may not have the richness of difference, but for some couples this can be a worthwhile trade-off.

Sixty-nine per cent of problems are unresolvable

John Gottman provides a very interesting statistic that fits in right here. From his ground-breaking research studying 'normal' or 'successful couples', he found that 69 per cent of conflict is about unresolvable, perpetual problems.[30] That is a lot to not be able to sort out.

Much of this 69 per cent results from this tendency to be attracted to people with different personalities who have different ways of doing things, of approaching issues and of tackling life generally. Personality traits are stable over many years, so the problems that follow from them are stable over a long period too.

After 30 years of marriage, my wife and I still have arguments about what I consider to be my exemplary driving style. Did I mention how she likes driving in fast cars – only if we do not accelerate quickly, let alone go fast?!

As it turns out, my wife and I have opposite personalities on the four dimensions of the Myers Briggs personality profile. In short, we could not be more different personalities. It is the same for our interests. I like restoring old cars. Penny likes to cook. If I try, I apparently do it wrong. Penny cannot stand the smell of grease. There is no overlap here. I would be happy if I never had to step into a kitchen again. The upside is that she always has sporty, safe and reliable cars to drive and I am spectacularly well fed. Neither of us would have it any other way, but our personality differences lead to regular conflict.

Understanding that so much conflict is a normal consequence of partner selection is critical. My clinical experience is that the highest marital satisfaction occurs when couples have different personalities and interests *and* they are good at conflict resolution.

While the skill to resolve conflict helps, what is even more important is an awareness of these processes at work. In short, while opposites attract making for richer, more rewarding relationships, this causes the problems we have just covered and many more. The antidote is to *know* you are opposites and that your pairing has happened for an important reason.

Fortunately, Penny is a psychologist who has also done a lot of training in relationship therapy, so we have a head start. It also means we have thoroughly road tested every strategy that we teach the people who come to see us.

While this is not a book on relationship therapy, I will give you a quick crash course on this issue. In a nutshell, there are three key ways forward around points of perpetual conflict:

1. Recognise that the fight is over an item of perpetual conflict. It doesn't hurt for you and your partner to take some time to list the things that habitually come up again and again, so that you can more readily identify them and be ready not to overreact to them.

2. Second, work hard not to let it escalate to the point where you become mean to each other. Saying something, preferably out loud, like, 'Ah, this is one of

    our points of perpetual conflict,' is helpful to reposition the issue and remind yourself to be patient with your partner.

3. Third, agree to disagree as soon as possible and look to reconnect as soon as you can after the conflict, so it only brings the relationship down for minutes, not days.

Gottman found that couples who are good at this third point more quickly move to what he calls 'repair attempts'. These are signals to your partner that there are no hard feelings, that you recognise the issue is not a deal-breaker and that you want to reconnect and move on in the relationship. In short, healthier couples don't hold a grudge.

Repair attempts come in different sizes. A little repair attempt is something like, 'What are we doing for dinner tonight?' A big one is to genuinely apologise for something you did, like, 'I'm sorry I got so angry with you before. That was uncalled for.' Other repair attempts include non-verbal affection, like a hug or doing something helpful for your partner.

What this figure of 69 per cent teaches us is that we cannot avoid conflict in our relationship – it is normal. Rather, we need to make sure it doesn't escalate and that we get the relationship back on track as quickly as possible.

In the chapter on defining love, I wrote about two key elements of true love. Just to remind you:

> True love is the feeling of being fully accepted by another who knows you intimately and who is committed to nurturing both your personal growth and their own.

One of the things we need to fully accept is that our partner has a personality that we were drawn to because it complements our own. Full acceptance means not getting annoyed at them for being different. Indeed, full acceptance means welcoming their differences because they will broaden our perspective, which leads to better decision making and a richer life.

As I mentioned, my wife and I more than complement each other: we are complete opposites. For example, my wife needs closure on an issue. She wants any uncertainty behind her so she can fully focus on the next issue. I like to keep it open as long as possible while I consider the options and take the pressure off having to make a decision before its deadline.

This causes conflict – particularly on big projects like building a new house. To her, I am just not dealing with things. To me, she is pushing unnecessarily.

It is important to remember that *no personality style is better than another.* They all have a time and place where they work best, and are the best fit with the situation at hand. The same applies to the workplace. The diversity in our personalities allows for a good fit with any of the varied roles that life requires of the human race. Equally, each personality style has its limits, where the fit is not so great.

My strategy of letting problems sit while I consider all the options, or do more research, can lead to a better decision. But it can also mean that I let problems accumulate and this can create unnecessary stress as deadlines approach. Stress can then lead to hurried, poorer decision making as the deadline forces a decision. Penny's strategy of wanting to sort a problem out sooner can also create stress from the sense that it must be solved now, when in fact there is more time. But when it is resolved sooner, that does free us up to give our full attention to the next problem.

When we accept each other's personality style, and capitalise on it, the magic happens. We negotiated the following: we sort tasks and problems by deadlines, well in advance. We plan to have the tasks done before the deadline, but not too much before, so we have some wiggle room. Then we sort by complexity. Simpler tasks we get done sooner, so we can cross them off the list. For the more complex tasks, we give ourselves until closer to the deadline.

This combined approach is superior to what either of us would have done on our own. Our personalities mean that we focus on different ends. I ensure that complex problems get maximum airtime. Penny ensures we are ticking off the tasks that can clog up the system. This is what full acceptance looks like. It only took us more than twenty years to perfect it!

As well as this critical role of accepting our differences, there is a particular antidote to the conflict that follows from butting heads around our differences.

The ultimate antidote to conflict

I was at a seminar on couple therapy many years ago. The author and therapist Wally Goddard was giving his trademark entertaining presentation when he mentioned something that did not quite make sense to me. He said he believed the single most important ingredient in a great relationship was patience. I sat there thinking, *What about big things like love, care, trust, loyalty, integrity and respect?* I was familiar with Wally's work and have been quoting him to my patients ever since I came across his particularly entertaining talk on love languages. So I knew it was unlikely that he was wrong. It took me some time to work out why he was so right. He only made a few comments about it and then moved on in his talk, but what he said got me thinking. Why would Wally rate patience as number one, ahead of all else? Then I got the fullness of what he was saying.

If it is present, patience is the final common pathway of all interactions between a couple. It is the final filter through which all other things have to pass.

There is little point to being loving and caring if it is delivered with impatience. The person on the receiving end will simply not feel the love or the care. The same applies to trust, loyalty and integrity. Patience is about the way we interact, the way we deliver our care on a day-to-day, moment-by-moment basis. How loved can a partner feel if we fly off the handle?

Equally, if you are patient with your partner whenever you interact with them, they will feel considered and respected. Most of all, they will feel heard. Not feeling heard is one of the most common issues that couples come to see me about. I spend a lot of time trying to get people to appreciate the importance of just letting their partner finish what they want to say without interruption, of hearing them out.

Too often, we humans try to have our way simply by not letting our partner say what they want to say – as if stopping them from saying something stops them from thinking or believing it. It is as though giving their words airtime will disempower us. Bringing patience front and centre into our interactions forces us to become a good listener, allowing our partner to feel heard and validated.

From another angle, I see one partner shut the other down from a fear that hearing them out will mean that they will have to agree or apologise. They are often surprised to find how much their partner can tolerate lack of agreement if they have been heard. This is true for all of us. Most of us are intrinsically okay with people not agreeing with us, but we want to exercise our right for our different opinion to be heard. Patience creates room for all of this.

The two parts of true love are full acceptance and the commitment. Earlier, I looked at how acceptance of our partner's personality plays out. Now let us talk about a practical application of commitment.

Being patient is not easy, particularly after a long, stressful day. It takes work. In particular, we need to be mindful in the moment, reminding ourselves, 'I need to be patient now, because I am committed to this relationship.' It is a good example of how true love is more about commitment than it is about a feeling.

Remember from our discussion on defining love – commitment is what carries a decision over time. So, we need to commit to work to be patient when we are experiencing feelings that are contrary to patience. Think here of feelings like frustration, irritation and, of course, impatience. This is how the commitment of true love works.

When people lose a loved partner, through death or divorce, they often talk to me about how they miss the quirky things their partner did – habits like eating noisily, leaving their underwear on the floor or biting their nails. As I listen closely, what I am often hearing is that these things often annoyed them earlier in the relationship. But these differences defined their individuality; they defined the person they loved. Over time, they also came to love these annoying things about their partner.

To be enriched by our differences and to not have them swamp the relationship, we need something more than good conflict management, acceptance and a commitment to patience. We need to have alignment on certain key issues. In particular, we have to be aligned in our relationship vision and our values. A failure to be aligned about where you see the relationship going, and the values in which you both believe, creates conflicts that can be too great for a relationship to survive.

In the next two chapters, Jiveny will dive into these issues.

Discovering true compatibility: Why values matter

JBW

I'm waiting for a woman who will love me for the man I
am ... pretending to be.

– Arj Barker, Comedian

By now you have probably wondered, 'If dating is an evaluation
process, then what are we looking for in choosing our life-
partner?'

People often tend to have shopping lists of what they want
in a partner. The problem is that sometimes we can make
the mistake of selecting criteria that are limited by our own
world-view without leaving space for the exciting unknown.
This can lead us to narrow our options a little too much and
discount a perfectly good match. While it is fine to put a few
deal-breakers on your list, like 'must not be a smoker' or 'must
not lack ambition', we don't want to get too carried away with
a super-specific list of desires and deal-breakers. After all, good
things can come in unexpected packages. It is also important

to note that, in order to properly 'evaluate' a potential partner, there is no substitute for investing quality time into getting to know a person.

Throughout this chapter, I also want to acknowledge that everyone will be looking for different things according to their own personality, values and priorities. As discussed throughout this book, dating is about finding a good match for *us* – someone who complements our own unique individuality. We all have different strengths and weaknesses, and our awareness of our own failings and strong points can also help to inform our 'criteria'.

With this in mind, the first few questions upon which we must spend some time reflecting are 'What kind of loving relationship do I want to experience?' and more specifically, 'What is most important to me in a partner?' In other words, what characteristics of a partner could help to balance you out?

Effectively, the more we can clarify what we want to create and experience in our future, the easier it will be to find a suitable partner. This is why it is so important for us to be single for some time and explore ourselves and our desires as an individual.

Aligned vision and values

As we have seen, opposites attract – especially when it comes to personality and interests. However, in some aspects alignment is definitely necessary. Research led by renowned relationship therapist Dr John Gottman, who we met in the last chapter, tells us that an alignment of vision and values is one of the most important factors predicting long-term compatibility in relationships. These two things can be make or break for most couples.

A vision is a plan, with varying levels of detail, for the voyage one would like to create and experience in their lifetime, while values are the moral compass that will steer the ship along the way. More specifically, a value is a guiding principle that is central to the way in which we live our life. Values inform our beliefs, actions and our aspirations. When we take the time to consider what we really want for our future, *before* we get into a relationship, we can use this as a compass to find a partner who complements our vision.

Harmonious pairings of both vision and values are important for long-term relationships – *very* important. This is because misaligned vision and values is a recipe for major, recurrent conflict, usually over some of the most important decisions that a couple must make together. This kind of conflict is quite different from the normal healthy conflict that builds a relationship. On the flipside, when we have a reasonable degree of value alignment, both partners will often naturally play a more supportive role for each other – without having to compromise or renounce their own core beliefs.

Let's consider a big value: the importance of family. There is a very big difference between people who value family at a high level and those who do not. Those who value family will most likely want to have children. They are also more likely to want to interact with the extended family on a regular basis. In short, they like spending their leisure time around family members. They are also more likely to canvass members of the extended family for advice and support.

At the other end of the spectrum you have people who want no children and want to spend their leisure time travelling or with friends. If they do have children, they are happy to have the children cared for by others most of the time and to take holidays without them. They want to keep their personal business separate from their extended family and make their own decisions or consult the relevant professionals. Often these people have grown up in families run by less functional parents, so their desire for separation is healthy and understandable. You can see how this would create issues if we had a couple from each end of this spectrum attempting to create a life together.

So how do you evaluate where your potential partner sits on this spectrum? By exploring discussion points (although probably not during your early dates!) such as:

- Do you want kids or not?
- If so, how many? (Two is different from five.)
- If you have kids, are you expecting that both parents will continue to work or do you want one parent to stay at home and look after them?
- How much would you see your parents as being involved in child care?

Another key vision question is where do you want to live? In the country or in the city? Acreage living is completely different from life in an apartment. This also relates to how much you want to engage with your local community. There is a big difference between living on a remote rural property, versus a small town with a close community or a high-rise apartment building in a big city.

As we explore these issues, we need to be creative and approach these discussions from a gentle, playful perspective. If you can, use a social cue from a movie or news story as a trigger to open the conversation. What it should not be is an interrogation.

Alignment can mean not feeling strongly

If two people in a relationship have different, strongly held positions, it means that someone is going to have to compromise, which may lead to more conflict or resentment down the track. Fortunately, there will often be one person who does not feel very strongly about an issue and is genuinely happy to go along with the other.

We need to be careful, however, to ensure the other person is 'genuinely happy' to go down a particular path. This is why we may need to revisit these issues more than once. Listen and look carefully to how your partner reacts. In the infatuation phase, partners are generally overly accommodating. In some ways, it is best to work this out during the power struggle phase because this is when you will hear what your partner really thinks.

Granted, often even in our late twenties we aren't entirely clear on what we want. The opportunity here is to co-create a life together. Indeed, it is through taking the time to trial and experiment with what we *might* want to do in life that we are able to get a better sense of what we *actually* want. Exploring this with a new partner also provides more insight into what we can create together, rather than just asking outright what the other person wants. This should be approached as a fun, interesting subject to explore as you enjoy the process of co-creating a life together.

As we have seen, 69 per cent of conflict in relationships is actually unresolvable. The key here is to make sure that *what* we argue about are not core values like whether to have children or how each other should be living their life – but smaller things such as where the toaster lives on the kitchen bench or the best way to peel a potato.

In the following sections, we share some examples of values for you to consider and how they might impact a long-term relationship. It is important to remember while reading this that the depth of one's values can sometimes only be revealed in time. Just as importantly, some values are only worked out as we mature, in and out of a relationship (this is one of the reasons why getting married later in life has a lower divorce rate). When dating, we need to actively explore the vision and values of our potential partners by watching, listening and asking questions about what they see in their future. This can take time, but it will save a lifetime (literally) of big arguments.

Dedication to personal growth

There is a saying in the coaching world: 'You're either green and growing or you're ripe and rotting.' In other words, life requires continuous growth. The question is whether you value personal growth. Is it something you seek out or does it just happen to you?

Being a bit of a personal development junkie myself, growth has always been an important value to me, so I have always been on the lookout for a partner who can grow with me. To me, that means someone who invests in dreaming, reflecting and learning from their mistakes in the name of becoming the best they can be. A partner who is willing to take ownership of their flaws and work on their issues. After all, if we are not growing together, it's only a matter of time before we start growing apart.

The fact that you are reading this book suggests that you probably value growth too, which is why I would suggest that you want to find a partner who is also interested in growth at some level – someone who values new ideas and is interested in becoming a better version of themselves every year.

Of course, some are more committed to this idea than others, and that is okay. Fortunately, you do not need to both have a rabid yearning for growing at the fastest possible rate. The point is that if only one of the couple is interested in growth and the other has an aversion to it, this will lead to problems down the track.

Personal growth is built around a preparedness to be self-aware and to confront ourselves – not necessarily while others are present, but certainly in the safety of self-reflection. Not surprisingly, individuals in successful couples tend to look at themselves when there is a problem in a relationship. Unsuccessful couples generally blame their partners. Accordingly, being in a relationship with someone who has the preparedness to confront themselves with self-awareness and growth means you are off to a strong start.

How can we evaluate this? In the early days it can be useful to notice some of the following aspects:

- Do they read non-fiction/self-help books, listen to empowering podcasts or watch useful YouTube videos?
- If not, how do they react to you doing these things? Do they think it's interesting or silly?
- Do they have goals and ambitions?
- Are they interested in talking about personal growth and how to live a more fulfilling life?
- If they are, are they walking their talk?

The key is to learn to spot the fakers from the real deal as there are certainly people out there who consume impressive amounts of self-help and personal development content but fail to put it into practice. This is the difference between someone being *interested* in personal growth and someone being *dedicated* to personal growth. The latter means actually walking the talk. It is fine if they only take baby steps – but there must be steps.

This often becomes clearer after you've been dating for a few months – then you can start to see a fuller picture:

- Are they willing to apologise and take responsibility for their role in things?
- Do they take action towards their goals or just talk about who they wish they could be?
- Are they humble at least some of the time and willing to admit when they are wrong or make a mistake?
- Do they value learning new things or having new experiences?
- Are they willing to invest in themselves?

Once we've witnessed how a potential partner values their own growth, we can be more confident that this trend will continue into the future.

Fun

Let's face it, life can get challenging. In these moments, being able to share a joke with your partner can certainly help to ease the pain of tough times. In fact, we *need* fun to take the edge off life's demands, stresses and calamities. Particularly when there is stress within a relationship, laughter can often be the quickest road to reconnection.

This doesn't mean that we aspire to a life without stress – good luck with that! Rather, it is through cultivating a life with regular fun experiences that allows us to recharge and bounce back, in the face of life's stressors. When there is no fun between stressors, even the most resilient person will ultimately crack. We now know this about Post-Traumatic Stress Disorder (PTSD): everyone breaks given enough major stress, it is only a matter of when. This is why we all need to stop and have fun. Reading a good book is fun, watching a good comedy is fun, a day at the beach or bushwalking, or kite-surfing, or water-skiing – you get the point.

Fun also relates to our sense of humour. Having a good sense of humour seems to be important to all of us. In one study, 94 per cent of people claimed to have an 'above-average' sense of humour. Amusingly, this is the first time in history that only 6 per cent of the population make up the norm! Bringing this back to potential relationship values, people who value fun are more likely to make time for fun as well as bring a spontaneous energy of playfulness to the day-to-day mundane. This attitude of playfulness is ideal when it comes to fun.

The catch is that playfulness sometimes requires vulnerability – the vulnerability to put ourselves out there, be a bit goofy and experiment. Often this sense of vulnerability can get in the way of us expressing our true playful nature (especially in the early dating phase if we're trying to present ourselves as cool, calm and collected). Yet when we give ourselves permission to be playful – and potentially embarrass ourselves – we become more real, and real is relatable. After all, it can be pretty hard to have a genuine laugh with your guard up!

This does not mean we have to find someone with a stand-up comedy–level sense of humour. It is more important to enjoy your company with each other and find ways to laugh and play together in your own way.

Partner considerations for someone who values fun include:

- Are they willing to let their guard down and get a bit silly with you?

- Do they enjoy making you laugh?
- Are they able to laugh at themselves?
- Do they laugh at your jokes, or at least not ridicule you for trying?
- Do they make time for fun?
- Do they think of fun things to do?
- If not, are they at least happy to come along and have fun when you organise it?

Other values to consider

Of course, there are many values that might be important to you which we haven't covered here. Below are some others you might like to consider:

- *Work/leisure balance.* Are we happy working 80 hours a week, over six days a week? Or is it important to be home in time for dinner with the family and not work on weekends?
- *Education and learning.* Is ongoing career development important or just acquiring general knowledge? Is one partner prepared to support the other and allow for the sacrifices that follow from periods of ongoing education?
- *Religion/spirituality.* Is each partner comfortable with allowing the other to explore their spiritual interest and learning? In what direction will the children be taken, particularly if each parent has very different beliefs?
- *Political attitudes.* While you don't necessarily have to have the same political alignment, you may have problems if you live on the opposite side of politics from each other and these are strongly held views.

- *Parenting values.* If having kids is important to you, how do you envision parenting them? This can catch couples unaware, as they both automatically resort to using the parenting strategies used by their own parents. Often this happens when kids are annoying their parents. From this stressed-out position, conflict is even more likely.
- *Self-care and mental health.* What importance will be given to self-care (e.g. diet, exercise and self-care) and how will this be prioritised?
- *The environment.* Are you concerned about the environment? How will this impact your day-to-day living? What sacrifices are you each willing (or unwilling) to make?
- *Aesthetics.* How much importance will be given to art, music, literature, drama and other cultural pursuits?
- *Travel.* Do you enjoy overseas travel or have no interest in leaving home? I have met couples in the past where one values travel and the other does not, which leads to tension because they cannot enjoy the experience together. A solution is that they travel with friends rather than a partner – but will the other person be okay with this? And then there is the way you travel that may have to be negotiated – one may want to see everything there is to see in a new country, while the other may want to relax by the pool on holidays.

Remember that there is no right or wrong around any of these values. Indeed, it is impossible to rank them all equally as they all require an investment of concern, time, money and effort, which come in limited quantities.

It is okay for each partner to prioritise some values more or less than their partner. The key is to have some alignment on strongly held values – meaning there is a sense of respect, tolerance and understanding about why that value is important to the individual and to keep communicating openly about it.

Look out for strongly held core values. You can imagine how politics, religion and parenting could become major issues if each person had strongly held, but opposing values. For example, there is likely to be significant conflict when both parents with strongly held, opposing religious beliefs want their children brought up in their religion.

As mentioned earlier, where one partner does not have strong views and is genuinely prepared to align with their partner, there is certainly a workable way forward.

Making friends for life:
Six qualities to consider

JBW

Happy marriages are based on a deep friendship.

– John Gottman

In addition to aligned vision and values, we suggest that there are six qualities worth nurturing if you want to develop a strong and healthy relationship with a partner. This is where we bring together much of what we have already touched upon in this book. These six qualities are reliability, influenceability, trust, empathy, preparedness to raise issues and a long-term view. These are also key qualities that make for a very strong, lifelong friendship.

When reading this list, it is important to remember that a lot of these qualities will only reveal themselves in time, so it pays to be patient. These qualities may also express themselves in a very different way from what we might at first expect. Once again, bringing an attitude of curiosity and detachment will help us to get the most accurate reading.

While we are suggesting that you do go looking for these things in a potential partner, the reality is that many of these qualities are built together over time. It is truly a wonderful experience for a couple to hold each other to account (although it may not feel like it at the time) and gently encourage each other to grow into the spaces where they are weakest. On the other hand, it is dangerous to marry someone for their potential when there are no signs of growing or changing, holding on to the hope that one day they will evolve into the person we want them to become.

Where does this leave us? It means that we want to see proof of a capacity to grow, change and co-create before we commit to the long term. This takes time. It is one reason why we want to wait ideally three years (as we have discussed, it can be less the older you are) before having children together. This gives you time to experience your partner's capacity to grow into the aligned vision that is important to you as a couple.

Reliability

Reliability is a key pillar for a strong friendship. Knowing that you have someone you can call upon to be there for you when you need help is a great comfort. As my father talked about in his TED Talk on preventing divorce, a lack of reliability is one of the biggest risks in a relationship. In particular, those of us who intend to have children need to know that we can rely on our partner to be there for us and our kids when we need them.

On a basic level, when we have previously made plans, we need to be able to feel that we can rely on our partner to follow through with them. As we become parents, there will inevitably be more and more important times when we need to be able to trust our partner to show up reliably. Building a sense of reliability in your relationship will undoubtedly save you a lot of anxiety as a parent. There is a big difference between knowing your partner will be there to pick the kids up from school and not being sure but hoping they do.

Reliability also comes into play when we are sick and incapacitated. How good is our partner at stepping up and looking after us during these times? (A quick side note here: when we are sick, it is critical that we clearly and explicitly explain to our partners what it is that we need from them. Too often people expect that their partner will work it out, then judge them harshly if they get it wrong. The only excuse for not being explicit is if you are in a coma!)

In short, we want to have the sense that our partner has our back – that they will be there for us when we need them, at least to the best of their ability.

We can evaluate reliability from early on in a relationship by considering the following:

- Do they follow through on their commitments?
- Do they show up when they say they will?
- Do they return your missed calls or respond to your messages within a reasonable timeframe?
- How well do they communicate when plans have to change?
- Do they call or text to let you know when they are running late?
- Do they make you feel safe?
- Do they build you up in front of others?
- Can you rely on your partner to stick up for you when you are in a situation where you might be verbally attacked by other people?
- Are they there for you when you are sick?
- Perhaps most importantly, when you call them to account, do they step up their game?

Remember, what we tolerate in the early days of the relationship (when people are often on their best behaviour) we will have to tolerate into the future. If a potential partner develops a pattern of flaking on you at the last minute early in the relationship, just think what could happen down the road if you had a child together.

Influenceability

'Influenceability' is a term that describes a couple's willingness to respect each other's opinions and allow themselves to be influenced by each other for the good of the relationship. It is about cultivating a mindset of 'we' instead of 'me'. In friendship, there is often a natural degree of influenceability when we talk through our problems and go to our friends for advice. Research shows that this is just as important, if not more so, in romantic relationships.

The good news for today's women is that it is no longer normal for the man in a relationship to call all the shots. In fact, John Gottman's previously mentioned research, which involved a long-term study of 130 newlywed couples, shows that there is a strong link between influenceability and long-term relationship success, particularly when men allow themselves to be influenced by their partner.[31] Yes, it is equally important for women to accept influence too; however, the research shows that when there is an influenceability imbalance, it is nearly always the men who are at fault. (It is not often you have research backing up a statement like that!) According to Gottman, a massive 81 per cent of marriages ended when the males were particularly unwilling to allow their partner to influence them.

During the evaluation process, this involves exploring whether or not your partner actually listens to you and cares about what you have to say. This is especially important when it comes to decisions that may have an impact on the future of your relationship.

For example, let's say your partner gets a new job offer on the other side of the country. Do they discuss it with you, acknowledging the implications of accepting it? Or do they just accept or refuse it without considering you or your opinion? Do they make significant financial decisions without discussing them with you? Do they decide to buy a new car and 'surprise' you with it?

Often people make unilateral decisions because they fear their partner will not hear and respect their views, but in acting from this position they deny their partner the same right. Our partners may need to be reminded that just as we want them to hear us, we are on their side and willing to hear them out and consider what is best for them, rather than just imposing what we want.

Factors to consider when exploring influenceability include:

- Do they ask for your opinion on things?
- Particularly if they are making a decision regarding something about which you have obvious expertise, do they ask for your advice?
- Do they listen to you and consider your perspective on more important issues?
- When you are in a relationship where you have combined finances or liabilities, do they consult you before making major purchases?

Trust

Trust is a central part of love. The essence of trust lies in how carefully we deal with our partner's vulnerabilities. If our partner shares their insecurities with us, do we keep it secret from others or do we throw it back at our partner when we are angry?

Of course, this is a two-way street. To build intimacy and trust, we all have to take the risk of giving our partner sensitive information to see how they deal with it.

In a 2012 study, Ahmet Uysal and his team explored the correlation between people who keep secrets from their partner and how this impacts on their relationship.[32] Not too surprisingly, they found that couples who shared more of their inner world tended to trust each other more than those who had a tendency to conceal things. Other studies have established that self-disclosure in relationships is reciprocal – that is, the more we open up, the more our partner is likely to follow suit.

You have probably seen this dynamic play out on TV a thousand times before. It's a classic storyline where someone is hiding some very important information from their partner, such as a huge debt or an illegitimate child. When it comes out, the relationship justifiably goes downhill. The following are some signatures of trust:

- Do they keep your secrets?
- Do they use your sensitive information against you?
- How long does it take before they reconnect with a repair attempt when they get angry?
- Do they share their internal world with you, or do you feel that they keep significant things from you? (Men in particular often need to take some time to process what is happening before they can share, so make sure to allow space for this.)
- Do you feel they are on your team?

Empathy

Empathy is another key to being a good friend and partner. It is our ability to do two things. The first is to put aside our emotions for a moment and make some space to connect to the other person without judgement. The second is to be able to step into their shoes, as much as one can. Typically, we need to ask questions to draw out what they are feeling.

Think about it from your own experience. Sensitive questions can show us, in a particularly powerful way, that our partner is tuning into our wavelength and that they care enough to go deeper with us. As discussed in the chapter on true love, nurturing our partner starts with empathically connecting with where they are at. This is about finding a partner who makes us feel both loved and looked after.

While it is great if our partner can recognise that we need empathy without us having to ask for it, that is the icing on the cake! In a healthy relationship, we need to become good at asking our partner to take some time out to give us some empathic support. When your partner has also had a tough day, or is stressed by family issues, it is too much to ask them to intuitively read your non-verbals. We need to say something like, 'Hey Babe, I'm going through some things here. Can I have ten minutes of your time to share?'

Often we tend to think of men as struggling with empathy, but sometimes women can also be quite insensitive to the emotions of men, meeting their vulnerability with sarcastic throw-away lines. I see this kind of behaviour as a response to the societal expectations placed upon men to be 'the strong ones'. If a man is emotionally vulnerable or expresses an insecurity (which the woman chooses to interpret as weakness), she can sometimes feel threatened by this. It's this reactive response to feeling threatened that can lead to bullying within the relationship – a flawed attempt to get men to 'man up', ignore their emotions and resume their position as 'the strong one'.

It is also an example of how the first step in empathy is to put aside our own emotional responses and our own agenda. Instead, we want to ensure our partners – male, female or otherwise – feel safe to express themselves, including their wounds, hurts and insecurities. When we respond to our partner's vulnerabilities in a bitchy or insensitive way, we encourage them to conceal their true feelings and train them up to be emotionally unavailable.

Accordingly, we need to see how good our partner is, over time, with putting aside their emotions for a bit and asking questions that will tune them in to where we are.

The following questions will give you some indication of a partner's empathy:

- Are they willing to comfort you and give you emotional support when you ask for it?
- Do they take the time to try to understand what you are going through?
- Do they try to understand why something might have upset you?
- Do you feel your concerns make sense to them?

The caveat here is when both of you are under similar pressures, meaning that neither of you have the bandwidth to be there for the other. This is why the death of a child brings so many relationships undone. If you are both very stressed, acknowledge this openly and discuss how you are going to rejuvenate each other and the relationship. This could be a time to take a weekend away together or put off less critical demands to give you both time to recover.

Preparedness to raise issues

No one likes conflict, yet a relationship without conflict is not a very intimate relationship. When exploring how we might share our life with another, disagreements are bound to come up. And it is actually a good thing because relationship growth is in many ways driven by conflict. Conflict highlights what we need to work on to build a better relationship. Often, conflict is a signpost that says, 'Hey, we need to address this so we can get on our way to a better relationship.'

When we use the term 'conflict', we are not talking about big fights, but rather about the differences of opinion and sometimes misunderstandings that will inevitably crop up in a relationship. This is healthy conflict. The bigger problem is when one or both partners intentionally avoid this healthy conflict. Left unspoken, disagreements will fester into resentment, and resentment turns into distance and distrust.

Remember earlier when we pointed out the tendency for our unconscious mind to avoid dealing with issues – the idea that every big problem was a small problem once? That is what we're talking about here. Instead, we want to commit to the opportunity presented by healthy conflict. As long as things don't get disrespectful, contemptuous or violent, an argument grants us an important opportunity to get to know our partner better. It is a way to tear down the walls we have silently built around ourselves, which would otherwise be a barrier to a deeper connection. Without addressing conflict, those walls will just keep getting taller and stronger, and it may not be until you get dumped that you realise how big they have become – or that they were even there.

But when we can address conflict, accept the discomfort that comes with it and talk through an issue to find some kind of resolution – perhaps a better strategy for the future, or even just agreeing to disagree – we tend to bond more deeply with our partner. Over time, the connection grows stronger because we learn that a disagreement has nothing to do with breaking up. This also adds to our sense of 'containment' within the relationship – the capacity to resolve conflict without being concerned that going into it threatens the survival of the relationship.

Given that conflict drives growth, we want to uncover some of the following:

- Does our partner tend to address or avoid dealing with issues that may lead to conflict?
- How does our partner deal with conflict?
- Are they quick to react and get aggressive?
- Do they shut down? Are they avoidant, what is known as 'stonewalling'? Do they stop talking to you? Or can they have a reasonable conversation where both of you can safely share your fears and concerns?
- At the very least, are they committed to learning how to navigate conflict in a more functional way?

A long-term view

As we wrote about when looking at Edward C. Banfield's research in a previous chapter, one of the keys to success in life is having a 'time perspective'. In other words, people who think the furthest down the track tend to have the most success in achieving their goals and living a fulfilling life. Bringing this back to relationships, a partner who has a long-term view is also much less likely to engage in an impulsive affair because they consider the longer term impact it will have on their relationship.

Alcoholics Anonymous uses this in one of their core teachings. They get the person to consider how they will feel *the next morning* after they start drinking. It is a simple manoeuvre to combat the natural inclination of the unconscious mind to ignore the longer term consequence of our actions.

Things to consider with a potential partner include:

- How much do they plan ahead and talk about their future?
- How much do they consider the long-term implications when making a decision?
- Are they able to delay immediate gratification – putting off rewards until the work is done?
- Are they willing to ignore short-term distractions in pursuit of a long-term goal?

Leading the way

As discussed in the introduction to this chapter, it is not that we have to find a partner who is already a master of all of these qualities – many of these things can be cultivated together as your relationship develops. What is more important is to find a partner who can recognise the importance of developing these skills over time.

It is also important to work on nurturing these qualities in ourselves. For example, if we want to find a partner who is reliable, we first need to commit to being a reliable friend – at least to the people to whom we are closest to in our lives. If we want to find a partner who is influenceable, we need to be willing to seek and hear advice from others regarding big decisions. If we want to find a partner who is empathic, we need to practise empathy in our day-to-day lives. In short, we will become better at recognising and keeping potential partners who have these qualities only if we are developing them in ourselves.

I cannot stress this point enough. We need to lead the way. Only then can we ask our partner to bring more, to match us.

It took me almost ten years to find a partner who could meet me on all of these levels. *Ten years* of active soul searching and dating! As I have shared with you, there were certainly moments of doubt and despair, when I questioned whether someone like this could even exist.

It was only with the gift of hindsight that I realised there were many lessons that *I* needed to learn in order to attract, claim and keep such a partner – lessons that were better learned with other people because it meant I could leave my mistakes behind me while taking the learning forward. So much of this was an internal process of reflection, acceptance and forgiveness as I learned to develop these skills in myself.

It also meant being a bit picky – not in a nasty way, but in a 'conscious decision' kind of way. Dating different people – many of whom had strengths that I loved, along with weaknesses for which I wasn't ready to settle – allowed me to learn from my mistakes and prepared me to navigate a much healthier relationship the next time as I reflected on the patterns I was playing into. As my experience grew, I realised that relationship growth does not happen when only one person is willing to put the effort in, and the first person we need to look to is us.

The other thing that we need to remember when choosing a life partner is that they have a history – and it can tell us a great deal about who they are.

The past tells the future

GBW

Study the past, if you would divine the future.

– Confucius

The past, the present and the future walked into a bar.
It was tense.

– Lex Martin

When it comes to how a partner – male or female – will be likely to function in a relationship, the best indicator is simply what has gone before. People do change; however, they most readily change in a negative direction as they become sad and/or bitter from having had traumatic and painful experiences. The more resilient and naturally positive the person is to begin with, the less frequently this occurs.

My patients in couple therapy often went into a relationship hoping their partner will change for the better. But as they say, hope is not a plan. To change in a positive direction requires something more than day-to-day life. Indeed, there are three things that bring about meaningful change in people's lives: therapy and/or a committed pursuit of personal growth; confrontation with death (through a terminal illness or death of a loved one); and a religious conversion (which can have mixed results).

So, while people can change, in the absence of these three forces past behaviour still remains the best indicator of future behaviour. As a relationship therapist, I spend a lot of time asking questions about the past to identify where the areas of difficulty lie, so we know what to focus on in therapy.

Let me reduce 25 years of asking these questions down to a crash course in taking a relationship history. Of course, when people come to see me, they expect me to ask lots of questions. I recognise that it is way more difficult to get away with this on a date. Fortunately, one of the big advantages of the online dating world is that it starts with the premise that you are strangers. You are there to get to know each other. This does allow us to get away with asking more direct questions than happened in the past.

An interesting and surprising finding in this regard is that men are more likely to answer intimate questions early on in an online discussion, than they are later face to face. I encourage my female patients to make the most of this, asking questions like, 'So, tell me about your family – what are they like? How do you get on with them? Are your parents still together? If yes, how do they get on? If no, who are you closest to?' For men and women, if you can get around to asking about their relationship with their opposite-sex parent that is always a very revealing subject.

People generally respond positively to people who are genuinely interested in what they have to say. This is your first job: be a good listener. Pay attention. Not only are they more likely to open up, but it is in your best interest to listen and learn.

What to ask about

Below is a list of the key things you ideally want to explore with a potential partner. Keep in mind that these are not questions for the first date, but certainly aim to start exploring them around date three.

- We are interested in the potential partner's relationships, past and present, at three levels:
  - relationships with previous partners
  - relationships with friends
  - relationships with family.
- We want to know whether our date is capable of long-term relationships. This is defined as at least more than 12 months and typically around 24 months.
- When did their last relationship end and how long was it? What ongoing contact are they having? We want to get a feel for how they broke up, how aggressive things got versus how amicably the situation was handled.
- What were the main issues? It is no big deal to ask questions like:
  - So, what brought things undone?
  - How long had things been shitty for?
  - How ugly did the breakup get?
- Finally, do not put too much weight on any one point – we need to look at the whole emerging picture.

Listen carefully for a sense of how angry or sensitive they are/were towards their ex as they talk about this. How someone answers these questions can be just as informative as what they say. There is a big difference between somebody who will happily discuss these issues and one who changes the subject quickly or outright refuses to go there.

Another thing to remember is that a lot of quite normal men, in particular, do not see the point of exploring these issues too deeply – particularly if they are painful. This is perfectly understandable. Why would somebody want to get into painful issues if this was not going to help in any way? Women are generally much more practised at this, and appreciate the value of unpacking an issue in order to process it and move on.

A man who has been in therapy is a real bonus here, as they can usually appreciate the benefit of understanding these forces that have pushed us in a direction that may not be healthy. It is not weakness that takes a man into therapy; it is courage. Most men are simply not prepared to endure the discomfort of self-evaluation that comes with therapy.

Anger versus aggression

In talking about people's previous breakups, we want to get a sense of how aggressive a potential partner can be. Let me give you a crash course on this subject. It is beyond the scope of this book to go into any great detail, but the essence of it can be explained quickly. Let's start with a critical distinction.

Anger is healthy. Aggression is not. Anger is not just an important and normal emotion, it is a necessary emotion. Anger simply tells us that we have been treated unjustly and need to do something about it. We need to stand up for ourselves. Anger comes from a good place. It comes from a sense that we deserve better.

Aggression, on the other hand, is completely different. It is unhealthy and unproductive. As well as physical aggression and intimidation, other forms include verbal aggression, such as swearing, and non-verbal aggression, including yelling. Anger does not have to lead to aggression. The goal is to express it assertively with respect for the other person.

In trying to gauge what happened in a breakup, an informative question – if you can get away with asking it (use a gentle voice) – is, 'How bad did the fighting get?' You will have to make a bit of a judgement call, as low levels of aggression such as raised voices and criticisms are so common that they are not deal-breakers. Anything more concerning, though, and you should run as fast as you can.

The one important exception is if the person in front of you says that they did not return the aggression, even in the face of it from their partner. Provided this is true, you are looking at somebody who is good at controlling their own aggressiveness. The truth is that we all have the capacity for aggression as it is a critical part of self-defence. Accordingly, this is about our ability to control it when faced with aggression from another.

Are they over their ex?

One thing you need to be particularly interested in is whether they are over their last partner or the most important relationship they have had to date (as this may have been prior to the last one). Questions you can ask include:

- Who was the love of your life? The one who got away?
- Do you think about them often?
- Do you wish you could get back with them?
- Would you take them back if they came knocking on your door?
- Do you find yourself comparing men/women that you have dated since with that person? (A degree of this is normal.)

Questions like these will give you an idea about whether or not the person has fully moved on, or a part of their heart is still attached to their lost love. Take note of what they say, then go away and reflect on it to work out whether you think they have moved on. It is tough if you really like a potential partner but it is clear they are not over a lost love. Relationships are challenging enough without this added complexity.

The best thing to do is to say something like, 'I really like you, but it seems like you are not over your ex and I can't compete with that. I'm not going to wait around for this to change, but if you do move on from them, feel free to get in touch with me down the track.' You could also gently add, 'In the meantime, it might help for you to go and talk to someone about it. In fact, if you're willing to do that, I would be keen to catch up down the track, if I'm available, to see where you end up.'

The last line is up to you, but anyone who is prepared to go to therapy to work out their relationship issues is someone worthy of a second look. You might continue to see them on a non-exclusive basis. This is simply because genuinely committing to therapy to look at oneself is perhaps the best possible asset to bring to a relationship.

We can use a similar strategy for other issues that are deal-breakers for us. Perhaps the trickiest issue is addiction. If you really like someone but it is clear they use too much alcohol, marijuana, cocaine or MDMA, let alone stronger drugs, run. It is a much bigger job in therapy to get people to give up an addiction. Moreover, addictions typically mean there are significant underlying issues at work.

Fascinating research has found that rats get addicted to drugs like heroin and cocaine *only* if they do not have other rats to interact with. Indeed, it is very difficult to get a rat addicted to these substances if they have other rats around with which they can engage. In short, to get a rat addicted to these substances you have to take away something more valuable – the experience of being part of a community with other rats.

My clinical experience aligns with this. Those who end up addicted to these substances have typically been isolated at some level from family and peers and have turned to these substances for solace, to self-soothe, to treat their lack of connection. Interesting research is revealing that the opposite to addiction is not sobriety per se; it is connection that allows sobriety. I have come to see that the power of AA (the organisation not the battery) resides more in the connection between the attendees than any other single factor.

Unfortunately, once the habit of the addiction is in place, not even love is enough to bring the addiction to an end. This is because of the nature of addiction – the powerful, intimate relationship between these substances and the neurophysiology of the human mind. It is a neurochemical bond, built around habit, that in turn creates powerful neural circuits, that love alone cannot break.

Computer games are another version of this addiction. In large doses, they create even further isolation from family and friends, which can be difficult to reverse. Now that these games offer partners to team up with from around the world, they can provide an illusion of connection. Unfortunately, though, this distant connection rarely has a future, and decreases the need to connect with people who are more readily available for building a relationship.

For these reasons I would not recommend waiting around for somebody to overcome their addiction – partly because you can only be sure after a year or more that they are really over it.

Is there someone you're not over?

Of course, the other side of this coin is that you may need to take some of this medicine yourself. Getting out and dating can help us move on. If, however, you find yourself thinking of your ex as you are dating someone else – particularly if you find yourself repeatedly comparing them – it may well be that you are not over your ex. If you have a lost love who still occupies an active role in your heart, you may need to go and see someone to help you move on. In simple terms, this is grief work and it is relatively straightforward therapy.

For this, I use Eye Movement Desensitisation and Reprocessing (EMDR) with great success. This is one of only a couple of effective therapies for bringing unresolved grief to an end quickly. Typically, if it is uncomplicated, we can do this in around half a dozen sessions. Psychologists all over the world are trained in this therapy. Jump online and search 'find a psychologist'. For example, in Australia this will take you to the www.psychology.org.au/Find-a-Psychologist page, where you can search for a psychologist nearby who does EMDR and relationship therapy.

Working the questions into dates

To give you a feel for taking a relationship history, let's eavesdrop on one of my sessions with one of my male patients who, after fifteen years of several unsuccessful relationships, was wanting to do it differently.

'So, what did you do differently this time around?' I asked.

'I did what we spoke about last session. As she spoke, I just looked at the emotion behind what she was saying. I just asked myself, "How caring is this person?" She was telling me about how her best friend's boyfriend was injured in a car accident.

She was so matter of fact about it all. It was not even his fault, but she appeared to have no empathy for him. Just to be clear, I asked how she felt about it. She said something offhand like, "He'll get over it," and she has known him for three years. She is smart and pretty, but I realised that I was lining up for yet another relationship with a woman who is emotionally unavailable. No thanks.'

'Well let's not make up our mind too quickly.'

'You haven't heard the rest of the story yet ...'

Ben was telling me about his experience on a date recently after I had explained to him in earlier sessions how to begin to assess the emotional availability and maturity of the woman he was dating.

At 32, he had been in therapy with me for a year or so. He was broad-shouldered and well-muscled. His chiselled jaw, almost too-intense bright blue eyes and a well-paid job, made him an attractive prospect for the opposite sex – at least superficially. He had almost made it as a pro footballer, but now he just played on weekends to keep fit. He was a man's man. (I was surprised when he committed to the abstract, emotional world of therapy.)

Ben grew up in a family with a violent, alcoholic father who was eternally defensive and critical. His mother was never there for him as she dealt with her own unhappiness in her sad marriage. They separated when Ben was around fourteen.

So there were Imago factors at play. With other men, Ben had a tendency to be overly suspicious and move into an aggressive stance too readily – which had been helpful on the football field. With women, he was not aggressive; however, he did hold back from allowing himself to get closer to them. This meant that women had often become unhappy with him as the relationship failed to grow and deepen. On one hand, he wanted the love his mother had never given him but was fearful of going there in case he was abandoned, as he was by his mother. At other times, as he mentioned, he found himself unconsciously drawn to play it safe with women who were not emotionally available.

As well as working with me individually, he had also attended one of my weekly groups that focused on making sense of relationships. He was a surprisingly psychologically minded, emotionally intelligent man, and he had come a long way towards understanding himself. He was ready to do things differently. He was ready for greater intimacy.

One of the things I had suggested he do was look at how much the woman he was dating cared about the other people in her life. If you want to get an idea of how much someone will connect with and care for you, look at how much they care about others. This includes ex-boyfriends.

'And did you ask her about her past relationships?' I asked Ben.

'Yes, but I couldn't remember all the questions to ask that you and I spoke about. I asked her how many serious relationships she had been in and then I asked her about the longest one.'

'Did she seem to mind you asking these questions?'

'As you know, I was concerned about that, but I don't think so. It was only our third date, and I said something like, "I'd like to get to know you better, given that we've both said we're wanting more than a fling. Can you tell me a bit about your past relationships?" She just said, "Sure, what do you want to know?" so it was kind of set up okay. Given we met online, I think she saw it as a reasonable thing for us to do, as we'd started off as strangers.'

'Do you think she felt like you were interrogating her?'

'No. I made some jokes about how I was thinking of becoming a therapist in my spare time, because they seem to get paid a lot of money just to sit and chat. She laughed and told me not to give up my day job. I said that in the past I'd never thought about these things and I really didn't know my partners. This time around, I want to really know them. She seemed to like that. The other thing I said was that she could ask me any questions too and I would happily answer them. But she didn't appear to have any, or didn't really care enough to get to know the real me. I found that off-putting. When I stop and think about it, it was like she was not interested in looking to see me.'

'Did she think you were a bit weird, as a guy talking that way?'

'You know, I was worried about that, but no she actually said it was cool to have an ex-footballer interested in relationships that way. You were right – women seem to like the mix of being one of the boys, a bit macho and then being able to talk about feelings and what I want out of a relationship. Rather than those things making me look weaker, they seem to respect it.'

'And what did you find out?'

'It was also a bit of a worry. She said she'd had five serious relationships and her longest relationship was only ten months. Didn't you say that emotionally healthy people by her age should at least be able to hold down a relationship for over a year?'

'How old is she?'

'She's 29.'

'Yes, by that age she should have had at least a couple of relationships that have lasted longer than a year. If she was in her late teens, or very early twenties, we could overlook it, but not at 29. The same goes for holding down a job.'

'Well I know that is not a problem, she's been in her current job for three years. That was easy to find out. When she was talking about her job, I just asked her how long she had been doing it for.'

'What did you say she does?' I asked.

'She's a debt collector for a credit card company.'

'You generally need to be fairly thick-skinned and a bit tough to do that job well. Is she good at it?'

'Yes, she's one of their most successful collectors. I think she might be a little too good at it.'

'How do you mean?'

'Well I think that's what I've seen in her. She can be sweet, but then she's really tough underneath. I think she kind of lures you in.'

'Okay. Did you ask her how the last relationship ended, how she was getting on with her ex?'

'Yeah. She said she just ended it cold. Deleted him from her phone and refused to take his calls. Has had no contact with him since.'

'Did she say why it ended?'

'She said they just grew apart and one day she realised she didn't want to be there anymore. It sounds like she didn't work on it at all, she just checked out.'

'Yes, that could be a concern – but there will, of course, be more to the story.'

'Yes, I know. Don't worry – I haven't forgotten your advice not to put too much weight on any one thing and then to check what they say out over time. To be honest, though, between her relationship history and her lack of empathy, I'm not sure I want to waste any more time with her. Besides, from my online dating account I have a few other women wanting to date me.'

'How were you thinking you might put that to her?'

'I'm thinking I'll tell her she's a cold, heartless bitch and that's not quite what I'm looking for! Just kidding. No, I thought I would say that I just want to date some other women first before I take our relationship to the next level. I did tell her right at the outset that I was wanting to take things slow to get it right this time. I've told her that while I'm wanting a long-term relationship, I'm not prepared to rush into something until I'm confident it has a reasonable chance of success.'

Yes, Ben was an unusually good study. (There's not much point in quoting those who were not!)

Ask their friends

Asking a potential partner about these things can be a bit of a challenge. This isn't so much the case with their friends, who are often more than happy to tell you about your potential partner's back-story – particularly over a few drinks.

A very helpful indicator of the kind of person with whom you are getting into a relationship is the nature of their friendships and their friends themselves. For this reason, you want to get to meet their friends as soon as possible. Fortunately – and understandably – people will usually let you in to meet their friends before they will introduce you to their children (if they have them) and family.

There is a huge parallel between how a person treats their friends and how they will treat a partner. If they have opposite-sex friends, this can be even more informative. What you are looking for here is not complex. You are looking to see whether or not you like their friends and how well your potential partner treats their friends. Their oldest friends can be particularly revealing, as they know your potential partner well.

A conversation with these friends (alcohol does not hurt – more for them, less for you) can give you a significant heads-up on how they treat both their friends and their previous partners. You're looking in particular for their loyalty and how much their friends can rely on them. The more time you can spend with your potential partner's friends, the more valuable information you will gather.

Having no friends is a major red flag. If nothing else, it means they are going to be overly dependent on you to meet their needs. We all need to be able to turn to friends to meet needs that partners simply cannot, and should not, have to meet. Not being prepared to introduce you to their friends is also a red flag. There can be a variety of reasons for this – for example, they could be ashamed of them or ashamed of you, neither of which is good news.

Equally, it is not important if your potential partner does not have lots of friends. In fact, it can be more of a red flag if they have lots of 'friends' but no deep connections. Most of us do very well when we just have a couple of people we call close friends. Given the time needed to invest in close friendships, it is most likely that you will be able to count them on one hand.

One final point. You do not necessarily have to like or get close to their friends, but do remember that you will have to spend time with them.

Keep it fun

As you can see, some questions are more important and should have more priority than others. Too much too soon and it can be hard for it *not* to look like an interrogation, and dating is meant to be fun.

The power of being a couple is that when one is in a funk the other can give you a lift. Note that 'fun' is only one letter away from 'funk'! Partners can rekindle old, established neural pathways around playing as a kid with a good friend. It's not about having a crackup sense of humour, it is about a readiness to play.

A recurring theme in this book is that of how we need to co-create a good relationship rather than find it. Jeffrey Hall at the University of Kansas researches the role of humour in relationships. His reassuring findings can be summarised thusly:

> 'That people think you are funny or can make a joke out of anything doesn't seem to matter that much. Also, there is no particular advantage to creating or appreciating humour ... neither is particularly strongly related to satisfaction overall. Instead, what really matters is the humor that couples create together.'

While misery loves company, this only really works if all parties are fine with being miserable. So, keep an eye on your potential partner's preparedness to have fun. And, again, this works both ways – you have a responsibility to bring as much playfulness to the relationship as you can.

Overall, this has been a guide to the kinds of things that you want to explore over time. It is more important that you relax and have fun with your partner and let this information come out gradually – but we are talking weeks rather than months. You will find that the more fun you are having the more likely your potential partner will be to open up. Indeed, if you are not really connecting and having fun together, then the answers to these questions become rather irrelevant.

Whether it is asking questions, being vulnerable or having fun, timing is everything. In the relationship space we call this pacing. Let's examine it a little more closely.

The thrill of the chase

JBW

When I want to end a relationship I just say, 'You know,
I love you. I want to marry you. I want to have your
children.'

– Rita Rudner, Comedian

Perhaps one of the most overlooked ideas in the dating world
is the concept of *pacing*. Pacing is all about moving at a similar
speed to a new romantic acquaintance, not rushing too far
ahead of them or lagging behind.

Think of two people dancing the tango. In order to make it
work, each dance partner needs to step in time with the other:
step forward too much and you might dance your partner out
of the room (and not in a graceful way); take no steps forward
at all and there is no dance. It is important to pace a potential
partner because moving too fast or slow can spoil the enchanted
tension of attraction, like a fruit bitten into before it is ripe or
once it has begun to rot.

Proposing to move in together or talking about kids after
just a couple of weeks into a whirlwind romance might reflect
the intensity of feelings you feel, but is also likely to scare off
a new flame. Many people will be confronted by this kind

of conversation too soon into a relationship – and with good reason! A potential partner will often freak out when they think the other person is reacting to some hidden, perceived promise, simply because it is just too early to know each well enough.

On the other hand, when you are months into a new fling but unwilling to consider your playmate's attempts at making it official, you might be moving too slow. Pacing is all about reading where your potential partner is at and how fast they are wanting to take things, and synchronising your pace – even if you want to rush in. This means regularly stopping to take stock of any feedback. Most of all, it is about reciprocity.

Setting the pace

In today's age of dating apps and hook-up culture, pacing or matching a potential partner is often about making sure we don't move faster than is safe and appropriate. The thing is, often when we start to like someone, it's too early to know who this person really is and whether or not they are worth committing to – particularly if we are looking for a serious relationship.

The dance of love is a delicate thing; if we can't keep in time we will tangle and fall. But match our partner at every step and it becomes a magical dance filled with romance and meaning. In order to master the art of dating, pacing is key. This is not about playing games, it's about protecting ourselves from unnecessary heartache.

In truth, the most treacherous time in a relationship is the initial stages of dating where there isn't much of a buffer to cushion our mistakes. Without having developed a history together, challenging moments and seemingly insignificant triggers can often send a new flame running. Often when we see a few qualities we like in a person, we can be quick to jump to conclusions. 'OMG, he likes the same music as me – we must be soulmates!'

Unfortunately, the more we *decide* we like this person, the more we tend to invest. And the more we invest, the less we are willing to fully acknowledge warning signs that might pop up along the road to relationship. Moreover, when we over-invest, things often become unbalanced very quickly.

Diving too deep too fast tends to put a new partner on a pedestal, which can feel uncomfortable for the person we are dating. And while we might think we are helping the bond grow, we are not actually doing ourselves, or them, any favours. This kind of behaviour can quickly have us slipping into the territory of unrequited love.

One of the most common statements I hear from both men and women is that their date went from 'zero to 100' way too fast. 'He seemed like a great guy, but then he got all needy, wanting to see me all the time and it just turned me off him.' I hear stories like this all the time from both sexes, and often the person they were dating sounded like a good option until they jumped the gun and fell heart over head in love.

This rushing into romance is the antithesis of pacing. It is often founded on the projections we cast on the people in our lives, rather than based in reality. I've been there too. When sparks fly, the mind can get excited and often look for ways to lock things down. This is when people go crazy in the name of love. Our minds crave certainty and 'sure things' – tempting us to live in an imaginary future with our potential lover despite the logic that tells us to keep it cool. Keeping an eye on the feedback and reciprocity of a connection is how we avoid prematurely fizzling out, and other problems.

Once again, dating is a kind of evaluation process. It's a good idea to keep an eye on how you and your potential new partner pace each other as the flame smoulders, to make sure that it doesn't get smothered or burn out of control.

Keeping the spark alive is much like starting a fire. We need to start with a flame, small twigs and leaves as well as oxygen to allow things to breathe. As the flame grows, we can then start to add bigger sticks to the fire – gradually building it up until it can eventually sustain a log. But if you put a log on the fire too soon, it can smother the flames and the spark will quickly die out.

Exactly the same is true of pacing; it means building a relationship piece by piece. If you've ever wondered why a new flame fizzled out too soon, while it could have just been a mismatch, another possibility was that the connection you were building was not paced. In dating, each stick we add to the metaphorical fire is a step forward, a symbol of our energy and investment. And with each step forward we should be looking for feedback. Is this person meeting me on the same level? Are they investing as much as I am?

Some ways to work this out include:

- When I look at our text history, who's writing the most?
- How does the time it takes for me to respond to texts compare with theirs?
- When I flirt, how do they respond? In kind? Or awkwardly dismissive?
- Are they as interested in my life as I am theirs – for example, paying attention and asking questions about my life?
- Are they fully present with me when we spend time together?

- Am I always pushing for the next date or do they make just as many plans?
- Do they make the effort to put forward new and interesting date ideas or are we always doing the same thing?
- Do they come to my part of town as often as I go to theirs?
- Do they respect my time as I do theirs? Are they often arriving late to a date or checking their phone?

These are just a few things to consider in the initial dating phase. And if you find you are investing more, perhaps it is time to pull back and see what happens. Do they make more effort or just let the connection die?

Noticing how a potential partner behaves towards us can also give us far more reliable information than words. The other person's actions and non-verbal cues provide us with the best feedback about where they are at and how much they are willing to invest in a connection at this point in time.

Embracing tension

When it comes to dating, I believe there are two overarching components that play into our initial attraction and desire towards someone. This dipole is *warmth* and *tension*. These two factors are the push–pull of pacing.

Warmth is all about creating a likeable connection – being friendly, approachable and someone people want to be around. *Tension* involves creating a bit of space for suspense and mystery. It's these two qualities combined that keep us coming back for more.

If someone is all warmth with no tension, we tend to put them in the 'friend zone'. We might think they're nice, but not really interesting in a romantic way. On the other hand, if someone is *only* creating tension, it might be interesting in the beginning, but without a good connection, chasing them can seem like a lot of effort with very little return. Taunted by this, we are likely to lose interest or possibly spiral into a frustrated toxic outburst.

You know that old adage 'treat 'em mean, keep 'em keen'? Essentially, it's about creating tension. Ever tried to put it into practice (with someone you are actually into) and have it backfire? I certainly have – playing things so cool the connection freezes over. At the time I didn't realise I needed warmth too.

Yet if you've ever dated someone and gently distanced yourself from them but still found them coming back for more, it's probably because you were being kind and tactful (warmth) in the way you pushed them away (tension). This is the cocktail of warmth and tension.

A common problem is that most people are uncomfortable with tension, so they seek to avoid, disperse and destroy it. This goes back to our natural discomfort with uncertainty – because that is essentially what tension is. It is the not-knowing mixed with hope for what we want. It is our curiosity piqued, leaving us with a strong desire to know more. It is our interest in something we don't fully understand, a question to which we don't yet know the answer. But we want to – badly. So much so that we get intoxicated by the thrill of it.

In its essence, tension is essentially about leaving things a little bit open-ended so there's something to come back for. Rather than a clear yes or a clear no, it's a 'maybe' or a 'not yet'. In other words, it is something to hope for. And people *love* something to hope for.

In this way, tension is actually the birthplace of our desire. Content creators know this – it's what gets us so hooked on TV series and movies. They play with tension while we get high on the mystery and hope for a satisfying ending. And good romancers know this too. Casanova, Cleopatra, Don Juan and Marilyn Monroe were all masters of playing with tension. In short, tension is an aphrodisiac.

In the movie *A Beautiful Mind* the character John Nash (who was a brilliant mathematician but lacked any social skills) approached a woman in a bar and said, 'I don't know exactly what I'm required to say in order for you to have intercourse with me, but can we assume I have said all that, and essentially we're talking about fluid exchange, right? So, can we go straight to the sex?'

Talk about going from zero to 100! This is dating without tension – the absence of flirting. It's unromantic to say the very least. When there is no banter and no build-up, we are left with expectation and coercion.

Great tension, on the other hand, is what gives us that feeling of 'butterflies in the stomach' as we get to know a potential partner. It is the little thrill that comes with flirtatious teasing and a sense of playfulness. It is the slow seduction of getting to know someone date by date as we learn new things about them. It is our secrets slowly shared and savoured. Once again, the journey is the destination.

There are various ways we can play with warmth and tension, sometimes even at the same time. My friend Margot demonstrated a great example of this one day when we were out at brunch. When we went up to pay at the end of our meal, our waiter asked, 'And how was everything?' Instead of just saying 'good', Margot said with a smile and a glint in her eye,

'Oh the food was *terrible*, I really struggled to choke down that second order of hash browns ...'

From the sidelines, I watched the waiter's energy completely change. He went from being a little aloof and just going through the motions to looking up, smiling and bantering along with Margot's playful ruse. In short, they got flirting and even ended up exchanging numbers.

This exchange exemplified a great balance between warmth and tension. Her warmth was projected through her body language, expression, eye contact and the warm and playful tone in her voice. The tension was held by her unexpectedly sarcastic answer (we loved the meal) and this answer certainly got her more attention than it would have if she had just said 'good thanks'.

Another key aspect of tension involves mixing things up a bit. It is about being unpredictable in a way that adds fun and novelty. Bear in mind that too much tension is also not good. Tension is best served with a side of warmth – playfully and flirtatiously. It is also crucial that the tension does not go on for too long and that it comes to a resolution. We are able to resolve tension with our partner through physical affection, understanding conversations and following through with what we have suggested we might do. Tension that never gets resolved, like a fight that never ends or a build-up of romantic potential that never gets fulfilled, can end up pushing a new flame away.

Of course, it is only natural that some tension will build up when we are dating – excitement, anxiety, differences of opinion and sexual tension – and it's important to acknowledge it and monitor how it is dealt with during the dating process. The way in which you and a potential partner resolve the tension that arises – whether playfully or painfully – gives you vital information about whether to keep investing in the connection.

Why am I telling you this? First, because I don't want you to be afraid of tension. I want you to enjoy it and not let the uncertainty that comes with it drive you to evolve a relationship too fast. In order to pace a new connection, we need to get comfortable with tension.

Second, when we play with tension, we amplify chemistry. When tension is held well, we feel intrigued, which feeds into our attraction towards this person. Then, when the tension is eventually resolved, we feel closer. It's as if we have been on an odyssey together – a hero's journey through the dark night of uncertainty – and lived to tell the tale. Having lived through this, we tend to value the connection more than if it was just handed to us on a silver platter.

Some examples of positive tension include:

- flirting
- friendly teasing
- playfully answering questions with another question
- allowing your talents and special qualities to organically reveal themselves over time
- sharing contrasting opinions – not in a put-down way, but in a way that embraces the full spectrum of the colourful world that we live in
- holding back from sex and in the meantime playing with the sexual tension by saying 'Not yet' – in some ways it's clearer than 'No'
- being a little unpredictable and spontaneous
- spending time apart so that you have more things to talk about when you spend time together
- creating a surprise for your new flame and teasing them with it – for example, telling them days in advance, 'I've got a surprise for you' and only giving

them clues. Of course, when you say you've got a surprise, it's important that you actually put some effort into creating a genuine surprise that they are likely to appreciate and enjoy.

Remember that the key to using tension well lies in combining it with lots of warmth and friendliness. It is this essence of warmth that mitigates the risk of the tension backfiring. For example, when it comes to playing with sexual tension, there is a big difference between totally avoiding physical contact (which could be interpreted as cold and total disinterest) and still being affectionate by kissing and cuddling. This is the difference that warmth makes.

I also want to make it clear that this concept of tension comes with a responsibility warning. Use it mindfully. It is not about leading people on or playing too hard to get. If you are not into someone, please be kind and let them know clearly. But if you are interested in someone, and you want to up the ante a little bit, tension is a great way to pace the connection and deepen the attraction.

We always recommend taking this slowly, and in the very early days it might be better not to commit too quickly, as the next chapter explores.

Dating around

JBW

> I know you dream of flowers, but first you must plant
> the seeds.
>
> – Beau Taplin

Perhaps one of the biggest hindrances to pacing is our
propensity to put all our eggs in one basket too early. When
we *finally* meet someone with whom we see the potential of a
future, it can be all too tempting to stop dating other people
and focus all our attention on this special one.

Instead, we want to perfect the art of 'low-pressure dating' –
a series of casual dalliances where we can hang out and get
to know different people without it having to mean something
serious. After all, this is the phase before we are exclusive,
which is the point – we are free to date others. It is important
to make the most of this freedom to avoid the problem of serial
monogamous dating that we mentioned earlier.

The key word here is *casual*. This period of casual connection
buys us time to gather insight into how much to invest in the
relationship as we discover how trustworthy, genuine, sensible,
mature, reliable and downright awesome each new person in
our lives *really* is.

Dating around in this way gives us more perception and possibilities to consider. The more we're exposed to different people, the more we learn about the traits we do and don't want in a lover. This can really help us to uncover the values and qualities that are most important to us when choosing a life-partner.

When we put all our focus on one person (before there has been a mutual discussion around commitment), it can be *very* difficult to pace. Despite our best intentions to take things slow, our romantic zeal can often take over and encourage us to move much faster than what is actually appropriate. But when we are dating around, we don't have a lot of time to spend obsessing over just one person. Why James hasn't replied to a text we sent three hours ago, doesn't matter as much as it would if he were the only person we are seeing, because Jack is already asking when he can see us next.

In this way, dating around acts as a reminder that we have options. We feel less of a need to pursue someone who is acting distant or to settle for someone out of sheer loneliness. Instead, we feel more desirable and confident, which constructively translates to attractiveness. Of course, we want to be responsible in navigating this. I'm not by any means encouraging you to lead people on. If you're definitely not at all interested in someone as more than a friend, make that explicitly clear.

On the whole, dating around is about exploring flirtatious friendships, which is why it helps to spend time with different prospects in casual scenarios. Forget going to the movies or meeting for dinner and drinks; instead go to the museum. Take a walk in the park. Have brunch together. Play basketball. And mention to them from the beginning that at this stage you are just dating around and enjoying life as you get to know different people.

If the thought of explaining this to others brings you any

anxiety, know that it's really not a big deal. As the American actor and author Cindy Lu writes in her book *The Four Man Plan*:

> It can be surprising to find that most men are not bothered by the fact that you are dating other men, but instead relieved and or intrigued. It may bug them at first and they may even step away for a moment, but it also makes them think about whether or not you are worth fighting for.[33]

I have also found this to be true.

Again, there is a difference between dating around and sleeping around. People will often tolerate the former but rarely appreciate the latter. Which is why when it comes to jumping into bed with a new flame, I encourage you to make a considered decision.

Check in with yourself honestly:

- Your lust and desire might be there but what about your heart?
- Are you *really* ready for this? Or are you feeling pressured by others' expectations?
- Do you actually want to 'do it' or is there a part of you that is motivated by other reasons?
- Can you sit with the sexual tension or are you just trying to defuse it?
- Is the other person investing as much as you at this stage? And if not, how much will it hurt you if the other person starts to pull away after you have slept together?

Again, this relates to the concept of pacing and protecting your heart from unnecessary heartache.

The other advantage of dating around is that it helps to create a subtle shift in our mind. No longer are we focused on divining whether a particular person is 'the one'. Instead, we need only consider, 'Do I like this person enough to see them again?' This relieves us of a lot of pressure and anxiety – particularly with online dating, where it can sometimes feel like a job interview – *You're single, I'm single, what are we doing here if not looking for a life-partner?* This kind of sentiment is a very effective tension killer that is almost guaranteed to murder the fun of dating and offset any natural chemistry.

Here are three core principles to dating around:

- *Focus on having fun.* Bring an essence of curiosity as you allow yourself to be (casually) romanced by different people.
- *Stay open to different kinds of people.* Even though you may not feel a fierce attraction at first, ask yourself, 'Do I like this person enough to see them again?' If so, keep hanging out on a casual basis – you never know where it could lead.
- *Practise safe sex* (duh!). Take your time before jumping into bed with someone. Remember that you are more likely to regret jumping into bed together too soon than holding off a bit longer. In the meantime, relish the tension, play with it and enjoy it – there is so much fun in that!

Slow and steady wins the race: The five-date rule

Perhaps the best example of managing tension in a relationship lies in how we navigate having sex for the first time. In order to fully integrate pacing and dating around, we generally need to get more comfortable with taking things slowly. Sometimes this might even involve making an internal agreement with ourselves to hold off sexual intimacy and any form of commitment to each another until a specified period has passed – for example, five dates. I recommend four dates as a minimum, but the number of dates you choose to wait is really up to you.

I call this the 'five-date rule'. Again, this is more about hanging out together than counting to five with expensive dinners. When I was getting to know my husband, we would often meet up just to play music together.

The beauty of this approach is that it provides a sense of certainty for the mind, along with the space to really get to know someone *before* we get too emotionally entangled to make any sane decision around how much to invest in a new flame. This is how we cultivate a 'slow burn'. To put this into perspective, if you're seeing each other once a week in the beginning (and then twice a week as things progress) this five-date milestone can be achieved within the first month of getting to know each other. If things are moving slower than that, it may be a sign that a person is not very invested in developing the relationship.

By committing to a specified period of time before jumping into bed together (and sticking to it), we stop ourselves from getting carried away and projecting too far into the future (the biggest premature killer of relationships). This makes it easier to maintain the essence of curiosity, without the weighty expectation of a particular outcome. Of course, during this time we can still flirt, date, kiss, cuddle and see other people, but we want to refrain from having sex while we suss this potential 'other' out.

I know this might sound a little old-fashioned in our modern age of hook-ups and one-night stands, but if we're really looking for a deeper and more lasting connection, it pays to take our time to get to know someone first. We can't always see the warning signs of a partner's character right away, and it hurts to find that we've invested our time, energy and love into a person who's not ready to match us on it. Also, if we are dating around we don't want to be sleeping with more than one person at a time as this can really complicate things. If you are seeing multiple people, I would suggest taking things even slower with most of them.

As a woman, choosing to take things slow often surgically removes the guys who are just in it for the sex. It also helps to weed out the guys who are likely to let us down or hurt us in the future as it requires them to decide whether they really want to get to know us.

So often women complain that men are only after one thing! Of course sex is of interest to men – they have testosterone to contend with. Forgive him that his DNA was built to drive the survival of the human species for both genders. In fact, be more concerned if they have little interest in sex! The bigger question to look at is, 'Is he interested in the rest of me as well?' The best response when a guy we like puts pressure on us to get sexual is not 'No'. It is, 'Not yet'. This is a great example of playing with the tension as mentioned in the previous section. (Of course, if you've decided it's never going to happen, then make it a 'No'.)

'Not yet' also gives us the all-important time to check in and see whether our vision and core values are in alignment, which as I've mentioned is one of the most influential factors of a successful relationship. In the long run, it's this kind of 'earned attraction' that keeps the passion alive and builds a sturdy foundation for an ongoing relationship. 'Not yet' avoids the uncomfortable position of having to make a quick decision about whether or not we get sexual, or risk bruising egos and ending the relationship unnecessarily.

The thing is, when we let a guy move too fast, we cannot distinguish them from the kinds of guys we have been disappointed by in the past. We might even get confused between liking him as a whole person and enjoying the sexual connection. On the flipside, when men show a genuine willingness to take things slowly, it takes the pressure off and makes women feel much safer as they are clearly here for more than just the sex.

By the way, this 'five-date rule' does not mean hiding or suppressing your sexual desire altogether, but rather demonstrating – in elegant ways – that you have control over it, can play with the tension and are prepared to wait for the right person.

For the record – and there has been some confusion around this in the past – I do not recommend telling your new date about this rule outright at the start. The moment you tell someone about a hard and fast rule like this, you will likely kill a lot of the sexual tension that can otherwise be an asset to your growing connection. Besides, telling a new date about this rule sets you up for a very awkward fifth date!

Instead, see this 'five-date rule' as more of a personal challenge for yourself. My invitation to you is to find fun ways to get comfortable with the tension and maintain the illusion of taking things date by date so you can really get to know each other without the pressure of future promises hanging over your head. Overall, the 'five-date rule' means that instead of rushing into things, we actually take the time to first get to know each other as friends and human beings. This is essential in order to have a truly intimate relationship – the basis of true love.

Ultimately, pacing a new partner as we date around and developing a slow burn allows us to feel safe about opening our hearts to the possibility of a real, deep and sexy kind of love. And to do that responsibly, we need to feel that we know who someone really is, whether we can trust them and that we are right for them. Again, this is all about building the intimacy and trust of true love and this requires vulnerability. Let's take it further as we look at how it fits into dating.

The power of vulnerability

JBW

> You don't measure vulnerability by the amount of
> disclosure. You measure it by the amount of courage
> it takes to show up and be seen when you can't control
> the outcome.
>
> – Brené Brown

It was midday and I was on my way to a first date with a guy I'd been crushing on for a while. *Finally* I was about to go on a date with someone I was *actually* interested in! I had already spent over an hour preparing, blow drying my hair, doing my makeup and carefully choosing the 'right' clothes to make an impression. It was a lunch date and we were meeting up at an organic café in a hip part of town. I was both excited and nervous – although you probably couldn't tell when I walked in the door, as I was well practised in the art of the poker face.

This was me at twenty years old. At that stage of my life, I thought the key to nailing a first date was to present myself as cool, calm, capable and independent. When it came to dating, my strategy had always been to keep my cards close to my chest lest someone discovered the goofy, sensitive little girl within. So I told him stories of my solo travels around the world and my plans to start my own business. When we parted ways at the end of the date, I thought he liked me.

Unfortunately, he never called me again. Little did I realise that my seduction strategy was lacking one vital ingredient: *vulnerability.*

But who wants to be genuinely vulnerable (especially with someone you are just getting to know) in this era of social media show reels? Even at the age of twenty, when social media was still getting started, my peers and I were very quickly becoming familiar with the push to create an online persona that was virtually flawless. Now, with online profiles often being the first point of contact for many modern daters, we can easily get stuck hiding behind these masks of invulnerability as we set about proving to the world that we are a good – no, 'perfect' – catch.

The irony is that in the process of striving towards perfection, we tend to alienate ourselves from our potential mates by withholding the very parts of ourselves that make us human and relatable. More often than not, this kind of approach to dating leads us to miss out on a true connection because we simply can't get beyond each other's masks.

If we are going to form a lifelong relationship with someone, we need to show them who we *really are* and what we *really feel*. This is important to make sure that our partner is aware of our likes, dislikes, hopes and fears, and can relate to us with that in mind. As explained earlier, without creating intimacy, how can we ever expect to create true love? As renowned vulnerability and shame researcher and author Brené Brown reminds us, 'Embracing our vulnerabilities is risky, but not nearly as dangerous as giving up on love and belonging and joy – the experiences that make us the most vulnerable.'[34]

Empowered vulnerability

While vulnerability is an important ingredient of long-lasting love, the concept of vulnerability itself doesn't always get the best rap. We tend to associate vulnerability with weakness – the expression of our fears, insecurities, past hurts and wounds. Yet this is really only half the picture because sometimes it can feel *just* as vulnerable to express our boundaries, our desires and even our pleasure. It is important to recognise that vulnerability comes in many shades, and as we attempt to understand the power of vulnerability in relationships, we need to acknowledge all of them.

But what if we express our frustration with a new date's aloofness and they ghost us? What if we share our secret desires in the bedroom and our partner does not want to see us anymore? What if we moan with uninhibited pleasure and we get laughed at for making a strange sound? *What if, what if, what if* … It is for this reason that the act of vulnerability – being willing to be witnessed in our truth – requires us to be courageous while picking the right person at the right time.

Furthermore, empowered vulnerability means embracing the full spectrum of vulnerability – the lighter aspects as well as the heavier ones. It means balancing the sharing of our fears and insecurities with the equally vulnerable expressions of our desire, pleasure and everything in between. Expressing each of these in a paced, discerning way becomes the difference between deepening a connection and scaring someone away.

This also means taking responsibility for our experiences – not playing victim to them, but owning our role as a player in the game of life so we can grow, evolve and become better. It is this willingness to grow and learn that takes the weight and burden out of sharing our truth and makes the difference between offloading onto someone and letting someone into our life.

Still I see many people playing at extreme ends of the spectrum when it comes to incorporating vulnerability into one's dating life. At one end we have the 'Ice Queen' (or King) archetype. This is what happens when we have sworn off vulnerability altogether. Remember when I wrote about how I used to ignore the men I was attracted to, hoping in vain that they would come over to talk to me? This is dating without vulnerability (I wasn't willing to let men see my interest or my desire to connect with them) and it gets us nowhere.

The hallmark of an Ice Queen is her cool, calm, collected composure. She maintains her poker face most of the time and because of this tends to come across as quite serious (and not much fun). Often this mask of invulnerability is really just a default protective mechanism – an effort to protect ourselves from rejection – so we keep a lid on our emotions. The Ice Queen (or King) might succeed in creating some attraction with a potential partner in the beginning because they are mysterious and strong. However, often this connection struggles because without exposing any vulnerability (in an empowered way), there is no 'humanness' to connect with.

On the flipside, while some people find it difficult to ever trust someone enough to share even small vulnerabilities, others find it a little too easy to open up as soon as someone is listening. This leads us to the other end of the spectrum, where we have the archetype I like to call the 'Bleeding Heart'. This is the reckless over-sharer – the friend who mistakes disclosure for vulnerability, thoughtlessly sharing their emotional baggage with anyone prepared to sit still long enough.

In some (rare) cases, this can create a bit of attraction in the beginning, but in the lucid morning light of a potential long-term relationship, merciless oversharing can often begin to feel a little too much for one person to handle. It tends to feel 'heavy' for the listener, who is often not well equipped to support the Bleeding Heart in the moment, let alone the long term. It becomes a particular point of contention when the over-sharer shows no commitment to personal growth – to doing something about their issues.

In contrast, while the Bleeding Heart is often comfortable expressing their fears, insecurities, past hurts and wounds, often they lack boundaries. The Ice Queen or King, on the other hand, is often a little *too good* at establishing their boundaries. They are unlikely to divulge their fears, insecurities, past hurts and wounds because pretending they do not exist is part of their protective strategy. Similarly, they will typically steer clear of sharing their pleasure and desire because that also feels too dangerous.

The traditional stereotype of masculinity, men who are strong and silent about their emotions, is an example of an Ice King – never needing to share his vulnerabilities or feeling unsafe to do so. However, current rates of male suicide, depression and anxiety show just how little truth there is to this notion that men are invulnerable and don't have feelings. In a toxic environment, where such toughness is demanded of men (and to a lesser extent women), it can feel quite unsafe to express weakness or vulnerability. For generations, men have gone to the grave with their gruff exterior intact, never daring to reveal their true hopes and fears. Thankfully, times are changing in the modern era with a new emphasis on emotional intelligence, therapy, the blossoming of men's and women's groups, and other cultural safe spaces.

All this said, for someone with a great fear of opening up, to successfully share their vulnerability requires two things: a trustworthy listener and a bold speaker. All the safe space in the world won't induce us to share our vulnerability unless we are willing to speak up ourselves. And speak up we must if we wish to share enough of ourselves that our partner genuinely knows our likes and dislikes, hopes, dreams and fears – the foundations of intimacy.

But how do we navigate the extremes of over- and under-sharing? I've coined the phrase 'empowered vulnerability' for this purpose. It means sharing our vulnerability (speaking up) at the same time as retaining our power (not looking for a hero). I define this as *exposing our vulnerabilities to build intimacy, from a place of courage.*

For some readers, this may sound like a contradiction in terms. How can we be both powerful and vulnerable at the same time? I argue that this seeming contradiction exists mainly because vulnerability is often viewed as a synonym for weakness. However, while vulnerability addresses our weaknesses, it has nothing to do with being weak. The challenge of personal growth begins with confronting ourselves and admitting our weaknesses. This takes courage. Cowards do not look closely at themselves for fear of what they will see, let alone share this with others.

White lies and lullabies

For many people, it's not a big problem to tell a few small lies in the spirit of getting along. For example, on a first date your potential partner might say how much they love the *Lord of The Rings* movies, and because you think they're cute you find yourself agreeing that they comprise an unsurpassed masterpiece. But be careful: you might find yourself spending dates two and three in a movie marathon getting through not only the original trilogy but also *The Hobbit* movies ... this is the punishment for white lies!

Not only can telling the truth about yourself and being open about your opinions avoid hours of viewing tedium, it can also create more positive tension and attraction when you offer a contrary opinion to that of your date. While we might think we are lulling someone into a sense of connection with our little white lies, often we are setting ourselves up for greater disconnection in the future. Finding out what your partner really thinks of your taste in music three months into a relationship can be much more disconcerting than it would have been on date three. Besides, no one wants to date a pushover who agrees with everything and does not have their own opinion or feelings about anything. In fact, holding well-thought-out opinions and putting them on the table can display to a potential partner that you have an ability for critical thought and friendly debate.

This is an attractive feature: you don't simply agree with the people around you, instead you find the courage to share that *Star Wars* has never been your cup of tea. Or how you could not care less about who wins the World Cup.

Drip-feed to create intrigue

Sharing your personal taste is an example of being vulnerable, albeit with small stakes. When it comes to sharing our hopes and fears, we enter the vulnerability big league, which means it is even harder (and more important) that we open up to a new partner about these things.

However, as in the previous chapters about pacing, this doesn't mean that we need to lay all our cards on the table right away. As in poker, we need to carefully place our chips on the table round after round, so we are sure of our position before we declare ourselves 'all-in!' (Unlike poker, we want to leave our poker face at home.)

I remember once, many years ago, I'd formed a connection with a lovely man – someone I could really talk to – during a group weekend away. He in turn shared openly with me. We spoke for hours and hours about our past, our future, our troubles and our joy. By the end of the weekend, we knew practically everything about each other; it almost felt as if we'd been together for months. As we parted ways, I suggested we meet up again – in a romantic sense. What he said in response taught me a valuable life lesson. 'Maybe not. I don't think this is the best way to start a relationship.'

I was hurt at the time, but looking back much later I can see that he was absolutely right. Having shared everything about each other in our first meeting, there was no mystery left. On top of this, maybe this oversharing had been overwhelming. We already knew all about each other's dreams and vulnerabilities. This rapid closeness had skyrocketed us into the 'friend zone', stifling attraction and the possibility of a romantic relationship.

While it can be easy for some to reveal all their issues as soon as they have an attentive ear, we must avoid the temptation to spend too much time talking about our insecurities and wounds too soon. Not only can it cheapen the bold act of sharing our intimate fears; it leaves little to be discovered down the track. This is the mistake the Bleeding Heart makes again and again. Unless you're looking for someone with a hero complex who wishes to come and save you from yourself, you will be pushing emotionally healthy people away. This is because expressing vulnerability should be paced, just like the development of the relationship. It's good to gradually open up over time – or, as I like to say, 'drip-feed to create intrigue'.

Besides, you may have already noticed that it does not really work just to sit someone down and tell them why we are so awesome (or flawed). After a few minutes of that, it can seem like you are bragging or seeking some kind of stamp of approval or, worse, reassurance. But if we can learn to *drip-feed* and take time to let our story unfold – the good and the bad, our preferences and dislikes – over multiple encounters, we create real *intrigue* because there is mystery and interest (positive tension) along with drip-fed clarity around the kind of person we are. This approach allows the conversation to become much more of a journey as we go deeper into the layers of who we are and what we appreciate in this world. It also leaves our date with a natural sense that there is more to be uncovered.

Be willing to be exposed

Notably, Oxford Languages online defines *vulnerability* as 'the quality or state of being exposed to the possibility of being attacked or harmed, either physically or emotionally'. The key word here is 'exposed'. When we open up to a friend, a date or a partner, we are exposing ourselves – and it is a risk.

Still, it is essential that when we are potentially building a lifelong relationship, we show our partner who we really are so they know who they have to match to. How can you both work out if you're a good match if you're not seeing the real person? One way or another, we need to expose ourselves. I cannot emphasise enough that the key is to do it in a paced way.

This is where working out the pacing really comes into play. It involves exposing ourselves bit by bit and reading the feedback, so we can learn to discern when it is appropriate to open up and trust our new partner with this special information. Watch closely how others treat what you share. You are looking for them to handle it with care. Over time, as you see them do this, you can start to give them more and more of yourself in a paced way. Hopefully they will do the same. It also means being aware that no one else can save us from ourselves. We are the authors of our own story.

The phrasing of our vulnerabilities is important too. There is a huge difference between talking at length about how your ex failed you, versus how you were hurt by your last relationship but also learned a lot. Following a negative experience with what you have learned from it is the best way to not just talk about the painful things in our lives, but also models this to our partners. It says, 'Sure we can talk about the bad stuff, but we do so with the purpose of growing from it.'

Knowing how to time and phrase the sharing of our own strengths, weaknesses and complexities is crucial to pacing and empowered vulnerability. We learn this intuitively by acknowledging the feedback, including non-verbal signs of interest and support. This allows us to create the foundation for that much needed sense of 'containment' as we build the house of a healthy relationship brick by brick. Containment is what will hold the relationship together when the conflicts and stressors inevitably arrive.

Of course, if you've done a few cycles around the sun, you've probably had some experiences in the past where your vulnerability was not met with the attention it deserved. This can often leave us with some confusion about how to express our vulnerability in appropriate ways. We have to be prepared to be disappointed – not everyone is going to be able to hold us in our vulnerability the way we would like. This is why I encourage you to start with small things (interesting but not-a-big-deal-I've-already-processed-it kind of things) instead of laying your whole life story out on the table.

If our partner receives these vulnerabilities well and listens without trying to save us and without making fun of our experiences, we may choose to open up more, thus forging a resilient bond. As we continue to feel respected in sharing our vulnerabilities, we can become more certain that we've found a trusted partner – and if things go really well, maybe one day we'll have no secrets left.

Remember, a key element of building true love is being fully accepted as we are. This means that without empowered vulnerability, there can be no true love. Keeping our power while expressing our vulnerability is about staying safe while dating, and it is an important strategy for finding a lifelong partner.

Not the marrying time

GBW

> To say that one waits a lifetime for his soulmate to
> come around is a paradox. People eventually get sick of
> waiting, take a chance on someone, and by the art of
> commitment become soulmates, which takes a lifetime
> to perfect.
>
> – Criss Jami

Meeting my future wife on that sunny day in July really
pissed me off. Our eyes met over a crowded psychiatric ward.
Encouragingly, neither of us was an inpatient. It was the very
first day of the beginning of my new career – indeed, my new
life. It would lead to me making the biggest decision of my life
and immerse me in the only specialty of medicine that fired
me up.

I was only six months out of finishing my internship and
of being registered as a real doctor. I had just landed a job as
a trainee psychiatrist. As a hospital registrar in training, your
pay jumps dramatically, commensurate with the fact that you
are now responsible for, and in charge of, the medical running
of your ward. I reported to a consultant psychiatrist who was
typically only physically on site two or three times a week.

If shit happened and I did not call the consultant, the buck stopped with me. It was a big responsibility. Medical students on placement, interns, resident house officers all report directly to the registrar, as do nursing and allied health staff on medical matters. Training registrar positions are more difficult to get than non-training positions, simply because there are fewer teaching hospitals.

If patients got worse, or died – and they did, for one reason or another – everyone looked to the registrar first, as the most senior, full-time, on-site doctor. It was a position of pride and anxiety in equal measure. Having only been working as a doctor for eighteen months, with only one three-month term in a psychiatric ward, I just didn't know how much I didn't know, which was awesome for me (not so much for the more experienced nurses and allied health staff around me).

I was the youngest trainee psychiatrist in the state, largely because I had made it clear that this was the only specialty in medicine in which I had any real interest. Being a general practitioner scared me to death. The terrifying part was recognising conditions that were serious but could present similarly to minor conditions, which had to be sorted in fifteen minutes – sometimes less – without the huge resources of a hospital behind you.

General practice was a world I understood well from knowing my father's work. Besides, all through medical school I had heard comments of respect for my father, who was an 'old school GP' (these guys delivered babies and routinely did some surgery – unheard of now), who also relieved as a flying doctor to remote Australia. There was no way I was going to compete with him!

It was the mid-1980s, the economy was booming, the world was at peace, the Cold War was cooling off and we were all blissfully ignorant that we were screwing up the environment. Life was great.

On this stage, at the age of 25, I finally had status, my own place, money and a cool car – a classic '69 Mercedes convertible. For the first time in my life, I felt I was ready to get out there and meet women at the highest level of the game.

So, there I was being introduced around the psychiatric unit of this large city hospital. I was taken to the other psychiatric ward by the director and that is where I was introduced to my future wife. This was so annoying! The last woman I wanted to meet was my future wife. What was she thinking, being there like that? Showing up then!

Penny was the psychologist attached to the other psychiatric ward at the hospital. It was one of those tragic attractions at first sight. Only later did I appreciate just how much she was like my mother. Just like my mother, she was unusually smart, independent and a free thinker. Also like my mother (who raised four boys with a workaholic husband), she was perhaps too independent and did not really need a man in her life unless he was worth it.

The first time I visited her parents' house, I had the very weird experience of walking into a house that was furnished with almost identical carpet and fittings to my own parents' home. It added a whole other dimension to that sense of feeling that you have known this person forever. It was like I had grown up in a parallel universe to hers. We later found out that we were born in the same year (she is two months older, so I call her the 'cradle snatcher') at the same hospital and delivered by the same obstetrician.

The more I got to know her, the more I saw her depth, her sensitivity and her capacity to care. This soft side was balanced by a sharp wit and a unique preparedness to be her own person.

She later revealed how she had not had a serious relationship for the preceding couple of years. After two serious long-term relationships, she was clearer about what she was looking for in a serious partner and did not want to just date people for the sake of having a boyfriend. I had never seen a woman do that before. She was ready to find a long-term partner and was not prepared to continue dating when the necessary ingredients were not there.

Which was just even more annoying! I had just entered my prime on the dating scene. Unfortunately we were a great match. We had completely different personalities and interests, but our vision and values aligned, as did our education and socio-economic background. Neither of us had any strongly held conflicting core beliefs, particularly when it came to family, parenting, politics or religion. And we made each other laugh!

The age of commitment

Surprisingly, there is not a lot of research on the point in their lives at which men are most ready to consider marriage and why. Overall, we know that this age has increased by roughly a decade since the mid-1960s, with men now getting married in their early thirties with their brides being a couple of years younger than them. But this does not tell us the whole story.

If there is a phase during which men are most ready to marry, this is fairly critical information for women who are interested in settling down. One of the most revealing studies comes from John T. Molloy. While Molloy is not a hard-nosed scientist, he is a market researcher – which is perhaps even more relevant to this particular space. For his book *Why Men Marry Some Women and Not Others*,[35] he and his team interviewed around 6000 people over eleven years to answer this question.

This included 2500 just-married couples and 1000 singles, with a control group. These are huge numbers that give his findings credibility.

He found that it was not so much about the 'why' as it was about the 'when'. Men have an 'age of commitment' – that is, a period in their lives when they are most prepared to settle down.

Molloy's team interviewed many single men to find a distinct pattern. Indeed, annoyingly, my story is apparently very common. As we blokes start to earn decent coin we can finally afford to be noticed. He writes:

> All of a sudden, they have a nice car and an apartment and an income. They're reluctant to even consider marriage for a few years, because they want to sow their wild oats.

As you would expect, this means that men who earn significant income from a younger age, such as tradesmen, are prepared to consider marriage at an equally younger age – Molloy found this to be around 26. But again, this is only after they have spent time on the singles scene.

For the majority of college graduates, Molloy found that it was not until around 28 that men will consider marriage. For those who have to undertake longer postgraduate training, like doctors, psychologists and lawyers, this gets pushed back further to age 30. The window then starts to close for men in their late thirties.

Of course, these ages are not set in stone. Molloy says 20 per cent of men will marry earlier and another 20 per cent will marry later. More important than these ages is understanding where the guy you are dating is at by considering these factors. The goal here is to get a feel for where your man is sitting relative to their age of commitment. Fortunately, it is not rocket science.

Men have clocks too

As you can see, while men are not so driven by a biological clock, we do have times when we are more ready to marry. There are signals to look for as the relationship matures. There should be a sense of progression. Search online for 'signs that a man is ready to marry' and you will be confronted by dozens of lists – some are 40 items long! Combining these with my own clinical experience, here are my top ten:

1. He is working in a job that is a meaningful career for him, and that he sees as his future.
2. He is not living at home (for some ethnic cultures, this is less of a concern).
3. He wants to live together (not just to save money).
4. He is there for you in hard times when you need support.
5. He talks about, and acts towards, the future on the basis you will be a part of it.
6. He wants to know the important friends and family in your life, and have you meet his.
7. You become his plus-one to important events.
8. He shows an interest in forming a family or, better still, in being a father.
9. The men he is close to are getting married.
10. He seems to be less interested in the singles scene.

These last two points have some numbers behind them. Molloy found that men followed suit once their peers started to marry; in fact, 60 per cent of recently married men had a friend who had married within the previous year (encouraging your partner's best friend to propose to his partner might be one of your best plays!). Men who are ready to settle down will start to withdraw from the singles scene. Molloy found that this withdrawal typically takes place over a period of 6 to 24 months before they meet their wife. This is a relatively easy subject to get a feel for. Just get your potential partner to talk about how active they have been in the singles scene. If they still have a lot of vigour and energy for it, move on. If their interest is declining, then you have a movement towards either permanent bachelorhood or getting married – which at least narrows the options somewhat. It is your job to work out which!

Equally, here are my top five signs that suggest it might be time to cut and run:

1. He is spending money for immediate gratification, e.g. on partying, or borrowing to buy a sports car while leaving him without the money to buy an engagement ring or move into a decent home with you.
2. He has concerns about losing money through a divorce.
3. He speaks badly of peers who are getting married.
4. He frequently breaks plans or is not planning to see you on the social days of the week, i.e. Friday and Saturday nights.
5. He sabotages the relationship when it's going well and you're feeling that you're getting closer, then reaches out when you start to give up on the relationship.

This last point of 'relationship yo-yoing' is confusing at first and reflects an underlying anxiety about intimacy. Over time the pattern declares itself when the blokes go missing just as you're feeling that you're getting closer. Then, when you get ready to move on (and they now feel safer) they are all over you.

The woman has to be more committed too

While understanding where a guy is in his life cycle is critical, so is one other factor. I love the story of the first two research assistants (who were sisters) who originally pushed Molloy to do this research because they could not find a man willing to settle down. After the first day of interviewing only fourteen newlyweds, Kelly[36] said she knew exactly what she was doing wrong with the men she dated. Molloy cautioned her that it was too early to know, but it would turn out that she was right.

What did she realise? She quickly saw that she was not dedicated enough to getting married to 'insist' on it. Impressively, once they applied their new understanding, both sisters were engaged within a couple of years.

As I see it, when it comes to marriage, while men may be responsible for the proposing (less so these days), women are responsible for the motivation for making it happen. We men are rarely in a hurry to get married, even when it is time to do so. We need women to gently encourage and support us through this scary life challenge. Indeed, it is helpful to get us to make a formal proposal, because it makes us feel that we had something to do with the decision! While point three of my top ten is the man showing interest in living together (undoubtedly, in part, in the hope of getting more sex!) this is the woman's cue to marry 'moving in' to marriage. It needs to be raised, even if it is kept more in the background. So, when I asked my wife if we could live together, she made it clear that the only basis on which she would do this was if it was with a view to marriage – a trial, as it were.

An extension of this understanding is that women who end up married do not stick around in a relationship that is not progressing, however slowly, towards marriage. Strikingly, Molloy found that 73 per cent of recently married brides admitted that they had put pressure on their man to make a marriage commitment, if not a proposal. Let's look at how to do this in a healthy, non-manipulative way.

A preparedness to move on

While they did not push for it early on, once marriage was on the table these women did not take it off again. Molloy found that over 60 per cent of recently married women admitted that if their partner had shown cold feet after they moved towards marriage, they would have made it clear that they would not wait around. The subtext was, 'marry me, or *else*'. The 'else' was that they would move on and find somebody who was ready to commit.

We don't deliver this message as a brutal ultimatum. In working with my patients, I suggest approaching this commitment in a firm matter-of-fact, that's-a-real-pity-as-I-will-have-to-move-on kind of way. They may say something like, 'It's so sad for both of us that you feel that way, as I just can't spend any more of my time in this relationship if it is not going anywhere, no matter how much we love each other.'

I often see patients who worry about putting too much pressure on their partner to marry. Obviously, we are now talking about mature, well-down-the-track, established relationships. In this situation, you need to know one way or another. This is particularly the case if staying in a dead-end relationship takes you out of the dating pool when you could be dating men in that high-yield window, particularly when men are in their early thirties.

In my experience, women are not pushing the point because of the fear of rejection and/or a fear of starting over again. In therapy, I will work through this with them, helping them to come to terms with accepting that an end to a relationship is not a statement of how good or bad they are; it is just a failed match. If it is not going to work out, you need to know sooner rather than later.

A principle I use a lot in my work is: *What makes a relationship healthy is a preparedness to leave it if it becomes unhealthy.* It may seem self-evident, but I have found that people are far more ready to complain than they are to leave in a reasoned, considered way, as it becomes clear that things are deteriorating. The key word here is 'preparedness'. There is a substantial list of reasons why we should leave a relationship, with being repeatedly hurt or abused at the very top. This way of seeing a relationship is built around the key concept of personal boundaries. It communicates to our partner that we require a certain standard of respect and love to give up the rest of our life for them. If you are not prepared to leave, no matter what, you are committing to stay in a relationship however unhealthy it gets. This is not a message you want to give to a partner. In effect you are saying, 'Don't worry about looking after me, I will stick around no matter how badly you treat me.'

Of course, boundaries have two sides. The other side is just as important, i.e. if you respect me and love me, I will commit to be here for you come hell or high water.

By operating from this principle of being prepared to leave, we still allow space to work on fixing the issues that arise in a relationship. We are just saying that there is a limit – a line in the sand when we part company and go our separate ways. This keeps people in their better behaviour and it starts back at this point when marriage needs to be put on the agenda.

I have long thought that the 'until death do us part' marriage vow, without qualification, was spectacularly unhelpful. I would abandon it in favour of, 'We will stay together for as long as we respect and care for each other and are prepared to work on this relationship.' Agreeing to 'until death do us part' can send the message that we will put up with our partner's shit no matter what. I think too many married men and women take advantage of this. Setting the boundary of being prepared to leave, is all about caring for and respecting yourself.

Along the same lines, Molloy gives us an insight into the women who are more likely to be able to get a man to commit. 'Women who married loved themselves more than they loved any man.' This is not about narcissism for a second; it is simply about self-respect and healthy self-love. Such a woman is simply not going to allow a man to muck her life around.

Equally, these women were not prepared to wait around once they realised that the men they were dating were not prepared to commit to them and meet their needs. They were not requiring the man to change; they were simply authoring their own life once they realised that, despite making their needs clear, their partner was not going to respond.

In truth, I think many men respect a woman more for voicing and standing by their desire for marriage, even if they are not keen to go there themselves. After all, it is hardly a surprise to us that women want to marry.

Older divorced men are a better bet than older never-married men

Let's now turn our attention to the older age cohort – a group with which I work closely. A couple of Molloy's findings are of particular importance to older single women.

Around their mid-forties, men who have never married are likely to become confirmed bachelors.

There is one interesting exception, and these are the men who were brutally rejected by women at a younger age. They are not confirmed bachelors as much as they are simply protecting themselves by not putting themselves out there anymore. Molloy found that early balding, being overweight, short or not socially sophisticated are examples of superficial flaws that can leave men being publicly and painfully rejected in their earlier years by women (who were concerned about their own image as projected by the man on their arm). Their egos have taken a beating and they are just not up to entering this arena anymore.

These men are the true diamonds in the rough, who can be polished into brilliance by a woman who takes the time to see who they really are and can look past these relatively minor factors when it comes to what is important in a long-term, loving relationship. Just bear in mind that these men will need significant encouragement and reassurance. I often see women make the mistake of continuing to overlook these men because they lack confidence and do not actively pursue the relationship.

Molloy speaks of how impressed he was by the men who had not married. They were rated as just as nice, as intelligent and as hardworking as their married counterparts. Some women seemed to have worked this out such that seven out of eight men over the age of 50 getting married for the first time, were marrying divorced women. Apparently, these women were prepared to marry these guys because 'they had already had a man who was tall or suave, and he hadn't made a very good husband'.

Look at their relationship with children

Don't try to convert a confirmed bachelor unless you gain a masochistic pleasure from taking on unwinnable, fruitless tasks. Men who are still bachelors into their forties and beyond often have decided to replace a woman with a career and/or more material gains. Even a pre-nup will not solve the problem because they are not as intrinsically interested in valuing or building a relationship as they are in building their assets.

A not insignificant number of men make this trade because they see work and money as more predictable, stable and under their control. Many of these men have a degree of intimacy avoidance, often resulting from having their heart broken or being confused by relationships, and that is not going to change without some intensive therapy.

While the statistics suggest that remarriage after divorce has high rates of failure, there is some complexity to this story. Yes, there are the men who are still angry and jaded by their divorce, or not prepared to look at themselves, or be more influenceable. These are the ones to dodge. If you are not sure if any of these apply to your man, look for these things, *after the infatuation phase is over*, and this will become clearer over time.

The good news is that, compared with committed bachelors, divorced men are a much better bet from middle age on. Having re-experienced the single life, many of these men are now convinced, once and for all, that married life is for them. And they are often more mature than they were when they got married the first time around.

So how do you work out who is who? As well as the tips and questions we have given you in the other chapters that talk about what to look for in a relationship, there is one particular point I want to add here. There is a very simple and powerful indicator when evaluating a divorced man as a potential partner. If he has children, look at how well he gets on with them. How close are they? Divorce is so common that it is effectively normal, and in and of itself cannot be used to judge a man's character. But how well he treats and relates to his children is incredibly informative.

While much of this particular chapter is directed at women in working us blokes out, this particular point is equally relevant to men. Look at what sort of a relationship your potential partner has with her children. How gentle is she with them? How much does she consider their needs? Equally, how good is she at setting boundaries with them?

Moreover, how much the children engage with and look up to their parent can be a powerful indicator of the kind of relationship that you are likely to experience with them going forward. Obviously, we do not introduce partners to children early in a relationship, but when you do get to meet them, a lot of information can be gathered by simply watching how they interact. Even before you meet them, look at how much of their life your potential partner puts aside to give their children quality time, or be there for them when problems arise.

A Penny for your thoughts

As you can tell, I was not happy meeting my future wife earlier than I would have liked. So what happened? Well, Penny could have saved Molloy a lot of time and written his book for him.

After a few weeks of running into each other around the hospital, I asked her on a date and we saw each other on several more. Sensing this woman was different, I nicely confused the issue on our second date by asking her how many children she wanted. Later, backtracking embarrassingly, I made it clear that I was not ready to settle down yet. Yes, I was Molloy's poster boy.

She made it clear to me that she was not interested in a casual relationship. Equally, she made it clear that she was not going to sit around and wait for me to sort my shit out. She matter-of-factly explained that she may or may not be available down the track if I decided that I was ready to look at a more serious relationship. Annoyingly, she seemed to be deadly serious. She put no pressure on me at all. She just made it quite clear where she was at and what she wanted.

Her independence, her preparedness to be her own person and not wait around, was exasperating and worthy of deep respect in equal measure. I think I lasted about six months. When I heard she had started dating a lawyer, I realised I really did not want to risk losing her and so I lost my nerve instead and decided that my single days were over.

The quote at the beginning of this chapter fits nicely next to what we have just discussed and also with arranged marriages and manufactured love. The fact that the majority of men marry when they are at a particular time in their life again highlights that partner selection is about forces quite different from stumbling across your soulmate. It is, indeed, more about 'the art of commitment'.

You can't require people to change, but you have a responsibility to ask

How Penny handled this with me brings me to the final point I want to make in this chapter, which relates to how to tell your partner that you are not happy with them at some level. Few relationship issues cause more confusion than this one. On one hand, partners can raise these issues in a way that causes significant resentment as the other person feels that they are not allowed to be who they are – that they are not good enough and have to change. On the other hand, I will often have one of the couple in my office saying something like, 'Oh, I don't have the right to tell them that they should change.'

In reality, it is unfair on a partner to *not* let them know what you are unhappy about. Particularly if you are going to continue to resent it. The trick is to deliver it from the perspective that you are not *requiring* your partner to change. You are simply stating what it is you would like to see change. You accept that it is up to them, and that they may choose not to make the change.

The reason why you have a responsibility to ask your partner to change is that it would be unfair on them to not be given the opportunity. I have seen people walk away from a relationship without making it clear to their partner what it was that they needed to keep them in the relationship. Often these people come from families where they were not allowed to voice their needs or did not expect them to be addressed if they did.

This is why, in the most successful relationships, people actually ask their partners, 'What could I do to be a better partner?' If you really want to reach for the stars, that is the question to step up to. For this reason, it is in our own best interests to check in with our partner and encourage them to tell us what they need from us.

Penny made it clear she wanted more in a relationship in a way that indicated she did not think what I was doing was wrong at any level. She was not judging me. It was just not enough for her to stay around. She was clear about what she wanted and would live with it either way, but one way had certain consequences for her. She left it with me to decide what I wanted to do.

Ultimately, you exercise total power to look after yourself by being able to leave if your partner does not make changes on issues that are potential deal-breakers. Nevertheless, you owe it to your partner to let them know what might cause you to leave, giving them time to rectify the situation if they can. This timeframe needs to be discussed and then followed up on. Typically it is days, maybe weeks but certainly not months.

For issues that are not deal-breakers, you can try something like, 'Of course I can't require you to change, but if you did XYZ I would really appreciate it.'

When you are on the receiving end of these requests, just keep one thought in mind. Nine out of ten times I see that how a partner wants their other half to change is generally for the better. We may not rate the issue as highly as our partner, but nevertheless it will make us a better person. This means we need to think seriously about what they are asking. To state the obvious, it never hurts to become a better person.

Sometimes, though, things simply don't work out. The match cannot be made. When this becomes apparent it is time to move on.

The art of ending: Breaking up

JBW

> Sometimes good things fall apart so better things can fall together.
>
> **– Marilyn Monroe**

> One of the best times for figuring out who you are and what you really want out of life? Right after a break-up.
>
> **– Mandy Hale**

Whichever way you cut it, breakups can be hard. Whether you're the one doing the breaking up or the one being broken up with, a breakup is often a time of heartache and confusion. What makes it worse is that most people are really bad at breakups by being unable to make a clean break or by cruelly disappearing without offering any scrap of closure. It is worth becoming skilled at breakups, however, otherwise we are likely to get stuck in a relationship that is not healthy simply because of our discomfort about breaking up.

Statistically, we are going to break up with everyone we date but one, so we had better get good at it!

When we discover an unsuitable match, we have the

opportunity to let that person go as easily and clearly as possible. Alternatively, we can string them along for months before vanishing from the face of the earth – that's a choice too. But, while ghosting often seems like an easy way out, and gathering the courage for an honest breakup chat can be daunting, when we've realised the relationship isn't working, it is important to break up cleanly and decisively.

Let's also make a distinction: when we refer to a 'breakup' we are talking about a relationship in which you got to the exclusive partner stage and which went on for a while – at least several months. While it can still be upsetting to disconnect after a few dates in the non-exclusive dating phase, this is usually easier for people as they either go off in different directions or maybe even become 'just friends'.

Generally, the longer we spend in a relationship with someone, the harder it is to break up – mostly because we have accumulated more memories and emotional attachments and, as mentioned earlier in this book, we have created 'constraints and investments', such as shared leases, joint bank accounts or a shared pet. Emotional attachments can be the hardest to kick because we habituate to having our partner around, and in our loneliest moments our minds turn to them.

This happens because until we move on we do not have an alternative reference point for love and intimate connection. In those lonely moments, it is often our natural response to think more of the best moments we shared than the issues that brought the relationship undone. Sometimes people mistake this as an excuse or justification to get back with an ex-partner who they have already realised is not a good fit for them, simply because they want the painful feelings to stop. But you broke up for a reason, right? An aching heart does not mean that breaking up was the wrong thing to do.

Even if you were the one who was broken up with, it is important to remember that the breakup was initiated for a reason and unless you can both commit to identifying and really working through the underlying issues, it is unlikely that it is going to be any better the second time around. The most significant factor in the failure or success of a renewed relationship lies in the reasoning behind why a couple decide to get back together. Is it because you and your ex have genuinely learned, grown and changed? Or more because you are lonely, bored or worried that you will never find love again?

If we do get back together with an ex, it is crucially important to learn from our mistakes and address the issues that led to the initial split. What are each of you prepared to work on and change this time around?

Sometimes when we renew a relationship, we get to enjoy a second honeymoon period as sparks are reignited. This can be both intoxicating and exciting, yet must not distract us from noticing whether there has been clear evidence of change. If the original problems are not addressed, it is only a matter of time before old issues re-emerge.

If you feel you might be at risk of getting back with an ex, it could be useful to write yourself a letter to remind yourself of your reasoning while it is still clear in your mind. It might begin, 'Dear Self, I want you to remember why we broke up ...'

Closure is overrated

So often, we have trouble moving on because we are still waiting for closure. Our mind wants a reason why it didn't work out. Especially when a relationship ends abruptly, a breakup can often leave us with a lot of mixed feelings and, in the absence of a clear explanation, our mind is likely to conjure up all sorts of stories.

The reality of dating is that we often don't get closure. Sure, you can ask for it, but we have no control over what the other person chooses to do with our attempts. Often, all we have to work with is the behaviour that played out at the end of the relationship. For example, if someone ghosts you, lets you down in a big way or breaks up abruptly without explanation, it is a pretty certain sign that they are not a match for you. Sometimes we can use these kinds of endings as motivation to let go. When we stop trying to explain or understand it and accept their bad behaviour as closure we can begin to move on.

As we discussed in the chapter about our mindset, when we try to guess the 'real' reasons why our partner left us, we often get it wrong. This is especially true in shorter relationships when we have less information to go by. Often there is nothing wrong with us at all – it is just about not making a match. As a rule of thumb, if you don't know why for sure, don't waste your emotional energy trying to guess unless the answer would make you a better person anyway.

When I think about some of my past relationships with exes who really let me down – and in some cases stomped all over my heart – at the time it was brutal and painful, and often resulted in months of recovery.

But each time I became a little wiser. With the gift of hindsight, I realised that if the relationship had ended any less painfully, I would probably still have had questions in my mind – like, *Was he the one? Where is he now? And what if things had turned out differently?* I realise now that it was actually seeing the ugly side of these relationships that led me to move on more readily. The hurt was closure – a very clear warning sign saying: *This person is NOT right for me!*

The complexity is, not all relationships end in heartache and not all exes hurt us badly enough to deter us from closing that door on them forever. Sometimes we might break up out of circumstance, such as when one person has to move overseas. These kinds of breakups have their own unique challenges. At other times it might just be a mutual decision based on incompatibility. The feelings might still be there, but you both know it is for the best. These are perhaps the toughest breakups of all.

Statistically speaking

The research suggests that between 30 and 50 per cent of couples who separate get back together after breaking up – often because they continue to spend time together post-separation. Please try to remember that the best person to console your partner after a breakup is not you. Literally anyone *but* you is better. This is because in trying to console a recent ex, giving them support will be experienced by their brain in much the same way as care and affection is experienced. Even on the giving side of this consoling, it can feel more like a caring relationship and draw you back in.

As Clint Elison[37] describes in his PhD thesis on this subject, for which he surveyed 214 heterosexual individuals who had recently gone through a breakup, with each breakup and renewal a couple tends to lengthen their relationship by an average of almost five months. Perhaps this is fine when we are young, but as our biological clocks tick on, we want to make sure that we are not wasting any more precious time with an unsuitable long-term match. Elison goes on to say that the most common thing respondents said about their relationship in hindsight was, 'I wish we broke up sooner.' This study also suggests that the longer the relationship, the more drawn out the breakup tends to be.

Not so surprisingly, there is also evidence to suggest that couples in renewed relationships are generally at a greater risk of recurrent relationship problems. A 2013 study by the Kansas State University[38] takes these findings further. It found that partners who have a history of breaking up and getting back together show a greater risk of repeating this pattern again and again. Moreover, couples who engage in an on-again-off-again relationship tend to accumulate 'greater constraints to permanently ending the relationship, greater uncertainty in their relationship's future and lower satisfaction'.

The study goes on to verify that although there is a possibility that some couples will get back together due to actual relationship improvements, most on/off couples that proceed to marriage do not have a relationship quality equivalent to that of couples without a history of breaking up.

Can we still be friends?

It is very common when we break up with an ex (especially when the decision is mutual) to express an interest in maintaining some sort of friendship – or at least the sentiment is there. But is staying friends with an ex really that healthy or realistic?

It depends on the circumstances. The deeper the feelings, the more likely it is that you or your partner will need a clean break in order to fully move on. It is only really when both parties have genuinely moved on that a healthy friendship can be established.

In Elison's study, individuals who had a more one-sided ending, resulting in less ongoing communication with their ex-partner, found it much easier to move on when interviewed after eighteen months. Those who had not found new partners often continued to engage with their ex on some level. They also expressed significantly more lingering feelings around their former relationship, such as confusion, hurt and sadness. In other words, continuous contact with an ex tends to slow down the healing period; the more we engage with our exes post-breakup, the harder it is to move on.

The healing period is the big issue here, as not having a clean break stops us from getting our head straight so we can fully move on to the possibility of a new relationship. The best thing we can do after a breakup is turn our attention to our support network of friends and family and take time to reflect, feel and process the hurt and grief of letting go. Equally, you need to leave your ex to get support from their network, no matter how limited – it is not your job! When it comes to a clean break, sometimes you have to be cruel to be kind.

This does not mean that you should never speak to each other again. It might just entail an agreement to reconnect when you're both feeling more secure as uncoupled individuals. For a true friendship to form, there first needs to be a complete break. We would suggest that this is at least three months. Obviously this is almost impossible to achieve if you have kids together. If kids are a part of the equation, do your best to create some boundaries around how you will interact with your ex during this transition period. This time of no contact should also include unfollowing your ex on all social media platforms. The last thing you need when you are trying to move on is to be bombarded with images of your ex living their life without you. It's also important to normalise this period of transition and be gentle with yourself. Especially if you are the one who got dumped, it will take time to process this change in trajectory and it is important that you allow yourself to grieve the loss of your partner. With that in mind, breaking up can be a real gift to your future as you take the time to reconnect with yourself as an individual and create the space to choose a new partner who is a better match.

What others really think: Listen to friends and family

GBW

> The biggest communication problem is we do not listen
> to understand. We listen to reply.
>
> – Stephen R. Covey

Kashif Afzal patiently explained to me why we have got it wrong in the Western world when it comes to choosing a marriage partner. We do not get it a little wrong: we get it as wrong as wrong can be. To be fair to this exquisitely polite, unassuming Pakistani limo driver, he was not actually arguing that we get it wrong – that was my interpretation. He was just answering my question about how this worked in his world.

'Of course, my parents should choose my partner. They have much more life experience than I do. I'm only 35.'

Now, that's not a sequence of words that you would hear in the West, particularly the last three!

Outside the big black BMW, the temperature was hovering on 40°C as he drove only a couple of metres behind the car in front at 140 kilometres per hour for the 90-minute trip from Dubai to Abu Dhabi. I was sitting up front, acutely aware that for my first trip to the United Arab Emirates I could learn a lot more from a man who drove people around for a living than spending the same time with a room full of local university professors.

I was familiar with the research showing the low divorce rates of arranged marriages – typically well under 10 per cent. As discussed when we looked at Epstein's work on manufacturing love, divorce rates remain low even when the partners in an arranged marriage integrate into divorce-embracing cultures, such as California.

We have to wonder what is going on – particularly when over 50 per cent of marriages on our planet are arranged – yes, even today. And, as we saw, over time they became happier than love marriages.

One thing that defines the human mind is the difficulty we have in stepping outside our 'normality'. Kashif had no awareness of my work and my writing on partner selection, and was speaking about his world with the relaxed ease that comes with sharing the bleeding obvious to an interested traveller. A few minutes earlier, he had been explaining that the traffic was heavier than usual because 1 September – a Sunday in this case – was the first day back at school after the summer holidays.

I had assumed that what he said could not be the case and was getting lost in translation, as obviously children do not go to school on Sundays. That was my normality. It turns out that in the Islamic world 'weekends' are Friday and Saturday, and the only person getting lost in the translation was me.

I was being shown just how arbitrary our normality really is.

'So, your parents can make a better decision than you?' I asked, to encourage him to elaborate.

'Of course, of course. My parents know me better than anyone. Who knows you better than your parents?'

I couldn't argue with that. Even parents who do not really know their own children intimately have a head start on the rest of the world.

He went on: 'My mother chose my brother's wife. She is not beautiful by the usual standards, but I have come to see her as one of the most beautiful, caring and wise people I know. Even though she is younger than me, I look up to her. I hope my mother can choose someone similar for me. It is not just my mother and father who will be involved; my siblings and aunts will also have a say. And then there is the other family looking at me. They know their daughter and they are also looking to see if we would be a good match.'

That was a lot of folks looking to see whether the match was a good one. More to the point, it was a whole lot more than the two people looking to make the match in a love marriage. As a side-note, it was interesting to see the not insignificant social pressure on these young 'non-lovers' to 'perform' as responsible potential marital candidates. This was a subtle, but consistent, force on young people to live with honour and industry.

'Do you get any say at all?' I asked.

'Sure,' he replied. 'They ask me what I'm looking for. I said I wanted a wife who is educated and around my age. Just two things. I don't want to be too demanding.'

I think he covered that one off! It was the shortest partner shopping list in history.

On the way back to Dubai, as luck would have it, I had another Pakistani driver (maybe not so surprising, given that Pakistanis and Indians comprise the largest group of expat workers in the UAE). What was a little more surprising, as I doubled the size of my study sample, was that his name was also Kashif! Apparently it's like 'John' in the Western world.

Kashif Number Two was also 35 (which did make me worry that 35 was a common age in Pakistan!), but there were two important differences. He was married – had been for eight years – and at 140 kilometres per hour, travelled a safer distance from the car in front. His English and interest in conversation were much less than those of Number One; nevertheless, I was able to prise some further information out of him.

When I asked how his parents came across his wife, he said that she was his cousin, five years his junior. With Number One's comments in mind, I thought about how, with a cousin, you would have two families considering the match between these two potential partners, who also knew each candidate well and each other's family well. This knowledge was then added to the 'life experience' that all these parents carried.

Number Two and his future wife had apparently had some influence on the decision, as they had liked each other for some time. Immediately, I wondered whether they were happier than their Western counterparts? When I enquired about this, Number Two responded, 'I moved here to Dubai after four years.' I wondered if this was a witty way to answer my question in the negative, but then I reminded myself that his English was not that good. Moreover, it is not uncommon in his culture to leave your country to find better paid work and he did return once a year in his holidays. He was planning to be away for six years.

I am not going to suggest that you abandon the love marriage, call your mother and ask her to let you know who you are going to marry. Which was pretty close to Kashif

Number One's plan. He told me how, during his next holiday home, he would find out who his wife would be – much as a mate might tell me how on his next trip home he would be interested to see who his brother was dating. He had no one in mind and he was leaving it entirely up to the family.

I am acutely aware of the argument that cultures which censure divorce or, worse still, stone women for leaving a marriage, effectively imprison people – typically women – in desperately unhappy, loveless relationships. Indeed, Number One explained that if a couple separated, the partner who was seen to be at fault can be disowned by *both* families.

There is however, a rather large lesson to take from the Kashifs' books. I would suggest that the hardest information to get in life is an objective view of yourself. Thanks to God Google, you can pretty much get information on anything you want, but try this search: 'Hey Google, how do other people really see me?'

Psychologists have studied how we all tend to see ourselves as better than we are. Excluding those people who have ferocious internal critics, the recurring finding is that the average person sees themselves as above average. In one study, 25 per cent of people believed they were in the top 1 per cent when it came to getting along with others. In another study of American and Swedish students, 93 per cent of US drivers said they had above-average driving ability (Swedish were more modest at only 69 per cent).

This is not a surprise, of course. This is just our unconscious doing what it is meant to do – giving us confidence to face the world. If it continually confronted us with all of our shortcomings, we would all become depressed rather quickly. In protecting us, it tends to overshoot, leaving us thinking of ourselves as better than we are.

The bigger issue is that this protective mechanism interferes with our ability to see ourselves, and all the parts of our personality and behaviours, for what they are. In turn, when it comes to working out how good a match we are to a potential partner, our self-blinkers make this very difficult.

However, that isn't the case for those around us who know us well. Even with some therapy helping us to achieve maximal self-awareness, we will still be some way from how people see us in reality. Moreover, in making a match with a potential partner, knowing yourself is a pretty key part of the equation. Let's dive a little deeper into the science of thinking we are better than we are.

The science of self-deception

A close second to knowing how others objectively see you is getting an objective take on your potential partner. I have lost count of how many times I have heard the following, in one form or another: 'After we broke up, my close friends and family told me how they could never understand what I saw in my ex. Why didn't they tell me?' Why indeed?

Some of us have made the mistake of attempting to point out to our close friend, brother, sister, son or daughter that their partner does not impress us. You know the response. At best it is a form of, 'You don't know them like I know them.' At worst it is a version of, 'I can't believe you don't trust my judgement,' as they then proceed to see less of you and more of their new-found flame who completes them.

The truth is that love really is blind. More accurately, we are looking at the way the mind defends its decisions when we have invested in something, or someone. This is cognitive dissonance in high gear. Add this blindness to those self-blinkers we are wearing, and you can see the magnitude of the potential for self-deception.

I find the science behind this self-deception, at which our unconscious excels, fascinating. Perhaps the best research was done by psychologists Justin Kruger and David Dunning in their 1999 study into the field of what is known as 'cognitive bias'.[39]

Their paper detailed what, not too surprisingly, is now known as the 'Dunning–Kruger effect'. It is one of my favourite peer-reviewed papers (which are typically tediously dry), as it starts with the story of a Mr Wheeler whose chosen career of bank robbing was not going to make him quite where he hoped: In broad daylight, without any attempt to hide his face, he casually walked in and robbed not one, but two banks in Pittsburgh in 1995. He was promptly arrested that night after the wonderfully clear images of him from the surveillance tapes were broadcast on the news. Even more unbelieving than he was unsuccessful, our bamboozled bandit exclaimed, 'But I wore the juice!' His cunning plan had been to rub lemon juice on his face on the spectacularly misinformed basis that it would make him invisible to the cameras.

The paper goes on to study a large group of students and evaluate how well they did on a series of tests. What made the paper famous was that the researchers then looked at how well these undergraduates thought they had performed against how they did perform. They tested logical reasoning, English grammar and, my favourite test, humour.

The first two areas were easy to evaluate, so how did they test humour? They took 30 jokes and contacted eight comedians (including one of my favourite comedians, Kathleen Madigan) and asked them to rate the jokes on a scale (1 to 11). For example: 'Question: What is as big as a man, but weighs nothing? Answer: His shadow' rated 1.3. A better joke, like the following (although a bit mean), rated 9.6: 'If a kid asks where rain comes from, I think a cute thing to tell him is, "God is crying". And if he asks why God is crying, another cute thing to tell him is "probably because of something you did!"' They then looked at how well the test subjects rated the better jokes as defined by the comedians.

They found the same results across all tests. The lower their score, the more the students got it wrong when it came to estimating their results. In essence, they found that the more badly people performed, the more they overestimated their performance. Indeed those who did the worst overestimated their performance by an average 50 per cent.

That is not a little bit wrong: it is a lot wrong. In essence, the incompetence that leads we humans to make mistakes equally prevents us from realising this very incompetence.

The equally surprising finding was that those who performed the best tended to under-estimate their competence.

So, it was with some foresight that Charles Darwin observed, way back in 1871, that 'ignorance more frequently begets confidence than does knowledge'. What this means for all of us is that when we are not expert at something, our lack of knowledge means we will think we know much more than we do.

Later research into cognitive bias has found that this 'illusory superiority', as it has come to be known, is widespread among humans, not just students overrating their driving prowess. In a survey of the professors at the University of Nebraska–Lincoln, 68 per cent rated themselves in the top 25 per cent for teaching ability, and more than 90 per cent rated themselves as above average. Imagine what the rest of us do! (To add insult to injury, the Dunning–Kruger effect suggests that these professors must have been particularly poor teachers!) Put in another way, this research is telling us that overestimating our ability is perfectly normal.

Remember when I suggested that our objective knowledge of our selves is the hardest knowledge to attain? It is *perfectly normal* for you to think you are better at evaluating potential partners, and how good a match to them you are, than is in fact the case. This is particularly so when you have an unconscious mind running its own agenda to heal itself.

Coaxing others to tell you what they really think

This is the lesson I am suggesting we need to take from the Kashifs of the world. Pursue your friends and family to give you their honest opinion of your new-found love. Maybe, we can improve on the arranged marriage approach?

What if we look around us for people who really are a good judge of character? It could be a parent, but it could also be someone else who knows us well. A neighbour, an aunt, a friend or your boss. People who have a track record of employing good staff are at the top of this list. And if they know us well, even though they may not give us this valuable information, they might just apply it to looking at how we would fit with a potential partner.

Of course, do not ask for an opinion from a family member who does not have your interests at heart (or who does, but is a terrible judge of character). In short, one of the cleverest and most powerful things we can bring to choosing a potential partner is looking to our friends and family for their evaluation of not just our potential partner, but how they would see us making a match with that partner.

The hard part is actually convincing people to be honest with us when it comes to giving feedback. The fact that it is so hard to get friends and family to give us feedback about a potential partner is not particular to this situation. As a culture, we are reluctant to give people negative feedback. Often the only time we find out what someone else really thinks about us is when we get them angry enough at us to trample this inhibition. While I would not advocate making people angry to access this information, it can be a way of finding out what the other person is really thinking. (But then anger can mean they overstate it, and we then throw the baby out with the bathwater.)

In two surveys of nearly 8000 managers published in the *Harvard Business Review*, 44 per cent of managers reported that they found it stressful and difficult to give negative feedback. Twenty-one per cent of managers avoided giving negative feedback entirely.

Feedback equals improved decision making. It equals intelligence. When it comes to relationships, it equals emotional intelligence – to my mind the highest form of intelligence. Without feedback, how much can we really know? Without feedback, how good a decision can we make?

One final consideration. There are a number of unmarried older women and men out there because they gave one person too much power in making this decision. Typically, it is a mother, but not always. This other person has reliably adopted the position that prospective partners are 'not good enough for my child'. There are women out there who have become completely disillusioned with the male of the species. Do not give anyone the power of veto – ultimately, the decision is yours. As mentioned, look for the people whose judgement you trust and who clearly have your best interests at heart, but make sure they don't have their own agenda.

So don't hold back from seeking out and seriously considering the opinions of friends and family when you think you have found that perfect lifelong partner. Encourage them to talk by making it clear that you genuinely value their opinion and that you will not be offended if they tell you something you may not want to hear. They have something very powerful to bring to this evaluation that you don't: a mind that is not yours!

When to stop and settle? Some mathematical advice

GBW

Ugh ... my boyfriend is taking forever to exist.

– Anonymous

As we come to the end of this book, let's turn to how to end your dating run and finally make a decision. Jiveny has spoken about how to end relationships that do not work out; now it's time to look at when to end your dating.

One reason that we need to stop looking is that FOMO on someone who 'might' be better can play nicely into the hands of an unconscious (or semi-conscious) anxiety about intimacy. Developing intimacy is risky and for those of us who are gun shy after having our heart broken, continuing to look can be a clever defence mechanism. By keeping on looking, we are not settling into a relationship enough to get our heart broken again.

Once you decide you don't want to be alone, you are in heartbreak territory and that is as it should be and always will be. Remember, fear-based decisions are the worst decisions.

Factor fear in, but never make it the basis for what you decide to do in life. Safe can be depressing. Safe can be lonely.

Typically, we humans don't like having to decide. There is a reason why decide shares the same Latin root as suicide and homicide. The Latin word caedere means to kill, to slaughter, reminding us that in order to decide, we need to kill off alternative options. What makes a decision hard is when we have more than one good and viable option to decide between. For the majority of us who are low on psychopathy, slaughtering a perfectly reasonable option is not something we like to do.

If there are not two or more competing options, then no decision needs to be made – so the way forward is clear. If there is only one flight to that city on the day you want to travel, no decision is required. But if there are ten flights that day, it's time to start slaughtering some options. Fine with flights, but what if we are talking potential partners? Add that to the endless possibilities that the online world offers and we have a ready-made excuse to not settle down.

Choosing a husband- or wife-to-be was easy back in the olden days when the sea was more of a puddle. In 1932 James Bossard published a study that introduced me to the lovely word propinquity. Propinquity refers to how geographically close we are to others. From studying 5000 marriages in Philadelphia he found that in a third of all marriages, the couple lived no more than five blocks from each other. Indeed, 17 per cent lived on the same block! Remember this is back when everyone avoided divorce and appeared to live happily ever after. So, with very limited choice, people married people and grew old with each other. As Bossard pointed out, 'Cupid may have wings, but apparently they are not adapted for long flights.'

With the advent of online dating, the average propinquity distance has grown to around 80 kilometres (over 300 city blocks), but as Cupid's wings become more adapted for longer flights, does the greater choice help us? Not if you look at divorce rates.

In *The Paradox of Choice – Why More is Less*, American psychologist Barry Schwartz highlights how greater choice causes us greater anxiety. While consumerism has spawned a range of products to meet everyone's individual desires, the resulting choice can leave us paralysed and unable to make a decision for fear of making the wrong call. What if there is another product out there that would better suit what I want and my particular tastes?

As we Tinderise people into products that you can swipe away at will, we are seduced into looking, looking, looking. But when should we stop looking and settle? Mathematician nerds, while maybe not going out so much (giving them more time to generously solve the problem for those of you out there dating endlessly) have found the solution. As it turns out this is an old mathematical quandary that has a name: Optimal Stopping Theory. Showing how old it is, it is also known as the Sultan's Dowry Problem, while the modern versions are The Secretary Problem, and, particularly relevant here, The Fussy Suitor Problem.

Let's use the secretarial version by way of explanation. The problem is that in hiring a secretary the employer wants to choose the best of the field of candidates. Ideally, one would run an ad for six months, interview a hundred secretaries and then at the end of the six months call up the one who interviewed the best and give them the job.

You can see the real-life problem here: too many time-consuming interviews, too many costly ads and at the end of the six months you call the best secretary, number forty-two and, of course, because she was so good, she now has a job somewhere else. An employer who was not paralysed with choice (or who understood optimal stopping maths) had snapped her up. At the other end of the spectrum, to avoid this problem, you could employ the first secretary you interviewed, because she presented so well, but then you lie awake wondering how much better again another out there might have been.

So, when is the optimal time to start looking to make a decision? More importantly to us, when does the fussy suitor start to think of settling? Those clever mathematicians have worked it out. The answer is 37 per cent. This is the point after which you get the most bang for your buck, or the best results for the time invested. You need to evaluate 37 per cent of the potential secretaries before you will have a useful, working idea of what good enough is in the current market.

For those of you employing secretaries this means you run the ad for a few weeks and then after interviewing 37 per cent of the shortlist, you hire the next better one. Better still if one of the earlier ones was better again, go back and see if you can grab them before someone else does.

So, how does this play out in the dating world? Let's step back a little. In evaluating what a healthy mother is, after some debate, psychotherapy researchers came up with the idea of the 'good-enough' mother. There is no perfect mother. All mothers will fail their children in some way (and even more fathers – I can say this because I'm one of them). Indeed, parents must not be perfect so that they fail their children. Let's go a little deeper on this.

The under-protective mother will have a child who has more accidents. The over-protective mother will have a child who is less emotionally resilient and less able to cope with life's challenges. A 'good-enough' mother fails her child just enough for them to not have a serious accident but enough so they get practice at rebounding after minor accidents and setbacks. They are prepared to get back on the horse after being thrown off. It is about becoming psychologically resilient. A good-enough parent is there for their child when a problem threatens to overwhelm a child, but they step back and give them gentle encouragement to rise above disappointments, and lesser problems, themselves.

So, in the same way the goal is to find a good-enough partner. We have seen in this book what arranged and manufactured love marriages tell us i.e. that there are many good-enough partners out there for us. Bosses who married secretaries that worked four metres away and Philadelphian residents who married someone on the same block, and lived happily ever after, teach us that we are not looking for a single fish in the oceans of the world.

Nevertheless, the astute reader will be wondering about the 'n' in the equation i.e. 37 per cent of how many secretaries, or suitors. We need to know the number of suitors to know when we have hit 37 per cent as it is after this point the game starts to get serious. This requires some estimations and approximations.

Say we start dating seriously around the age of seventeen after some school dalliances and we marry at the ideal age of 30 (which means you have probably met at around age 28), this gives us thirteen years in our dating life. Let's say we have a series of relationships lasting from six months to 30 months i.e. two and a half years. We also have time in between to recover from breakups and be single – along with some not so serious flings. Let's take out a total of 36 months, three years, for these periods. We're left with 120 months. Let's say we have two longer relationships totalling another 42 months, two of around twelve months, three of roughly six months and two of three months. Finally, as we think seriously of settling down, we have a longer relationship of two and a half years, i.e. 30 months.

If you add these up, you get ten partners (who have been selected out of many more dates). While these numbers are highly arbitrary, they approximate what I hear from people who get married in their early thirties (yes, I take a full relationship history from every patient or couple I see).

What our 37 per cent figure means is that after the first four relationships (40 per cent) that were long enough for you to get to know what you are looking for in a relationship (and how you want to be in a relationship), it is game on. With each subsequent potential partner you are becoming well qualified to make a call. Of course, there are other factors at play – a big one being that partner number five, for example, may not be ready to settle down at that point. You get the idea.

However, we need to take into account the point I made earlier in this book about the fact that our brains and personalities are still maturing right up until our early thirties. Getting married much younger than this risks you both growing, literally, in different directions.

The maths also tells us that as we gain further experience after we hit the 37 per cent point, we are now becoming more expert at the evaluation. So, by the time you have had six significant relationships you certainly have enough relationship experience to make a better decision. Of course, this does depend on our capacity to learn. In turn, this comes down to our desire to learn. If our mind is closed, if we do not realise that how people react to us has a lot to do with how we behave towards them, then even twenty partners will have nothing to teach us.

The optimal stopping problem mathematics can also be applied to dating a given individual. There is a point at which we will have sufficient information to decide if we have a first level match with a potential partner. Julie Ferman, our professional matchmaker you met early in this book, pushes people to have at least three dates – unless there is a powerful repulsion on the first date. If it takes five dates, as Jiveny has suggested before we go to the next level, optimal stopping theory says we need to have at least three dates before we are in a position to decide whether to continue or not.

Finally, remember that it is not about judging what is right or wrong in a person. Rarely are we in a position to judge this for sure. It is entirely about what works between a man and a woman, for a given couple, to make a functional match. What we are learning is what we want from our relationships, what our minimum standards and our deal-breakers are.

In short, if you're in your late twenties and have had relationships with around half a dozen partners, you do not need to be any more qualified to choose your partner. If you have been thinking about, and learning from, the ups and downs of these relationships, you are as ready as you will ever be to choose. The chances of finding a better partner if you keep looking improve, but not significantly. Most people seem to be okay with this as they start to experience a degree of burnout some time after that half-a-dozen point.

What is much more important than more relationship experience is increased insight into our Imago-based dating patterns. Look for that slow burn, seven-out-of-ten who is reliable, caring and committed and let go of those dangerous, oh-so-enticing nines and tens.

Decision time

GBW and JBW

Having a baby is like getting a tattoo on your face. You really need to be certain ...

— Elizabeth Gilbert

Thank you so much for sharing this road with us. While this book has focused on how to make a better decision when considering a potential partner, it aims to do more than just enable you to have the happiest relationship possible. Perhaps more importantly, it is about creating a more stable, loving world for the next generation to be born into.

The world is becoming more used to divorce since it became statistically a 'normal' state by the end of the twentieth century. Our legal, schooling, health care and social systems are much better at normalising this painful experience for the huge number of children affected by the separation of their parents. Nevertheless, children do best in a secure, loving family.

Fortunately, as the age and maturity at which people marry increases, the divorce rate has been decreasing. But even more than bringing a child into a healthy family, we want to teach them how to go on to create a stable, loving, long-term relationship. The most powerful way to teach this is by modelling it, living it and being immersed in it, from a young age. We believe that in this way we can reduce the divorce rate even further. We are looking to create intergenerational change. It has to start somewhere.

What if there is only one thing you need to do?

In this book, we have covered a large range of factors to consider in making the best possible, most conscious match. But what if you need to do just one thing?

Most loving grey-haired couples celebrating their diamond anniversary have not had the benefit of the advice in this book. Some of them may not be truly content and happy in their marriages. But what if some are? Could there be something singular that carried them to a happy ending?

Consider also the experiences of arranged marriages and the accounts of people falling in love just through spending time together and manufacturing intimacy in experimental settings. It leads to a sneaking suspicion that there could be a singular, overarching force at work in love marriages, arranged marriages and manufactured love marriages.

We suggest that it could be as simple as one word. A word that has been peppered through this book: 'commitment'.

Remember Professor Epstein, who researched how we could 'manufacture love' through various exercises in intimacy? What he found was that 'the most important factor was commitment'. We are not talking about a commitment to stay married no matter what. While this does have some benefits – it lowers the divorce rate and could give children a stable home – it can still leave the couple unhappy. And if there is overt, recurrent aggression, staying together does not actually give the children any benefits. If anything, it sends children the message that you should put up with remaining in a toxic relationship.

The commitment to which we refer here is a special commitment. What I think some wise couples have worked out is that if you both commit to truly love your partner, to accept and nurture them, you can overcome everything, including a less than ideal match. Just as importantly, you need to work out how to forgive and nurture yourself.

Remember that to commit means that we hold the course no matter how bad the weather. As we've discussed, let's remind ourselves what true love is:

> True love is the feeling of being fully accepted
> by another who knows you intimately and who is
> committed to nurturing both your personal growth
> and their own.

When we point it in the other direction, from the giving side, it becomes:

> To truly love another, you make them feel safe enough
> to be vulnerable as you fully accept them and commit to
> nurture their personal growth as well as your own.

We would argue that if two people commit to love in this way, and fully embrace it, then maybe true love may be enough to overcome ... pretty much everything.

Why write a book to cover all that we have, if it takes just one thing? The beauty of a book is that we do not have to reduce the complexities we have covered down to just one thing. The tentacles of love are many and far-reaching. They are worthy of taking the time to understand and apply, but we all need a head start.

That head start is a good, solid match. A match that has

aligned values and a shared vision with consideration to the various other factors that we have covered in this book.

Then, when whatever problems arise that might throw us off course for a while, we slowly but surely come back to accepting and nurturing each other – no matter what. This is the commitment. Remember, committing is what carries us through the challenges, knowing that we have made an informed decision. In nurturing ourselves as well, we recognise that we have to take the ultimate responsibility for our personal growth. While it is wonderful to have a partner to nurture our growth, responsibility for this is ours and ours alone.

The great sadness

We cannot finish this book without writing something on managing expectations as we head into a lifelong relationship. Expect tough times. Even when you have made the best possible match and you have committed to truly loving your partner, life will test your relationship. Financial difficulties, illness, job loss, a seriously ill child, greater economic or social crises – the list of stressors that can seriously impact a relationship over the decades to follow is long.

In a recent podcast with George, the interviewer said, 'I know we should expect bumps in the road after we marry.' Politely George pointed out that it would be more helpful to expect 'not just huge potholes, but maybe sink holes that an entire car can disappear into!' On top of life's tests, no one will challenge you more than a partner who knows you warts and all.

One problem is worthy of particular mention, though. Often one partner, and sometimes both, may feel unhappy with their own life. Common stressors are career obstacles (like being fired) or health problems. Working out how to live a satisfying, rewarding and meaningful life can get really tough. Indeed we would suggest that being troubled by life is the normal human state. Taking these troubles out on (or worse still, blaming) one's partner can be mortally wounding to a relationship.

Our partners are always an easy target. Not only are they the closest target, if we want to allow ourselves to be annoyed by them, there will be a constant supply of things we could react to. If we do this, something spectacularly unfortunate happens – in blaming our partner for our own unhappiness, we push away the very person most able to help us find a way to that satisfying, rewarding and meaningful life we so desperately want. I call this the 'great sadness'. Once we allow the great sadness to inhabit our relationship we are really screwed.

The reality is that we do not need lots of close, loving relationships to make life great. One is enough, two is even better, and with three you are set for life. A partner and a close friend or two, a child or two – awesome! To push away relationship #1 is very problematic. You need to have an excellent reason to do it.

The great sadness is that you are stopping the best person to help you find your way back from the darkness from doing so. It is 180 degrees the wrong way around. These are the very times we want to let them in, let their love help us find our way back home – yet we have pushed them away.

It is great if our partner appreciates that it's us not them, and much better if we can tell them, 'Hey, I'm a bit stressed at the moment, it has nothing to do with you.' This simple communication can save a lot of relationship pain. Without clarifying this, our partners add to our problem by reacting negatively to our impatience, as they become unnecessarily defensive.

Moreover, if we actively blame our partner when life is not working out, we push them away and we become less able to be loving towards them – remember, this is the most reliable way to access love when we most need it.

Either way, when one partner is doing it tough, the other needs to step up and carry the relationship. They need to recognise that their partner is going through a tough time and not take their impatience, and inability to care, personally. Equally, if one partner is angry, does the other partner de-escalate it? If one partner can do this, the relationship can survive to go on to grow into something special.

The research shows that it takes around ten to fifteen years for a relationship to grow into something approaching what it was that the couple got married for in the first place. In many ways, the simple trick is to keep the relationship going for long enough to get there! If we both bring a commitment to true love, the chances of getting there are so much greater.

Academy Award winner Gwyneth Paltrow tells the story of her parents, director Bruce Paltrow and actress Blythe Danner: 'I asked Dad once, "How did you and Mom stay married for 33 years?" He said, "We never wanted to get divorced at the same time." When two people throw in the towel at the same time, then you break up, but if one person's saying, "Come on, we can do this," you carry on.'[40]

Here Gwyneth is talking about how one partner carries the commitment to love when the other one cannot. When both partners commit to love truly, you have cover. Sometimes we need to be protected from ourselves. We only need one to carry us through the tough times.

This brings us to a singular question as you contemplate a life-long relationship: can your potential partner offer you true love as we have defined it here? Given that the way we have defined it here is not the way most people automatically think of it, you will probably have to introduce them to it – gently. Over time, do they accept this way of seeing love – and, more importantly of course, can they live it? Can they walk this talk? Can you?

Time is needed to work this out – time to 'find out' whether you can both embrace true love fully. And, more importantly, time to work up to becoming *more expert* at true love. Nadine Gordimer, who won the Nobel Prize for Literature, captured this idea simply: 'What is love? You learn only as you go along.'

We have suggested allowing a minimum of three years before having children (eighteen months if you are around 30 or older and your biological clock is ticking more loudly). Remember the recent research from the United Kingdom (discussed in the relationship phases chapter) showing that the average couple is now in a relationship for an average of 4.9 years before getting married. The total average time living together before marriage is 3.5 years. At best, these extended courtships allow couples to become more expert at loving. At the very least, they mean that marriage is entered into with very realistic expectations about what your partner will be bringing to the party.

When do you really need to decide by?

The time by which a couple must really decide to commit to each other long term is not at the point of marriage. It is when they decide to get pregnant. Yes, we know it sometimes happens by accident. It has always been that way and it probably always will. Fortunately, modern contraceptive options make the deciding version more likely. And yes, some people choose to have children independently of getting married. Some then choose to marry as well. Either way, the decision to have children is the real point of commitment. For many of us, it is also the beginning of our final maturation as adults. Parents don't grow children into adulthood; it is the other way around. When a parent has a child it requires at least one of them to become the adult!

Relationships are really locked down when the first child is conceived. Between marriage and the first pregnancy, you have a final period of grace. Breaking up in this phase has no more long-term psychological impact than any other breakup with someone you loved. The marriage certificate is immaterial in terms of the emotional impact. The moment you conceive that first child, you now have a third person impacted and a clean separation is impossible.

For these reasons, we often say the person we are really choosing is the 'other parent of our children'. We realise that not everyone wants children or can have them, but it is those who do want to have children that have the biggest responsibility to choose well.

But what exactly are we choosing? You can be forgiven for thinking we are choosing a partner. Yes, we have written a book about how to do this better. As we have said, choosing a good match is a great head start. But what we are not choosing is a great relationship. This has to be built.

We are really choosing who and what principles, what relationship vision, we *commit* to. *We need to choose to commit to true love, more than we need to choose a person to commit to.* From the place of mutual commitment to true love as we have defined it, we then build a truly loving, enduring relationship.

This also means that, more than anything else, we are looking for a partner who will match our preparedness to commit. From this position, we believe that a couple can build the kind of loving relationship that they desire. We do not find the love of our life; rather, we commit to loving a partner who will commit to true love in return. Then we co-create the love of our life.

We will not wish you good luck on this quest.

It is way too big a decision to leave to luck.

Select bibliography

Bach, Richard, *Illusions: The Adventures of a Reluctant Messiah*. Dell, 1977.

Banfield, E.C., *The Moral Basis of a Backward Society*. Simon and Schuster, 1967.

Banfield, E.C., *The Un-heavenly City: The Nature and the Future of Our Urban Crisis*. Little, Brown, 1970.

Brown, Brené, *The Gifts of Imperfection: Let Go of Who You Think You're Supposed to Be and Embrace Who You Are*. Hazelden Publishing, 2010.

Dandine-Roulland, C., Laurent, R., Dall'Ara, I., Toupance, B. and Chaix, R., 'Genomic evidence for MHC disassortative mating in humans'. *Proceedings of the Royal Society B* (2019), https://royalsocietypublishing.org/doi/10.1098/rspb.2018.2664.

Elison, C.C., Disharmony: Premarital Relationships Dissolution. PhD dissertation, RELATE Institute, 2010, https://www.semanticscholar.org/paper/Disharmony%3A-Premarital-relationship-dissolution-Elison/cd9d1d5537d4c7a6948392f6d8c8b4d9e210e409.

Frost, Jeana H., Chance, Zoë, Norton, Michael I. and Ariely, Dan, 'People are Experience Goods: Improving Online Dating with Virtual Dates'. *Journal of Interactive Marketing*, 22(1) (2008), 51–61.

Gilbert, Elizabeth, *Eat, Pray, Love*. Penguin, 2006.

Gottman, John, *The Seven Principles for Making Marriage Work*. Seven Dials, 2018.

Hendrix, Harville, *Getting the Love You Want: A Guide for Couples*. St Martin's Press, 1988.

Kosar, K.R., 'How an Idyllic Italian Village was Crippled by Family Centrism'. Zocalo Public Square, 15 December 2016, https://www.zocalopublicsquare.org/2016/12/15/idyllic-italian-village-crippled-family-centrism/ideas/nexus.

Kruger, J. and Dunning, D., 'Unskilled and Unaware of It: How Difficulties in Recognizing One's Own Incompetence Lead to

Inflated Self-Assessments'. *Journal of Personality and Social Psychology*, 77(6) (1999), 1121–34.

Len Catron, Mandy, *How to Fall in Love with Anyone*. Nero, 2017.

Lu, C. *The Four Man Plan: A Romantic Science*. Createspace, 2007.

Luo, S. and Klohnen, E.C., 'Assortative Mating and Marital Quality in Newlyweds: A Couple-Centered Approach. *Journal of Personality and Social Psychology*, 88(2) (2005), 304–26.

Matthews, Andrew, *Being Happy*. Being Happy, 1988.

Matthews, Andrew, *Follow Your Heart*. Seashell, 1999.

Molloy, John T., *Why Men Marry Some Women and Not Others*. HarperCollins, 2014.

Newton, Michael, *Journey of Souls: Case Studies of Life Between Lives*. Llewellyn Worldwide, 1994.

Pausch, Randy, *The Last Lecture*. Hyperion, 2008.

Rhoades, G.K., Stanley, S.M. and Markman, H.J., 'Should I Stay or Should I Go? Predicting Dating Relationship Stability from Four Aspects of Commitment'. *Journal of Family Psychology*, 24(5) (2010), 543–50.

Rosenfeld, Michael J., 'Meeting Online: The Rise of the Internet as a Social Intermediary', https://web.stanford.edu/~mrosenfe/Rosenfeld_How_Couples_Meet_PAA_updated.pdf

Rotz, D., 'Why Have Divorce Rates Fallen? The Role of Women's Age at Marriage'. *Journal of Human Resources*, 51(4) (2016), 961–1002.

Treisman, Deborah, 'Kristen Roupenian on the Self Deceptions of Dating'. *The New Yorker*, 4 December 2017, https://www.newyorker.com/books/this-week-in-fiction/fiction-this-week-kristen-roupenian-2017-12-11.

Uysal, A., Lin, H.L. and Bush, A.L., 'The Reciprocal Cycle of Self-concealment and Trust in Romantic Relationships'. *European Journal of Social Psychology*, 42(7) (2012), 844–51.

Wakimoto, S. and Fujihara, T., 'Correlation Between Intimacy and Objective Similarity and Interpersonal Relationships'. *Social Behaviour and Personality*, 32 (2004), 95–102.

Notes

1 E.C. Banfield, *The Un-heavenly City: The Nature and the Future of Our Urban Crisis*. Little, Brown, 1970.

2 K.R. Kosar, 'How an Idyllic Italian Village was Crippled by Family Centrism', Zocalo Public Square, 15 December 2016, https://www.zocalopublicsquare. org/2016/12/15/idyllic-italian-village-crippled-family-centrism/ideas/nexus; E.C. Banfield, *The Moral Basis of a Backward Society*, Simon and Schuster, 1967.

3 G.K. Rhoades, S.M. Stanley and H.J. Markman, 'Should I Stay or Should I Go? Predicting Dating Relationship Stability from Four Aspects of Commitment'. *Journal of Family Psychology*, 24(5) (2010), 543–50.

4 Harville Hendrix, *Getting the Love You Want: A Guide for Couples*. St Martin's Press, 1988.

5 Richard Bach, *Illusions: The Adventures of a Reluctant Messiah*. Dell, 1977.

6 Elizabeth Gilbert, *Eat, Pray, Love*. Penguin, 2006.

7 Michael Newton, *Journey of Souls: Case Studies of Life Between Lives*. Llewellyn Worldwide, 1994.

8 Mandy Len Catron, *How to Fall in Love with Anyone*. Nero, 2017.

9 D. Rotz, 'Why Have Divorce Rates Fallen? The Role of Women's Age at Marriage'. *Journal of Human Resources*, 51(4) (2016), 961–1002.

10 bridebook.co.uk, Marriage Report 2017, https://bridebook.co.uk/article/bridebook-co-uk-marriage-report-2017

11 This is appreciatively borrowed from the work of Harville Hendrix.

12 Andrew Matthews, *Being Happy*. Being Happy, 1988.

13 Andrew Matthews, *Follow Your Heart*. Seashell, 1999.

14 Randy Pausch, *The Last Lecture*. Hyperion, 2008.

15 Deborah Treisman, 'Kristen Roupenian on the Self Deceptions of Dating'. *The New Yorker*, 4 December 2017, https://www.newyorker.com/books/this-week-in-fiction/fiction-this-week-kristen-roupenian-2017-12-11.

16 When someone breaks off a relationship by stopping all communication and contact without warning or justification, as well as ignoring any further attempts to reach out or communicate.

17 When someone creates a fake social networking account with the intent of targeting a specific victim with abuse, deception or fraud.

18 When a 'crush' engages online or via text just enough to keep a person interested even though they do not intend to take things further – usually because they enjoy the validation.

19 Putting a date on the backburner because you see them as more of a 'Plan B'.

20 A culture of casual, sexual, non-committed encounters.

21 A 2010 study by Michael Rosenfeld of Stanford University found that roughly one in four straight couples meets online. See Michael J. Rosenfeld, 'Meeting Online: The Rise of the Internet as a Social Intermediary', https://web.stanford.edu/~mrosenfe/Rosenfeld_How_Couples_Meet_PAA_updated.pdf. For gay couples, Rosenfeld found that this proportion leaps to two out of three. While these figures may have increased in recent years, it is the ratio that is of interest and that Rosenfeld's research also suggests that there is very little difference between the quality of relationships started online or offline.

Notes

22 Jeana H. Frost, Zoë Chance, Michael I. Norton and Dan Ariely, 'People are Experience Goods: Improving Online Dating with Virtual Dates', *Journal of Interactive Marketing*, 22(1) (2008), 51–61.

23 John T. Molloy, *Why Men Marry Some Women and Not Others*. HarperCollins, 2014.

24 Pet Product News Staff, 'Study reveals diseases mixed breed and purebred dogs are prone to develop', American Veterinary Medical Foundation, 2018, http://www.petproductnews.com/News/Study-Reveals-Diseases-Mixed-Breed-and-Purebred-Dogs-Are-Prone-To-Develop.

25 A. Goris, 'Comment: The HLA Region in Multiple Sclerosis'. *Neurology*, 79(6) (2012), 544.

26 C. Dandine-Roulland, R. Laurent, I. Dall'Ara, B. Toupance and R. Chaix, 'Genomic evidence for MHC disassortative mating in humans'. *Proceedings of the Royal Society B* (2019), https://royalsocietypublishing.org/doi/10.1098/rspb.2018.2664.

27 S. Wakimoto and T. Fujihara, 'Correlation Between Intimacy and Objective Similarity and Interpersonal Relationships'. *Social Behaviour and Personality*, 32 (2004), 95–102.

28 As always, their names have been changed for confidentiality reasons.

29 S. Luo and E.C. Klohnen, 'Assortative Mating and Marital Quality in Newlyweds: A Couple-Centered Approach'. *Journal of Personality and Social Psychology*, 88(2) (2005), 304–26.

30 J. Gottman, *The Seven Principles for Making Marriage Work*, Seven Dials, 2018.

31 Gottman, *The Seven Principles*.

32 A. Uysal, H.L. Lin and A.L. Bush, 'The Reciprocal Cycle of Self-concealment and Trust in Romantic Relationships'. *European Journal of Social Psychology*, 42(7) (2012), 844–51.

33 C. Lu, *The Four Man Plan: A Romantic Science*. Createspace, 2007.

34 Brené Brown, *The Gifts of Imperfection: Let Go of Who You Think You're Supposed to Be and Embrace Who You Are*. Hazeldon, 2010, p. 6.

35 Molloy, *Why Men Marry Some Women and Not Others*.

36 I will call her that because that is her name ☺ – she was named in Molloy's book.

37 C.C. Elison, Disharmony: Premarital Relationships Dissolution. PhD dissertation, RELATE Institute, 2010, https://www.semanticscholar.org/paper/Disharmony%3A-Premarital-relationship-dissolution-Elison/cd9d1d5537d4c7a6948392f6d8c8b4d9e210e409.

38 Based on Amber Vennum, Rachel Lindstrom, J. Kale Monk and Rebekah Adams, '"It's Complicated": The Continuity and Correlates of Cycling in Cohabiting and Marital Relationships'. *Journal of Social and Personal Relationships*, 31(3) (2014), 410–30.

39 J. Kruger and D. Dunning, 'Unskilled and Unaware of It: How Difficulties in Recognizing One's Own Incompetence Lead to Inflated Self-Assessments'. *Journal of Personality and Social Psychology*, 77(6) (1999), 1121–34.

40 'Gwyneth Paltrow's Marriage to Chris Martin Has Seen "Terrible Times"'. *Huffington Post*, 2 May 2013, https://www.huffpost.com/entry/gwyneth-paltrow-marriage-terrible-times_n_3202926.

Dr George Blair-West is a medical doctor specialising in psychiatry, particularly relationship therapy, in Brisbane, Australia. George's writing career began more than 25 years ago with a series of scientific publications on suicide and depression while a senior lecturer with the University of Queensland. Magazine, newspaper articles and books followed on a range of subjects including the psychology of weight loss. His most cherished writing (prior to this book) is the award-winning *The Way of the Quest*, an inspirational historical novel that explores how to find meaning and purpose in life. George sees his most important work as preventing divorce through helping people to find enduring love (his talk on this subject on TED.com has had more than 3.5 million views). His writing is heavily influenced by his wife of 32 years, Penny, a clinical psychologist with whom he road-tests every relationship strategy he writes about.

Jiveny Blair-West graduated from Queensland University of Technology with a distinction in copywriting. After working in advertising, Jiveny found herself disheartened by having to work on campaigns she didn't believe in. Ready for a change, she left Australia and travelled the world for several years before returning to settle in Melbourne where she became a Credentialled Practitioner of Coaching through The Coaching Institute. Then, following in her parents' footsteps, she specialised to become a dating and attraction coach. In her work as a dating coach, she has helped many women unlock the power of sustainable attraction, in turn leading them to find wonderful partners. Her signature ten-week course, The Alchemy of Attraction, helps women to develop their relationship wisdom and empower themselves to take action and find true love. You can find all the details and join the program at jiveny.com.

The Alchemy of Attraction

A masterclass with Jiveny Blair-West

My wish for everyone is to attract a truly compatible partner who lights up your soul and shares your values. Not a fairytale romance, but a real-life love story. Someone who makes you feel nurtured and respected. Someone who is willing to work on their relationship with you to make it the best it can be. Someone who enjoys who you are and ultimately brings out the best in you (as you do for them). The kind of person you still love to be around long after the honeymoon period is over.

I've helped many women unlock the power of sustainable attraction, in turn leading them to find a wonderful partner. So you might want to consider joining my ten-week course, The Alchemy of Attraction. (Sorry guys, this program is strictly for women.) This is my flagship course where I teach you how to develop your relationship wisdom and empower yourself to take action and find true love.

Join me and we will take everything you've read about in this book to the masterclass level. You'll learn how to:

- deeply understand sustainable attraction (and how to avoid superficial attraction)
- identify the pitfalls that often prevent you from attracting good men
- communicate with and relate to men more effectively
- work out where men are at in their dating/marrying cycle
- understand and assert healthy boundaries with confidence and grace
- unpack and upgrade your dating strategy to improve your chances of finding a match
- embrace your inner siren and have more fun exploring the modern dating world

Head to my website www.jiveny.com to join the waiting list. I'll be giving preference to people who have read this book.

See you there!

Jiveny